U.S. Constitution

by Melissa Mandel, JD and Glenn Smith, JD, LLM

U.S. Constitution For Dummies®

Published by: **John Wiley & Sons, Inc.,** 111 River Street, Hoboken, NJ 07030-5774, www.wiley.com

Contents at a Glance

Table of Contents

CHAPTER 3: **Resolving Key Dilemmas with the U.S. Constitution** 37

CHAPTER 4: **Interpreting the Constitution** 49

PART 2: SETTING UP (AND LIMITING) NATIONAL GOVERNMENT POWERS 61

CHAPTER 5: **Constituting the Legislative Branch** 63

CHAPTER 9: Dividing Power between National and State Officials 117

PART 3: BROADLY PROTECTING CIVIL LIBERTIES 129

CHAPTER 10: Assuring Freedom of Speech 131

CHAPTER 11: Protecting Freedom from and of Religion 149

CHAPTER 14: Navigating Intimate Liberty and Privacy Issues....197

PART 4: PROTECTING PROPERTY, GUN OWNERSHIP, AND VOTING RIGHTS........................213

CHAPTER 15: Promoting Stability by Safeguarding Specific Interests 215

CHAPTER 19: Checking Government Power to Investigate, Arrest, and Indict 277

CHAPTER 20: Guaranteeing Fair Trials 303

Introduction

The United States Constitution affects every corner of American lives. Its provisions come into play on countless issues of international, national, state, local, and individual concern, including war, healthcare, election integrity, immigration, education, religion, fair housing, taxes, property ownership, protests, gun regulation, travel, marriage, and criminal trials. This remarkable document establishes the foundation of U.S. democracy. It has endured as the supreme law of the land, standing the test of time against evolving societal norms and unforeseeable technological advancements.

The Constitution establishes a government by the people, for the people; and participation is a bedrock principle of American democracy. We wrote this book to foster participation by making the Constitution accessible and showing you why it matters. We think you can find this book valuable, no matter what participation means to you; whether you aspire to become an informed citizen, a more knowledgeable student, or an effective voter; run for elected local, state, or federal office; seek an executive or judicial appointment; serve as a government attorney or staff member; or just satisfy your curiosity and understand what you see on the news.

We hope this book can provide you with the knowledge, confidence, and motivation to take part in fulfilling the promises of the Constitution's preamble: "to form a more perfect union" and "secure the blessings of liberty to ourselves and our posterity."

About This Book

Whether you're a Constitution expert looking for help describing complex issues in straightforward terms, a law student hoping to ace an exam, or a person who has questions about whether a government action violates their constitutional rights, you can find what you're looking for here. Read the book cover-to-cover if you want, but we think you more likely want to browse through the Table of Contents or look up a specific topic in the Index to get right to the heart of what you want to know. Like all *For Dummies* books, this one is designed to give you quick answers when you want them while providing more comprehensive coverage for those who have the time and interest. It may help you win arguments with friends (or at least help you understand when you lose!).

At the heart of it, the Constitution deals with granting and limiting government powers. We cover these topics extensively, looking at the constitutional text and its meaning as interpreted by the Supreme Court. We explain the tensions that arise between the three branches of government and delve into the details of the Constitution's system of checks and balances.

Individual protections feature prominently in the Constitution. We examine the Bill of Rights and look at how due process protects property and liberty interests, including civil rights. We also examine how the right to privacy has changed and how the Constitution protects people from unfair treatment by government figures.

The constitutional landscape is always evolving, so we keep you up to date by summarizing recent Supreme Court cases and describing unresolved controversies the Supreme Court may take up soon. (If you want to see the latest cases and decisions, check out the Court's website at https://supremecourt.gov.)

Foolish Assumptions

We assume a few things about you:

>> You have a basic understanding of the U.S. Constitution's history and role as the foundation of American democracy. (Although we do provide some big-picture historical information.)

>> You want to know about current constitutional issues and how the Supreme Court might resolve them.

>> You want to see how the legal landscape evolves when the Supreme Court interprets the Constitution and how societal changes can influence those interpretations.

>> You think a deeper understanding of the U.S. Constitution can make you better informed about current political debates.

Icons Used in This Book

Throughout this book, you see certain information set aside or highlighted in various ways. For example, we put some information in boxes on the page, called *sidebars*, which contain examples or discussions that may deepen your knowledge but aren't critical to your understanding of the subject matter.

In addition to sidebars, we use the following icons to flag certain material:

We use the Tip icon to give pointers, provide practical information, or describe a nuance or application of a principle to help you gain a deeper understanding.

Pay attention to the Warning icon. We don't use it much, but when we do, we're letting you know about a potentially dangerous area.

The Remember icon signals information that we think is important for your understanding and application of constitutional knowledge.

This one is for the geeks. Technical Stuff information is interesting and relevant to the discussion in a section, but it may contain technical information or legalese that you can skip if you want.

Beyond the Book

We think we've done a pretty good job describing the Constitution's articles and amendments in this book, but you can't get closer to the material than reading the Constitution in its entirety, which can give you a true sense of its breadth and durability. The Constitution is surprisingly short — it's about the length of a short story or a chapter in a novel. We encourage you to read it. The National Constitution Center includes an online version of the full text at `https://constitutioncenter.org/the-constitution/full-text`. And we offer other helpful materials in our online Cheat Sheet, which you can find by going to `www.dummies.com` and typing "U.S. Constitution for Dummies" in the search box.

Where to Go from Here

Now it's time to begin exploring the nuts and bolts of American democracy. If you're interested in the history of the Constitution and its relationship to other governments, start with Chapter 1. Chapters 2 and 3 are good starting points for those looking for information about the Constitution's organization and an overview of the main problems it tries to resolve.

If you have questions about what the president can or can't do, start with Chapter 6. To understand the Supreme Court's power to invalidate acts of Congress, check out Chapter 7. Chapter 9 is the place to look for answers on the balance of power between the federal government and the states.

Parts 3, 4, and 5 cover constitutional protections for individual rights. Start with Part 3 for details about the Constitution's role in maintaining civil liberties. Part 4 focuses on specific interests that the Constitution protects. And Part 5 provides answers to questions about constitutional protections during the criminal justice process.

1

Getting Started with the U.S. Constitution

Chapter **1**

Viewing the U.S. Constitution from a Broader Perspective

ourts and legal scholars start with the Constitution's text when they want to figure out what it means, but the words didn't come out of nowhere. They're the product of historical events; political, economic, and geographical disputes; and a diverse new country's struggle to unify and build a government around its common values.

In this chapter, we look at the big picture, placing the Constitution in context. You can read about how historical events created momentum for a stronger federal government that would still honor state's rights and individual freedoms. We also talk about what was going on at the time the Constitution was drafted, introducing the Framers and reviewing how the Constitution was signed, amended, and ratified. You can also see how the Constitution fits into the broader U.S. government system, including its relationship to federal laws and state constitutions.

A CONSTITUTIONAL TIMELINE

Here's a brief timeline to help you keep track of the chronology of the events that we examine in this chapter (some of these events overlap):

- **1215:** *Magna Carta,* a charter requiring the King of England to grant civil rights to his barons, goes into effect in England.

- **1688–1789:** The Age of Enlightenment, an intellectual movement focused on the power of reason, occurs in Europe.

- **1775–1783:** The American Revolution is fought and won.

- **May 10, 1776:** The Continental Congress passes a resolution for independent state governments.

- **July 4, 1776:** The Continental Congress signs the Declaration of Independence.

- **March 1, 1781:** The Articles of Confederation are ratified and serve as the country's first constitution.

- **May 25–September 17, 1787:** The Constitutional Convention is held in Philadelphia.

- **September 17, 1787:** Delegates sign the Constitution.

- **June 21, 1788:** The Constitution becomes the law of the land (replacing the Articles of Confederation) when New Hampshire becomes the 9th state to ratify it (a number required by the Constitution itself).

Convention participants greatly debated the process for ratifying the Constitution. Although some members thought ratification should require all states to vote in favor (which the Articles of Confederation required for amendment), others advocated for a simple majority. Ultimately, the Framers agreed on Article VII stating that nine states needed to ratify to make the Constitution law. They chose nine because that was the number of states that the Articles of Confederation required to approve certain important matters.

Understanding the Constitution's Predecessors and Influences

Throughout this book, we use *Framers* (with a capital *F*) to refer to the individuals in attendance at the Constitutional Convention and those who substantially influenced the first seven articles. Our references to *framers* (with a lowercase *f*) refer generically to the Founding Fathers and those who were instrumental in drafting any part of the Constitution, including the amendments.

Three major influences guided the Framers in how they chose the features of the new constitutional democracy (for more on the Framers, see the section "Getting to Know the Framers," later in this chapter):

>> Historical events — specifically, Magna Carta (Latin for *Great Charter*) and the Enlightenment (both discussed in the following section) — cemented the notion of inalienable rights.

>> Drafting and living under state constitutions for nearly a decade gave the Framers an idea of what worked and what didn't. (We talk about this aspect in the section "Noting the influence of state constitutions," later in this chapter.)

>> The failings of the Articles of Confederation demonstrated the need for a stronger federal government to manage areas of national concern (as discussed in the section "Reacting to the Articles of Confederation," later in this chapter).

Calling the document *Magna Carta*, instead of *the Magna Carta*, may sound weird, but it's correct because Latin phrases don't use definite articles.

TECHNICAL
STUFF

Tracing back to Magna Carta

The foundations of the Constitution began centuries before the first American colony. In 1215, a conflict erupted between King John of England and his *barons* (wealthy landowners). The king's authoritarian methods, abuses of power, and imposition of high taxes to fund unsuccessful wars ultimately led to a rebellion. The barons captured London and threatened to start a civil war if the king refused to agree to their demands.

King John agreed. The king and his barons entered into a pact called Magna Carta that limited the king's powers and specified that the king himself was subject to the laws. Magna Carta became a symbol of the ideal that government exists to protect its people and that it can't infringe their fundamental rights. Provisions in Magna Carta

>> Required the king to provide due process

>> Guaranteed barons the right to a jury trial

>> Protected barons from taxation without representation

>> Prohibited the king from imposing excessive punishment on his barons

The Founding Fathers, American Civil Rights leaders, and voting rights activists considered Magna Carta an important symbol of universal human rights, but it actually benefitted only a small number of wealthy elite landowners in England. These rights didn't extend to most serfs who, under the feudal system, were forced to labor on their lords' estates.

Bringing forth the Enlightenment

Centuries after Magna Carta (see the preceding section), English philosopher John Locke advanced the theory of *inalienable rights* — that all individuals have rights to life, liberty, and property, not granted by the government, but inherent in human existence. His ideas caught on quickly. Locke was one of several philosophers who contributed to the *Age of Enlightenment,* an intellectual movement in the late 17th and early 18th centuries in Europe that grew out of the *Scientific Revolution* (the emergence of modern scientific method and thought). The Enlightenment was a pivot toward knowledge and reason, away from religion and cultural tradition, as the foundation of government. In England, France, and Colonial America, Enlightenment philosophers criticized the idea of an authoritarian state and promoted the concept of a democratic government.

The Enlightenment saw government as a social contract. The movement envisioned a government that ensured freedom of religion, freedom of the press, and freedom from torture and other cruel punishments. French philosopher Montesquieu advocated for three separate but equal branches of government, giving rise to the concept of checks and balances. The Enlightenment's core ideas of human rights and political democracy led to reforms in England and to the French and American revolutions.

Using the past to inform their positions

Magna Carta and the Enlightenment (discussed in the preceding sections) strongly influenced the American colonists' movement toward independence and the type of government that the Framers chose to create. For example, the principles embodied in Magna Carta formed the basis of the Continental Congress's 1774 declaration of rights and grievances against King George III and inspired the American Revolution. And the 1776 Declaration of Independence strongly echoes ideals from Magna Carta and the Enlightenment as justification for American independence from England.

In the *Federalist Papers*, a series of essays written under the pseudonym Publius by statesmen Alexander Hamilton, John Jay, and James Madison to persuade citizens to ratify the Constitution, the authors referenced Magna Carta to explain the importance of a stable government to ensure fair legal processes. And the Constitution itself includes several fundamental rights rooted in Magna Carta, such as the right to a jury trial, the prohibition against cruel and unusual punishment, and the concept of due process.

The Enlightenment also foreshadowed the controversy over slavery that took place at the Constitutional Convention. (We describe this controversy in Chapter 2.) Some Enlightenment philosophers opposed slavery on moral grounds, while others justified slavery as an economic necessity; and many Enlightenment advocates were slave owners. At the Constitutional Convention, similar moral undertones framed the debate over whether slaves would count as people or property for purposes of taxation and representation.

Noting the influence of state constitutions

Some scholars believe that state constitutions were the primary influence on the U.S. Constitution. On May 10, 1776, Congress passed a resolution directing the colonies to "adopt such government as shall, in the opinion of the representatives of the people, best conduce to the happiness and safety of their constituents in particular, and America in general." This resolution served as a directive for states to work on writing their own constitutions.

Writing state constitutions was a daunting task because the colonists didn't have a template to work from. In England, the constitution was unwritten; it was a collection of laws amassed from tradition, acts of parliament, common law, and the monarchy. With no written constitution, the king could disregard or disobey the law without consequence. In America, government accountability was a priority that leaders believed could best be achieved by having written constitutions.

States spent the decade after the 1776 resolution creating various frameworks for constitutional democracy. State constitutions varied substantially based on the state's economy (agricultural or industrial), whether or not slavery was lawful, and variations in geography, size, and politics. Those years of writing and living under state constitutions served as an experiment of sorts to test drive the potential features of a new federal government. When the Framers gathered in Philadelphia in 1787, their collective experiences strongly informed their positions. State constitutions

>> Were cited in debates at the convention, pointing out provisions in different state constitutions that worked or didn't work

> » Provided the Framers with information about what was popular
>
> » Gave Framers a starting point to compromise
>
> » Allowed Framers to implement new ideas by combining features from different state constitutions

TECHNICAL STUFF

England granted self-governance to the colonies in charters, but it retained substantial power, especially over legislation and the judiciary. Some colonies created their own self-governing documents, called *colonial constitutions*. These charters and colonial constitutions influenced state constitutions in the same way that state constitutions later influenced the U.S. Constitution.

The 1780 Constitution of the Commonwealth of Massachusetts was one of the strongest influences on the U.S. Constitution. Drafted by John Adams, the Massachusetts Constitution followed the framework laid out in Adams's essay "Thoughts on Government," which called for three separate branches of government and a two-tiered legislature. The Framers of the U.S Constitution looked to the Massachusetts Constitution to decide many disputed issues. For example, in deciding whether the legislative or executive branch should appoint judges, it followed Massachusetts' lead by giving the power of appointment to the executive, with advice and consent of the legislature.

Reacting to the Articles of Confederation

The Articles of Confederation, ratified in 1781, served as the original constitution for the 13 states. But by 1787, the country was on the verge of economic and political failure.

In September 1786, delegates from five states met in Annapolis, Maryland, to discuss American trade policy. These representatives quickly realized the nation's commerce problems were too big to solve on their own. After the meeting, Alexander Hamilton wrote a report calling for a convention in Philadelphia the following May to amend the Articles of Confederation to give the federal government sufficient power to manage national affairs.

That meeting is what historians call the Constitutional Convention. Delegates at the convention quickly gave up on amending the Articles and spent the summer months hammering out the framework for a new government.

REMEMBER

The convention was held in secret, with no reporters or guests allowed, leading some at the time to suspect that delegates were plotting a conspiracy to overthrow the government.

The Constitution addresses the perceived weaknesses in the *Articles of Confederation,* the governing arrangement under which the states tried to operate starting in 1781. Most historical observers see the weak federal government created by the Articles as lacking sufficient power to unify the states; it couldn't

>> Regulate trade (or prevent individual states from trying to provide advantages to their residents and business interests over those in neighboring states)

>> Create a military

>> Collect sufficient tax revenue

Trying to execute federal policy by a legislative committee, rather than a separate executive function, was cumbersome, as was the fact that every state had to agree before the articles could be amended.

Specific provisions in the 1787 Constitution responded to each of the perceived deficiencies in the Articles of Confederation. For example, Chapter 3 shows how the Article V constitutional-amendments process allows less-than-unanimous supermajorities to change the basic governing document. And Chapter 5 notes that the first power that the Framers gave to Congress in Article I, Section 8, was an independent federal power to tax.

Getting to Know the Framers

State legislatures chose 74 delegates to attend the Constitutional Convention in Philadelphia between May 25 and September 17, 1787, but only 55 showed up, including representatives from 12 of the 13 states (every state except Rhode Island). Most of these delegates had been involved in drafting their state constitutions. Here are some Framers who had particularly noteworthy roles:

>> **George Washington (Virginia):** Previously commander-in-chief of the Colonial Army (and later the first United States President); selected to preside over the convention. Washington was one of seven from the Virginia delegation.

>> **James Madison and Edmund J. Randolph (Virginia):** Proposed the Virginia Plan, advocating for representation based on population, which favored larger states.

Madison also kept extensive notes about convention deliberations; made available after his death, modern interpreters use these notes to understand what the Framers did and didn't do, and why.

>> **George Mason (Virginia):** Played a key role in the Great Compromise proposed by Oliver Ellsworth and Roger Sherman (we provide a more detailed look at the Great Compromise in Chapter 5).

>> **William Paterson (New Jersey):** A New Jersey delegate who proposed a response to the Virginia Plan. The New Jersey Plan advocated for a one-house legislature and equal representation regardless of population, giving greater power to smaller states.

>> **Oliver Ellsworth and Roger Sherman (Connecticut):** Proposed the Great Compromise to settle the differences between the Virginia Plan and the New Jersey Plan. It included a *bicameral legislature* (an elected assembly consisting of two chambers), with equal representation in one chamber and population-based representation in the other.

>> **John Dickinson (Delaware):** Helped to craft the Great Compromise. He also advocated against slavery.

>> **Benjamin Franklin (Pennsylvania):** An anti-slavery representative, Franklin was 81 years old and the oldest delegate. Franklin's family once owned slaves but, later in life, his views changed.

>> **Gouverneur Morris and James Wilson (Pennsylvania):** Opposed slavery and participated extensively in the constitutional convention debates.

>> **John Rutledge (South Carolina):** Served on many committees and advocated for Southern interests.

>> **Charles Pinckney (South Carolina):** Instrumental in reaching a compromise to eventually abolish the international slave trade.

Not every delegate ended up supporting the Constitution as finally proposed. Both Mason and Randolph refused to sign the Constitution; Mason because it didn't include a bill of rights and Randolph because he objected to a one–person executive.

Adopting the Constitution

On September 17, 1787, the first draft of the Constitution was finalized and signed, but according to Article VII, it wouldn't become law until it was ratified by at least 9 states. Each of the 13 states called ratifying conventions to debate and vote on the Constitution.

On June 21, 1788, New Hampshire became the ninth state to ratify the Constitution, making it the law of the land.

The Constitution's *preamble*, or introduction, stated its noble goals: "We the People of the United States, in Order to form a more perfect Union, establish Justice, insure domestic Tranquility, provide for the common defense, promote the general Welfare, and secure the Blessings of Liberty to ourselves and our Posterity, do ordain and establish this Constitution for the United States of America."

As important as the Preamble of the Constitution is in setting forth the ideals of the newly created government, it doesn't create enforceable limits. (You can't sue your least-favorite government official for disturbing the "domestic Tranquility" of your household, for example.) But the Preamble does provide useful guidance to what the enforceable limits in the remainder of the U.S. Constitution mean.

RATIFICATION CONTROVERSY AND THE MASSACHUSETTS COMPROMISE

The contrasting Federalist/Anti-Federalist views generated significant writings and debates while states grappled with whether to ratify:

- **Federalists:** Leaders tried to convince citizens in their states to ratify the Constitution. They thought a strong federal government was necessary to promote national interests where the Articles of Confederation had failed.

- **Anti-Federalists:** Opposed the Constitution. They feared that a strong federal government would subjugate individual freedoms, much like the oppressive British government that they had fought against.

Many Anti-Federalist concerns were allayed by the Massachusetts Compromise on February 6, 1788, when Anti-Federalist leaders John Hancock, Samuel Adams, and others convinced Massachusetts citizens to ratify the Constitution on the condition that it would be amended to add a bill of rights.

Following through on the Massachusetts Compromise, James Madison introduced 17 proposed amendments. Congress adopted 12 of those amendments on September 25, 1789. On December 15, 1791, Virginia became the 10th out of 14 states to ratify the first ten amendments, giving the Bill of Rights the two-thirds majority it needed to become law. (Vermont became the 14th state on March 4, 1791, before Virginia voted to ratify.)

Fitting the Constitution into the U.S. Legal and Governmental System

The Constitution (including amendments) contains only 7,591 words, about the length of a short story. It takes an average person about half an hour to read it from start to finish, and for the most part, it's accessible and understandable (which doesn't mean it's crystal clear — people have debated its meaning for more than two centuries!). Grab a cup of coffee or tea (or other favorite beverage), find a comfortable chair, and read the full text of the Constitution. You can find a good copy on the National Constitution Center website at https://constitution center.org/the-constitution/full-text.

The following sections deal with how the Constitution fits into the legal and governmental pecking order in the United States. The U.S. government is based on constitutional supremacy, which means the Constitution stands above all other federal laws and policies. The U.S. Constitution also plays a role in how state and local officials can carry out state constitutions, laws, and policies.

Grasping federal constitutional supremacy

Article V of the U.S. Constitution declares that "This Constitution . . . shall be the supreme Law of the Land." This simple statement of *constitutional supremacy* is one of the document's most important design features. Judges and others use the U.S. Constitution as the basis for assessing the validity of all laws enacted, treaties made, presidential executive orders issued, lower court rulings handed down, federal regulations promulgated, and policy decisions announced.

Because the Framers opted for constitutional supremacy, the Constitution is sacrosanct; it sets limits on the power of even the highest ranking government officials in each of the three branches. Even in long-standing democratic countries that have *parliamentary supremacy* (meaning the legislative body holds absolute authority), such as England, the laws passed by the legislative body don't have to conform to any superior legal authority. What one parliament enacts, another can change or amend. (Hopefully, unwritten traditions may blunt that possibility.)

A notable feature of U.S. constitutional supremacy is that it promotes stability (or rigidity, depending on your point of view). Article V of the Constitution requires an extraordinary supermajority consensus over time to change the Constitution; two-thirds of both houses of Congress (a substantially higher margin than the simple majority needed to pass most ordinary legislation) must propose the same amendment text. After it gets proposed, three-fourths of the states have to ratify it. So, for better or worse, the enduring constitutional language can't change easily with any change in the majority.

The Framers designed the Constitution to last, allowing for change only upon the agreement of a *two-tiered supermajority* (two-thirds of both houses of Congress and three-fourths of the states). Modern efforts to amend the Constitution illustrate just how difficult officials find achieving the required level of bipartisan support in a politically diverse country. Take, for example, the 22nd Amendment, providing that "No person shall be elected to the office of the President more than twice."

For decades since the passage of the 22nd Amendment, most recently in January 2025, members of both political parties have proposed amending or repealing the 22nd Amendment to allow their party's incumbent president to remain in office after completing a second term. These proposals required

- Two-thirds of the House of Representatives voting in favor (290 votes)

- Two-thirds of the Senate voting in favor (67 votes)

- Three-fourths of all states ratifying (38 states)

It probably comes as no surprise that none of these proposals have even come close!

REMEMBER

In more than two centuries, only 27 amendments have been ratified. The first ten amendments (the Bill of Rights) were ratified as a package in 1791, and three amendments (discussed in Chapter 2) were enacted close in time in the immediate aftermath of the Civil War. The most recent was the 27th Amendment (preventing Congressional salary changes), which was ratified in 1992.

Reconciling the U.S. Constitution with the states

Constitutional supremacy has important implications for state laws. The Constitution imposes the obligation to follow its supreme provisions specifically on state judges — and implicitly on all other state and local officials — in the Supremacy Clause of Article VI, where it says "any Thing in the Constitution or Laws of any State to the contrary notwithstanding." All state and local officials "shall be bound" by the U.S. Constitution "and the Laws of the United States" made under the Constitution's authority.

Putting these clauses together establishes an important federal-versus-state hierarchy. The U.S. Constitution — and any constitutionally authorized federal statutes, presidential executive orders, court rulings, regulatory decisions, and policies — take precedence over state laws, and even the highest law of a state, its own constitution.

This supremacy means that the U.S. Constitution establishes a floor of constitutional protections below which states can't go (although they can build on top of that floor). For example, state constitutions and laws that racially segregated school children fell to the 14th Amendment Equal Protection Clause, as declared by the 1954 *Brown v. Board of Education* Supreme Court decision.

Chapter **2**

Getting the Basics of the U.S. Constitution

When the Framers scrapped the Articles of Confederation and began drafting the Constitution (which you can read about in Chapter 1), they had to think about how the various provisions would work together and how the new federal government would operate in relation to other government systems. Not only are the articles and amendments internally interdependent, but the Constitution itself is part of a larger government network that includes state constitutions, federal laws, and foreign constitutions.

In this chapter, you can see how the Constitution is organized and how it fits into the universe of governments and laws. We compare the United States Constitution to state and foreign constitutions and consider the Constitution's internal structure. As short as it is, the U.S. Constitution covers a lot of ground.

Comparing the U.S. Constitution to Other Constitutions

The Framers based the Constitution on a system of *federalism*, dividing and sharing power between the federal government and individual states. This non-centralization protects national interests while also safeguarding state autonomy.

In contrast to federalism, in a *unitary* system of government, such as the governments in the United Kingdom and Japan, a centralized government holds all the power. It may grant powers to other government units, but it can also rescind those powers.

State constitutions

The 10th Amendment to the Constitution explains the distribution of power:

>> **The federal government:** Has the powers specifically granted by the Constitution

>> **The states (and the people):** Have all other powers, unless specifically prohibited by the Constitution

The structural relationship between the U.S. Constitution and state constitutions is a lot like the structure of a quilt. Like a quilt's fabric panels, states are complete, independent, fully functioning units. They can vary greatly in size and have unique characteristics, but they're also part of something bigger, the federal government, which (like a quilt's stitching) connects the separate parts and enables them to function as a cohesive whole.

Although different states have different procedures for amending their constitutions, state constitutions are designed to be amended more easily. They cover more of the nuts and bolts of daily life and therefore need amending more frequently than the broader U.S. Constitution.

State constitutions can provide greater individual rights and protections than the U.S. Constitution, but they can't provide fewer rights or less protection.

Foreign constitutions

The U.S Constitution holds an important place among governments worldwide. It's the oldest surviving written constitution in the world. Its reliance on ideas from Magna Carta and the Enlightenment reverberated globally and inspired other countries to follow suit. (You can read more about the history of the Constitution in Chapter 1.)

SETTING MICHIGAN PRISONERS FREE WITH A SINGLE WORD

One provision of the Michigan Constitution illustrates how a state's unique history and priorities can create differences in the way courts interpret similar provisions in their state constitution and the U.S. Constitution:

- **And:** The 8th Amendment to the U.S. Constitution prohibits "cruel *and* unusual punishment," so a prohibited punishment must qualify as both.

- **Or:** A related provision of the Michigan Constitution prohibits "cruel *or* unusual punishment" which means it prohibits punishment that qualifies as either one or the other (or both).

Michigan courts have found that this one-word difference provides defendants with greater protection under the Michigan Constitution than the U.S. Constitution, opening the door to release for hundreds of previously life-sentenced prisoners. Based on Michigan's unique history of promoting rehabilitation, the Michigan Constitution also requires Michigan courts to consider whether the sentence promotes a meaningful opportunity for rehabilitation, a factor the 8th Amendment doesn't require.

Key differences exist between the U.S. Constitution and other democratic countries' constitutions:

- **Leadership:** The U.S. Constitution creates a presidential system, while some other countries (such as England and Canada) have a parliamentary system.

  In a *parliamentary system,* the citizens don't elect the chief executive (usually a Prime Minister), but rather the legislative majority selects one of its members to hold that position.

- **Rights:** The U.S. Constitution creates *negative rights* (rights to be free from government interference), whereas some other countries' constitutions (such as Spain's and South Africa's) create *positive rights,* such as rights to healthcare and education.

- **Length:** The U.S. Constitution is short, laying out broad, fundamental principles, whereas some other countries' constitutions (such as Mexico's) are much longer, more detailed, and specific.

- **Consolidation:** The U.S. Constitution is a single, comprehensive document, whereas some other countries' constitutions (such as England's) are derived from statutes, common law, history, and tradition.

Zeroing In on Articles I through VII

The Framers set up an entire new government in only seven articles. In the first three articles of the Constitution, the Framers established the legislative, executive, and judicial branches, including provisions to protect each branch from the others. The fourth article prescribes states' relationships to each other and to the federal government. And the final three articles establish the federal government as the supreme law of the land.

Congress is sometimes referred to as the first branch of government. Not only does it appear first in the Constitution, but to the Framers, the idea of a government by the people through their elected representatives was one of the Constitution's primary defining features.

Setting the legislature with Article I

The longest and most detailed of the three government-establishing provisions (which also include Article II and Article III), Article I creates a bicameral legislature that consists of the Senate and the House of Representatives as the result of the Great Compromise, which resolved the dispute between large and small states about representation. (We discuss the Great Compromise in Chapter 5.) Article I

>> Establishes equal representation in the Senate and proportionate representation based on population in the House of Representatives.

>> Provides that Congress can override a presidential veto with a two-thirds vote.

>> Limits congressional power to those powers expressly granted by the Constitution. (In Chapter 5, you can see how the Court has interpreted Article I to grant Congress the authority to carry out its enumerated powers.)

The Framers couldn't resolve the slavery dispute, so they compromised. Article I, Section 9, Clause 1 prohibited the federal government from limiting the importation of slaves before 1808. And Article I, Section 2 counted slaves as three-fifths of a person for purposes of taxation and representation. Both provisions became obsolete when the 13th Amendment was ratified in 1865.

Using Article II to outline the presidency

Article II lays out the rules for the executive branch. It includes the following topics:

>> Four-year terms for both the president and vice-president

>> The electoral college (later modified by the 12th Amendment, which you can read about in Chapter 17)

>> The line of succession to the presidency (later modified by the 25th Amendment, discussed in the section "Policy and Process Amendments," later in this chapter)

>> The minimum qualifications to serve as president

Before a president begins their term of office, they have to swear or affirm to the oath in Article II, Section 1, Clause 8, that they will "faithfully execute the Office of President of the United States, and will to the best of [their] Ability, preserve, protect and defend the Constitution of the United States."

Anyone who wants to serve as U.S. president must meet these three minimum qualifications. They must be a U.S. citizen by birth, at least 35 years old, and a U.S. resident for at least 14 years.

Article II grants broad powers to the president, including:

>> Designating the president as commander-in-chief of the military

>> Giving the president the power to pardon people convicted of criminal offenses

>> Enabling the president to require written opinions from department heads on any subject related to their duties

>> Negotiating treaties (subject to Senate approval)

>> Nominating ambassadors and judges (subject to Senate confirmation)

According to Article II, the president can appoint Supreme Court and federal judges, ambassadors, cabinet secretaries, and department heads, but only if they have the advice and consent of the Senate. Article II also provides that a majority of the House is required to impeach and two-thirds of the Senate is required to convict and remove the president (and others) from office for high crimes and misdemeanors, as we discuss in Chapter 6.

PARDON ME!

A full presidential pardon eliminates a person's conviction and sentence, effectively erasing their crime, like it never happened. Presidents also have the power to commute a person's sentence while leaving their criminal conviction in place. The pardon power is extremely broad, but the constitutional text builds in two limitations:

- A president can pardon only federal crimes; state and local convictions and civil penalties are outside the pardon power's reach.

- The president can't use their pardon power in cases of impeachment.

The presidential pardon and clemency powers promote two main objectives. They

- Serve as a check on the judiciary by providing a mechanism to relieve individuals from unjust criminal consequences.

- Provide an opportunity for mercy and national healing (like President Lincoln's grant of clemency for Confederate soldiers after the Civil War).

Establishing the courts with Article III

Article III establishes the judicial branch of the federal government. This article

- Creates a Supreme Court.

- Gives Congress the power to establish *inferior* (lower) federal courts.

- Specifies that federal judges "shall hold their Offices during good Behaviour" and prohibits Congress from reducing their pay during their time of service.

  We discuss the term *good behavior* in Chapter 7. In general, it means that federal judges serve for life, unless they're impeached and convicted.

- Lays out the Supreme Court's and lower-federal courts' jurisdiction.

- Gives anyone prosecuted for crimes other than impeachment the right to a jury trial.

- Defines *treason* as levying war against the United States or providing aid and comfort to its enemies.

Structuring the government in Article IV

Article IV describes the terms of the federalist structure of government, defining the relationship between the federal government and the states, as well as the states' relationship with each other. It

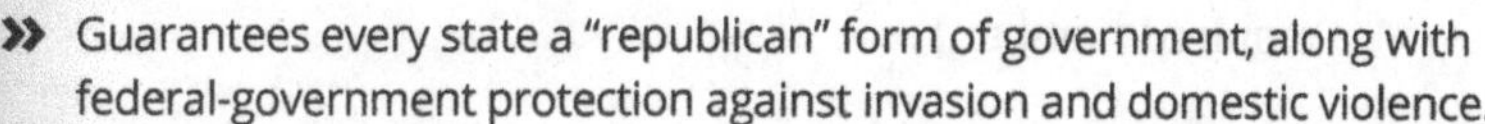

> » Requires states to recognize and honor (give "full faith and credit") to acts, records, and judicial proceedings of other states.

> » Guarantees that the citizens of any state enjoy the privileges and immunities of other states, allowing them to travel without fear of being discriminated against because they're citizens of a different state.

> » Requires states to extradite upon demand fugitives who committed crimes in other states.

REMEMBER

> Article IV includes the Fugitive Slave Clause, which required that states return escaped slaves to their slave owners; the 13th Amendment, which abolished slavery, made this clause obsolete.

> » Guarantees every state a "republican" form of government, along with federal-government protection against invasion and domestic violence.

TIP

> *Republican* in this context means *representative.* It has nothing to do with political parties, which didn't exist at the time the Constitution was drafted.

Amending the Constitution in Article V

Article V sets forth the amendment process for the Constitution. The Framers intentionally made it difficult to amend the Constitution in order to promote stability and continuity in the government and prevent frequent politically motivated changes.

Either two-thirds of both houses of Congress or a constitutional convention called for by two-thirds of state legislatures can propose an amendment. Then, either three-fourths of state legislatures or conventions in three-fourths of the states have to ratify the proposed amendment. Article V also prevents anyone from using the amendment process to deny a state's equal representation in the Senate.

Establishing national supremacy with Article VI

Article VI makes the following declarations:

>> The United States will honor agreements and obligations that existed under the Articles of Confederation, before the U.S. enacted the Constitution.

>> The federal government has supremacy over state governments.

>> Congress, state legislators, and federal and state executive officers and judges have to take an oath to uphold the Constitution.

Using Article VII for ratification

Article VII provides that the Constitution will become effective upon ratification by nine states. (Chapter 1 describes how the Framers settled on nine as the required number.)

Securing Freedom with the Bill of Rights

The Bill of Rights is the second main component of the Constitution, after the first seven articles (discussed in the section "Zeroing In on Articles I through VII," earlier in this chapter). In Chapter 1, we discuss the Massachusetts Compromise and describe how the Bill of Rights became part of the Constitution in 1791. In the following sections, we give a brief overview of the individual rights secured by the first ten amendments, divided in three categories:

>> Establish civil rights

>> Protect individuals suspected of or charged with crimes

>> Reinforce the Framers' core belief that states and individuals retain all other rights not mentioned by the Constitution unless expressly prohibited

The Bill of Rights applies to state governments, in addition to the federal government it initially sought to constrain, through *selective incorporation* (applying individual Bill of Rights protections to the states on a case-by-case basis), which relies on the 14th Amendment's requirement that states not deprive persons of liberty without due process (ratified in 1868; see the section "Expanding Freedom through Post–Civil War Amendments ," later in this chapter).

Establishing civil rights

Several amendments in the Bill of Rights focus specifically on the civil rights of individuals; for example

>> **Individual freedoms:** The 1st Amendment prohibits laws that establish a religion, prevent the free exercise of religion, restrict freedom of speech or of the press, or impair the right to peaceful assembly.

>> **Keep and bear arms:** The 2nd Amendment protects the right of the people to possess and carry weapons.

>> **Freedom from forced housing:** The 3rd Amendment protects individuals from the government forcing them to house soldiers.

>> **Due process of law:** The 5th Amendment prohibits government from depriving people of life, liberty, or property without due process of law, and prohibits taking private property for public use without just compensation.

>> **Jury trials:** The 7th Amendment protects a defendant's right to jury trial in civil cases.

Protecting criminal suspects, defendants, and prisoners

The Bill of Rights includes amendments designed to make sure individuals receive fair treatment in criminal matters:

>> **Restricted policing:** The 4th Amendment prohibits unreasonable searches and seizures and requires probable cause for search warrants.

>> **Trial protections:** The 5th Amendment requires grand-jury indictments for federal felonies, grants a privilege against self-incrimination, and prohibits prosecutors from retrying a defendant more than once for the same offense.

>> **Trial rights:** The 6th Amendment provides that criminal defendants have the right to a jury trial, that criminal trials must be speedy and public, and that defendants have rights to counsel, to be informed of the charges against them, and to confront witnesses.

>> **Punishment:** The 8th Amendment prohibits cruel and unusual punishment.

Preserving all other natural and state's rights

The last two amendments in the Bill of Rights lay out

>> **The people's rights:** The 9th Amendment provides that the absence of certain rights of the people from the Constitution doesn't mean the people don't have those rights.

>> **States' rights:** The 10th Amendment provides that the states retain any powers that the Constitution doesn't give to the federal government or prohibit to the states.

People sometimes mistakenly accuse state government officials of violating the Bill of Rights. For example, if a state or local police officer searches a house without a warrant, they might be challenged for violating the resident's 4th Amendment right to be free from unlawful search and seizure. But technically, non-federal police can't violate the 4th Amendment because the Bill of Rights applies only to the federal government, not state governments or their agents.

Expanding Freedom through Post–Civil War Amendments

For all the ground that the first two parts of the Constitution covered, Articles I through VII (see the section "Zeroing In on Articles I through VII," earlier in this chapter) and the Bill of Rights (discussed in the section "Securing Freedom with the Bill of Rights," earlier in this chapter) didn't resolve the bitter political dispute between proponents of slavery and abolitionists. Residents of Southern states relied on slavery to support their agriculture-based economy, while those residing in the more industrial-based Northern states largely opposed slavery on moral grounds.

During the Reconstruction Era (the period between 1865 and 1877), the federal government focused its attention on fixing the injustices that led to the Civil War (1861–1865). To rejoin the Union, Confederate states had to agree to certain conditions.

>> Rewrite their state constitutions at constitutional conventions in which all men could participate.

>> Ratify the 14th Amendment (flip to the section "Granting rights with the 14th Amendment," later in this chapter).

Ending slavery with the 13th Amendment

The 13th Amendment bans slavery, stating: "Neither slavery nor involuntary servitude, except as a punishment for crime whereof the party shall have been duly convicted, shall exist within the United States, or any place subject to their jurisdiction." On December 6, 1865, Georgia became the 27th state to ratify the 13th Amendment, giving it the necessary votes to become the law of the land.

TIP

Nearly 4 million slaves became legally free with the passage of the 13th Amendment, which prohibits private parties, as well as the government, from owning slaves. It's the only constitutional provision that directly proscribes private conduct.

Granting rights with the 14th Amendment

The 14th Amendment was ratified in 1868, three years after the end of the Civil War. This amendment includes specific provisions focused on reunifying the country after the Civil War and broad provisions designed to root out state-sponsored discrimination.

Diving into the 14th Amendment's Section 1

Section 1 of the 14th Amendment provides for birthright citizenship, protects privileges and immunities, and prevents states from denying due process and equal protection. Here's a breakdown of this section:

>> **The Birthright Citizenship Clause:** States, "All persons born or naturalized in the United States, and subject to the jurisdiction thereof, are citizens of the United States and of the State wherein they reside."

This clause ensured that everyone born on American soil qualified as an American citizen. Although the provision was designed to grant citizenship to former slaves, its broad language has been applied to anyone born in the country, including the children of undocumented immigrants.

The Supreme Court is expected to decide *Trump v. Barbara* in 2026, after we finish writing this book. *Trump v. Barbara* raises a question about the constitutionality of President Trump's executive order limiting birthright citizenship depending on the immigration status of the baby's parents. To see whether the Supreme Court has reached a decision, check out the Court's website at www.supremecourt.gov.

>> **The Privileges and Immunities Clause:** "No state shall make or enforce any law which shall abridge the privileges or immunities of citizens of the United States."

This clause prevents states from interfering with the rights that come along with United States citizenship.

>> **The Due Process Clause:** "[N]or shall any State deprive any person of life, liberty, or property, without due process of law."

The Due Process Clause provides three main protections (discussed in more detail in Chapters 13 and 14):

- *Procedural due process:* States must use fair processes before depriving individuals of life, liberty, or property. Generally, *fair processes* involve notice, a hearing, and a neutral decision maker.

- *Substantive due process:* States can't deprive individuals of liberty or property without legally sufficient justification.

- *Selective incorporation:* As noted in the section "Securing Freedom with the Bill of Rights," earlier in this chapter, the Supreme Court has found that almost all the provisions in the Bill of Rights apply to the states through the Due Process Clause.

>> **The Equal Protection Clause:** No state can "deny any person within its jurisdiction the equal protection of the laws."

Although the constitutional text refers only to states denying equal protection, the Supreme Court has held that the federal government must also provide equal protection because it's implied in the 5th Amendment Due Process Clause.

Covering Sections 2 through 5 of the 14th Amendment

Although Section 1 of the 14th Amendment tends to get all the attention (see the preceding section), the other sections contain important post–Civil War provisions:

>> **Section 2:** Fully counts all persons for purposes of representation, eliminating the three-fifths provision (see the section "Setting the legislature with Article I," earlier in this chapter), and penalizes voting discrimination by proportionately reducing representation.

The 15th Amendment, which you can read about in the following section, and later voting-rights laws have made Section 2 mostly obsolete, except to the extent it allows states to deny the right to vote to people who participate in crimes.

>> **Section 3:** Disallows holding public office to people who have engaged in insurrection or rebellion against the United States or given aid or comfort to its enemies (unless a two-thirds vote of Congress allows it).

>> **Section 4:** Reaffirms the government's commitment to honor obligations incurred during war, except those in aid of insurrection or rebellion, and disallows any claims for the loss or emancipation of slaves.

>> **Section 5:** Grants Congress enforcement power.

Securing the right to vote with the 15th Amendment

The 15th Amendment was the last of the Reconstruction–era amendments. Ratified in 1870, it states, "The right of citizens of the United States to vote shall not be denied or abridged by the United States or by any State on account of race, color, or previous condition of servitude." Its original purpose was to guarantee that freed slaves wouldn't face voting discrimination, but its enforcement provision led Congress to enact sweeping voting rights legislation in 1965 to ensure that government didn't infringe on the right to vote based on race.

A state, for example, violates the 15th Amendment when it imposes burdensome procedural requirements that impede Black voters in exercising their right to vote.

During the immediate post–Civil War era, Congress passed strong legislation to address both public and private discrimination, but the Court often limited Congress's powers. However, in 1968, in *Jones v. Alfred H. Mayer Co.*, the Court found that Congress had authority to enact a law prohibiting private persons from discriminating based on race in the sale or rental of property.

The law and the Court were slow to work against discrimination after the Civil War. For example, in 1896, in the case *Plessy v. Ferguson*, the Supreme Court held that racial segregation in trains didn't violate the Constitution if the segregated facilities were "separate but equal" (which they really weren't!). But times changed, and in the 1954 decision in *Brown v. Board of Education*, the Court held that segregation in public schools violated the 14th Amendment.

Using Amendments to Expand Voting Rights

Amendments that affect voting rights make up an important piece of the Constitution. Five amendments ratified between 1913 and 1971 expand classes of voters and remove obstacles to voting:

REMEMBER

>> **Election of senators:** The 17th Amendment, ratified in 1913, gave the people the power to elect senators. Article I, Section 3 of the Constitution (see the section "Setting the legislature with Article I," earlier in this chapter) provided for state legislatures to choose senators.

Members of the House of Representatives have always been elected by voters, as set forth in Article I, Section 2.

>> **Women's voting rights:** The 19th Amendment, ratified in 1920, gave women the right to vote. First introduced in 1878, it took decades of marches, protests, and legal challenges before final ratification.

>> **Rights for D.C. voters:** The 23rd Amendment, ratified in 1961, expanded voting rights for residents of Washington, the District of Columbia (Washington, D.C.), but specified that the District could have no more electors than the least populous state.

- » **Poll taxes:** The 24th Amendment, ratified in 1964, outlawed *poll taxes,* fees that some states required you to pay before you could cast your vote. This practice was discriminatory because, after the Civil War, Black people were disproportionately poor.

- » **Voting age:** The 26th Amendment, ratified in 1971, lowered the voting age to 18. The 14th Amendment had previously used the age of 21 as a benchmark for certain voting procedures.

Policy and Process Amendments

The category of amendments that we discuss in this section serve to clarify, correct, and explain government structures, processes, and dynamics:

- » **The 11th Amendment:** Ratified in 1795, establishes state sovereign immunity by prohibiting citizens from suing states in federal court.

- » **The 12th Amendment:** Ratified in 1804, requires electors to separately vote for president and vice president, and makes other changes to the electoral college.

- » **The 16th Amendment:** Ratified in 1913, grants Congress the power to impose and collect income tax.

- » **The 18th Amendment:** Ratified in 1919, prohibits the manufacture, sale, or transportation of liquor. (This amendment was later repealed by the 21st Amendment.)

- » **The 20th Amendment:** Ratified in 1933, establishes January 20 as the beginning and end of the presidential term.

- » **The 21st Amendment:** Ratified in 1933, repeals the 18th Amendment, ending Prohibition.

- » **The 22nd Amendment:** Ratified in 1951, limits presidents to serving two terms.

- » **The 25th Amendment:** Ratified in 1967, sets forth procedures for when a president can't discharge their duties and establishes a presidential line of succession.

- » **The 27th Amendment:** Ratified in 1992, prohibits members of Congress from raising their salaries until after the next election for the House of Representatives.

Seeing How the Different Parts of the Constitution Interact

Various parts of the Constitution often work together to achieve (or attempt to achieve) a just and fair democracy. For example, suppose a state government agency refuses to hire people from a particular political party. This problem implicates several parts of the Constitution:

>> **The Bill of Rights:** A person challenging the policy would likely claim it violates their 1st Amendment rights to express their political views freely. (We talk about the Bill of Rights in the section "Securing Freedom with the Bill of Rights," earlier in this chapter.)

>> **Article III:** The situation raises a constitutional question, so federal courts have jurisdiction, as Article III addresses (see the section "Establishing the courts with Article III," earlier in this chapter).

>> **Article VI:** This article (discussed in the section "Establishing national supremacy with Article VI," earlier in this chapter) maintains that states are responsible for enforcing the principles of the supreme U.S. Constitution.

>> **The post–Civil War amendments:** The 14th Amendment Due Process Clause (which you can read about in the section "Diving into the 14th Amendment's Section 1," earlier in this chapter) makes the 1st Amendment applicable to state governments.

But sometimes, the various parts of the Constitution clash. This can happen, for example, when a problem arises with one part of the Constitution, but another part (usually the power-granting or power-limiting provisions in the Articles) interferes with the government's ability to solve the problem. It can also happen when different parts of the Constitution conflict with each other when applied to a particular problem.

Trump v. Casa, 2025

President Trump issued an executive order limiting birthright citizenship by excluding certain people based on their parents' immigration status. Plaintiffs in three states filed lawsuits challenging the executive order. All three federal district courts granted *universal injunctions* that operated as nationwide bans on enforcing the order. The government challenged the universal injunctions, arguing that federal district courts lack the authority to impose nationwide bans not necessary to protect the parties in the lawsuits before them.

The Supreme Court agreed that the courts lacked authority, based on the extent of remedial powers that Congress (Article I) gave to federal courts (Article III).

The Court didn't decide whether the executive order on birthright citizenship was constitutional, but it's poised to issue this ruling in 2026. (If you want to find out about the Supreme Court's latest decisions, go to its website at www.supreme court.gov.)

The question of the constitutionality of the executive order provides an especially clear example of clashing constitutional provisions:

>> **Post–Civil War Amendments:** The underlying question is whether the executive order violates the 14th Amendment Birthright Citizenship Clause.

>> **Articles I through VII:** Presents questions about the authority of the president (Article II) to issue executive orders; the way in which Congress (Article I) has defined citizenship; and the courts' Article III authority to invalidate executive orders.

>> **Bill of Rights:** The underlying case implicates the 5th Amendment Due Process Clause (discussed in the section "Establishing civil rights," earlier in this chapter), raising questions about both procedural and substantive due process.

Bush v. Gore, 2000

The 2000 presidential election was extremely close, coming down to the votes in Florida. Under Florida election law, the state conducted a mandatory machine recount. Disputes arose between counties and precincts about how to count votes on punch–card paper ballots where the voter did not punch the card in a clean, complete manner, leaving the voter's intent ambiguous.

The Florida Supreme Court ordered selective hand recounts, but Bush successfully petitioned the U.S. Supreme Court to intervene and stop the recounts:

>> **Articles I through VII:** The case raised the question of whether the Florida Supreme Court's recount order created a new election law in violation of Article II, Section 1 (see the section "Using Article II to outline the presidency," earlier in this chapter), which gives that power to the state legislature.

>> **Post–Civil War Amendments:** The Court held that the Florida Supreme Court's recount order violated the 14th Amendment Equal Protection Clause because the inconsistencies in counting disputed ballots statewide would result in arbitrary line drawing that valued one person's vote more than another.

The Supreme Court determined that no fair recount could be conducted by the deadline when the state sought to certify its electors. George Bush's victory in Court meant that he would be the next president.

United States v. Nixon, 1974

Several members of President Nixon's White House staff were indicted on charges arising out of a burglary of the Democratic Party headquarters in the Watergate building. A special prosecutor subpoenaed recordings and documents from President Nixon about his meetings with some of the indicted staff members. President Nixon sought to quash the subpoena, claiming an absolute executive privilege to withhold records relating to confidential communications with his aides.

The Supreme Court held the executive privilege was limited and didn't protect the items at issue from being reviewed by a judge and potentially used at trial:

>> **Articles I through VII:** The Court rejected President Nixon's argument that Article II gives the president an absolute executive privilege. When balanced against the need for evidence in a criminal trial, the privilege extends only so far as to protect military, diplomatic, or sensitive national security interests. An absolute privilege, the Court held, would interfere with the role of the courts under Article III.

>> **Bill of Rights:** The Court balanced the executive privilege against the indicted staff members' 6th Amendment right to a fair trial and 5th Amendment right to due process, finding that those rights outweighed the executive privilege in this case.

Chapter **3**

Resolving Key Dilemmas with the U.S. Constitution

The Constitution is multidimensional. It defines the federal government's relationship with the states, foreign governments, and the people. It establishes a system of meaningful checks and balances within the federal government itself, delegating powers and setting limits on the three branches of government. And it ensures that the minority can't be drowned out in a system based on majority rule.

In this chapter, we look at seven main issues that the Constitution seeks to resolve. Each of the issues that we discuss in this chapter focuses on the tensions and conflicts that the Constitution strives to reconcile. If you read through this list of dilemmas, you may notice an interesting pattern: The Constitution often tries to strike a fair balance between competing interests, rather than subjugating one to the other.

Balancing Individual Liberty Against Societal Priorities

In Chapter 1, you can read about how Magna Carta and the Enlightenment contributed to the Constitution's basic premises that government exists to serve the people and that the people have certain universal human rights that the government can't take away. However, those rights aren't absolute; a government that functions for the benefit of the majority of its people must inevitably infringe on the rights of some.

This simple example illustrates this point: The Constitution prohibits the government from arbitrarily depriving individuals of liberty. But people accept the government's right to imprison people convicted of violent crimes because the convicted person's right to remain free must give way to the government's important role in protecting public safety.

Courts apply various tests to ensure that the government doesn't needlessly infringe on individual rights. These tests vary, depending on the individual right and government interest at stake, but they often involve weighing factors such as

» The severity of the infringement

» The importance of the societal interest that the government is seeking to advance

» Whether the government minimized the intrusion as much as it could under the circumstances

For example:

» Criminalizing speech that calls for unlawful action violates a person's 1st Amendment rights unless the speech is

- Directed to incite or produce imminent lawless action

- Likely to incite or produce such action

» The government can take private property for a public purpose under the 5th Amendment, but it must pay just compensation.

» When a law treats people differently based on their race, national origin, or ethnicity, it violates the 14th Amendment Equal Protection Clause, unless the law is narrowly tailored to serve a compelling government interest. For example, in *Loving v. Virginia*, the Supreme Court struck down a Virginia law prohibiting interracial marriage. The government asserted the law wasn't discriminatory because it applied to people of all races, but the Supreme Court found the law served no compelling government interest.

>> Under the 4th Amendment, police need a warrant to stop and search individuals, but an exception applies when the police have a reasonable suspicion that a person is armed and dangerous.

>> Criminal defendants have various 6th Amendment trial rights, but courts can decide not to reverse a conviction if they find that some type of error occurred during the trial but it was harmless beyond a reasonable doubt. If the Constitution required reversal for every mistake, cases would drag on and clog the system, preventing other litigants from getting their day in court.

Don't assume that courts always engage in this type of balancing when government action interferes with individual rights. The Constitution prohibits this type of balancing in certain cases. For example, the test for whether

>> A law violates the 2nd Amendment right to bear arms doesn't turn on the seriousness of the violation or the importance of the societal interest at stake, but rather on whether the law has an historical counterpart

>> Admitting a statement in a criminal trial violates the Confrontation Clause doesn't turn on the seriousness of the violation or the importance of the state interest, but whether the statement is testimonial

Empowering the Majority while Protecting the Minority

The Constitution establishes a system of majority rule. A majority of the electorate choose congressional representatives. Those representatives, in turn, vote on legislation that (with some exceptions) generally passes or fails based on a majority vote. But even in a system that favors the majority, protecting minority rights is essential to democracy. Without certain built-in safeguards, a winning party could simply vote a losing party out of existence.

Protecting minority rights is generally considered vital to preserving democracy, but some alternatives to majority rule can undermine democratic principles. For example, many people say that the electoral college undermines majority rule because it sometimes enables candidates who lose the popular vote to become president.

In certain situations, the Constitution protects minority rights or otherwise provides for a check on the majority. Some examples include:

>> **Amending the Constitution:** Amendments require two-thirds of the states to propose a constitutional convention, or a two-thirds vote of both houses of Congress to propose an amendment, plus three-fourths of the states voting to ratify. (Discussed in Chapter 2.)

>> **Senate representation:** By providing for every state to have the same number of senators (see Chapter 2), the Constitution balances the population-based representation in the House of Representatives and ensures that small states will be fairly represented in Congress, even though their citizens make up a small minority of the population.

>> **Convicting an officeholder of an impeachable offense:** Convictions require a two-thirds vote of the Senate on Articles of Impeachment passed by a majority of the House of Representatives. The supermajority requirement serves to prevent lawmakers from abusing the impeachment power and removing officeholders for political purposes. (You can read more about impeachment in Chapter 6.)

>> **Judicial review:** The Constitution enables a life-tenured judiciary to declare legislation unconstitutional, even when a majority vote passed the law. (Chapter 7 talks about judicial tenure.)

>> **Constitutional protection for certain rights:** Enshrining certain protections against government action into various parts of the Constitution without regard for majority approval (such as due process, equal protection, property rights, voting rights, and rights for criminal suspects and defendants) prevents the majority from trampling over important civil liberties.

Distinguishing Private from Public Action

The Constitution regulates government conduct, not private conduct (except for the 13th Amendment, which prohibits slavery or involuntary servitude by public or private actors). The State Action doctrine comes from the 14th Amendment's language that "no state shall deny equal protection or due process of law to any person." Under the State Action doctrine, for a party to establish a violation of their constitutional rights, they must show that a government official or employee — or, in exceptional cases, a private person sufficiently connected to the government — committed this violation.

Despite its name, the State Action doctrine applies to all federal, state, and local government officials and agencies.

The State Action doctrine clearly applies when elected officials, police officers, public-school employees, or prison officials acting within their official capacity commit acts allegedly violating the Constitution. But in other cases, the line isn't so clear. In one case, for example, a security guard who was working in his private capacity removed four people from an amusement park and arrested them based on the park's policy of excluding Black people. In it's 1964 decision in *Griffin v. Maryland*, the Court held the guard's actions violated the individuals' 14th Amendment right to equal protection because he was also employed as a deputy sheriff, so he possessed state-granted powers that he used to enforce a private policy of racial discrimination.

STATE ACTION THROUGH SOCIAL MEDIA

The widespread use of social media raises complicated questions about the interplay between state action and the 1st Amendment. In 2024, in *Lindke v. Freed*, a city manager blocked a Facebook user from his personal account after the user posted comments that the city manager didn't like. The Facebook user sued the city manager for violating their 1st Amendment rights.

The Court held a person's status as a public official doesn't mean that all their social media activity amounts to state action. Just as private parties can act with the authority of the state (such as the private-security guard discussed in the section "Distinguishing Private from Public Action," in this chapter), state officials can act as private citizens. Government officials have private lives and their own 1st Amendment rights.

The state-action determination involves a fact-specific inquiry. A government official's social media use constitutes state action only if the official both

- Possesses actual authority to speak on the state's behalf

- Purports to exercise that authority when they speak on social media

The Court emphasized the importance of the first prong, stating that the person must have actual authority to act on the government's behalf; it's not enough that the person appears to have authority. The Constitution's bedrock principle (that conduct must be attributable to the state to constitute state action) means that you must be able to trace the person's authority to the state through a statute, ordinance, custom, regulation, or usage.

Balancing States' Rights and Federal Authority

Strong state governments allow for choice, diversity, and experimentation in government policy, and they provide a necessary check on federal government power. But unchecked state power can obstruct national agendas, erode civil liberties, and create interstate conflict. The Constitution created a federalistic system, preserving the states as independent governments while creating a strong federal government empowered to handle matters of national and international concern. Still, inevitably, power disputes arise.

Courts resolve these disputes through various constitutional provisions, legal doctrines, and rules that have been developed to both protect and limit each government sphere. For example:

>> **Limiting federal powers:** Federal government powers are limited to those enumerated in the Constitution and those necessary and proper to carry them out; all others are reserved to the states (and the people).

>> **Relying on the Constitution:** It's the supreme law of the land, and federal laws preempt inconsistent state laws (but states are free to regulate matters left open by federal law).

>> **Letting the feds handle commerce:** The Commerce Clause grants broad power to the federal government, and the Dormant Commerce Clause doctrine (described in Chapter 9) prevents states from passing laws that undermine interstate commerce.

>> **Giving states a choice:** The federal government can't coerce state governments to enforce federal laws, but it can give them a meaningful choice to participate or decline in federal programs.

The tug-of-war between federal and state power is often heightened in disputes over issues that affect people's everyday lives, such as healthcare, immigration, and abortion. Recent examples include high-profile disputes about whether state officials can arrest federal-immigration officers for violations of state law while performing official federal duties and litigation over whether doctors can or must perform life-saving abortions when federal and state laws conflict over the legality of such abortions.

Balancing Executive, Legislative, and Judicial Power

In 1788, Founding Father James Madison wrote that the accumulation of legislative, executive, and judicial power in the same hands was "the very definition of tyranny." The Framers considered it critical to create three separate branches of government, and they developed a carefully interwoven set of checks and balances to curtail the abuse of power by any one of them. Table 3-1 outlines some of the ways that the powers and limits of the three branches of government interact.

TABLE 3-1   **Powers of the Branches of Government**

Power	Legislative	Executive	Judicial
Impeachment	Has the power to impeach but limited to removing and disqualifying public officials	Can't pardon impeached officials	Can convict impeached officials for criminal offenses Federal judges hold office for life but can be impeached and removed by the legislature
Passing laws	Has the power to pass laws and override a presidential veto with a two-thirds vote	The president can veto a law	Can declare a law unconstitutional
Treaties	Must approve treaties by a two-thirds vote	Has the power to make treaties	Can invalidate treaties to the extent they interfere with U.S. citizens' rights
Appointments	Gives advice and consent to the president	Can appoint ambassadors, federal judges, and U.S. officers	Can invalidate unconstitutional or unlawful appointments
Treason	Decides punishment for treason	Investigates and prosecutes treason	Can convict someone of treason
Federal crimes	Passes criminal laws	President has pardon powers	Can convict someone of federal crimes

Honoring the separation of powers was the Court's primary concern in the 2024 case *Trump v. United States*, when it set forth a new framework for deciding whether former presidents have immunity for crimes committed while in office. (It was a new framework because it was a new problem — it was the first time a former president had been indicted for crimes allegedly committed while in office.)

After his first term, President Trump was indicted on four federal charges alleging that, while still in office, he acted in various ways to overturn the results of the 2020 election. He claimed that he had absolute immunity for acts committed while in office; the government argued that presidents have no immunity for criminal acts.

The Supreme Court rejected both arguments. It held that presidents have absolute immunity for conduct within their "conclusive and preclusive" powers (apparently referring to the president's exclusive powers under Article II of the Constitution; see Chapter 6) and presumptive immunity for all official acts. They don't have immunity for unofficial acts. The Court emphasized the importance of ensuring that potential threats from the judicial branch (in the form of criminal prosecutions) or the legislative branch (in the form of laws that criminalize actions within the president's power) don't deter presidents from performing their duties.

The Supreme Court sent the case back to the District Court to make findings about whether President Trump's actions were official or unofficial. But that District Court hearing didn't happen; the prosecutor dismissed the case after President Trump won the 2024 general election based on a Department of Justice policy not to prosecute sitting presidents. So, at the time of this writing, the Court hasn't provided clarity on the difference between official and unofficial acts.

Balancing Constitutional Change and Stability

How long should the Constitution last? The Framers debated this controversial question, disagreeing about whether the Constitution should have a built-in expiration date or continue indefinitely. The debate raised questions on many fronts: philosophical, moral, political, and practical. The writings of two Framers present very different perspectives:

>> **Thomas Jefferson's writings:** Pondered whether a generation has a right to bind future generations. He famously believed that the earth belongs to the living and the Constitution should last only as long as a generation.

>> **James Madison's writings:** Show his contrary belief that the government needs a lasting constitution to protect rights and ensure that states can't erode individual liberties.

Madison's view carried the day. More than two centuries later, the Constitution is still the supreme law of the land.

Notably, changes to the Constitution have been few and far between — to date, only 27 amendments. The first ten, the Bill of Rights, were adopted at the same time in 1791. The 27th Amendment (limiting Congress's right to raise its members' salaries) was the latest to pass in 1992. (Turn to Chapter 2 for information about all the Constitution's amendments.)

Article V (also discussed in Chapter 2) makes amending the Constitution difficult but not impossible. Amendments require a two-step process:

>> **Proposals:** Two-thirds of both houses must propose an amendment or two-thirds of state legislatures must apply for a constitutional convention, in which the proposal gets made.

>> **Ratification:** Three-fourths of state legislatures must ratify or three-fourths of state conventions must ratify.

INTERPRETING OR AMENDING

The Supreme Court resolves controversies involving the Constitution by elucidating, clarifying, analyzing, and explaining constitutional provisions and applying them to the case at hand. This interpretive process is well-established within the Supreme Court's Article III powers (discussed in Chapter 7). But can it go too far? The debate falls into two camps:

- **Originalists:** Argue that when the Supreme Court issues a ruling that goes beyond the Constitution's original meaning, the rule it establishes essentially amounts to a constitutional amendment that didn't go through the proper process. They believe that the Constitution means today what it meant when it was first drafted. It doesn't change with the times.

- **Living constitutionalists:** Believe that the Constitution evolves to reflect a changing society and that formal amendments aren't required for the constitutional meaning to grow and develop.

A person's political party doesn't dictate their philosophy about constitutional interpretation. Whatever the issue and the outcome, the losing side often complains that the judiciary has overstepped its bounds and engaged in judicial activism by amending the Constitution.

Protecting Defendants and Public Safety

The Constitution is mostly hands-off when it comes to criminal law (although it does contain a few references to crimes and punishments, which you can read about in Chapter 6). For the most part, state legislatures decide what conduct qualifies as criminal and how to punish that conduct because protecting citizens is predominantly a state function that falls within the states' police powers.

Criminal laws and punishments reflect the state's unique priorities and law-enforcement concerns. For example, border states may have stricter laws and harsher punishments for drug crimes because they experience a higher rate of drug smuggling, while agricultural states may have more laws related to crimes involving crops and livestock than states that are more industrial.

TIP

The Supreme Court hasn't specifically defined the term *police powers* but generally recognizes that under the 10th Amendment (which provides that powers not delegated to the federal government are *reserved* to the states and the people, meaning the states and people retain those powers), states have broad authority to regulate matters involving public safety, public health, morality, and general welfare. (Flip to Chapter 2 for a breakdown of each amendment.)

Although the Constitution doesn't define most crimes and punishments, it does seek to ensure that criminal processes are fair. The criminal arena really highlights the power disparity between government and individuals, where police officers, prosecutors, and judges hold the power to arrest, imprison, and sometimes even execute people.

Guaranteeing fundamental fairness

The 5th Amendment Due Process Clause (which you can read about in Chapters 13 and 14) prevents the federal government from acting in ways that "shock the conscience" or are "fundamentally unfair." (As you can see in Chapter 2, the 14th Amendment contains a Due Process Clause that applies to the states and prohibits the same type of government misconduct.) Government actions that violate due process include

>> Pumping a person's stomach without their consent to retrieve drugs that they swallowed in order to obtain evidence to prosecute them for drug crimes

>> Failing to disclose to the defense that a key prosecution witness lied about being under a psychiatrist's care

>> Admitting clearly irrelevant evidence about a murder defendant's sexual history, extramarital affairs, and role as a wife and mother

Applying Bill of Rights criminal protections to the states

Using the concept of *selective incorporation* (described in Chapter 2), the Supreme Court has found that most (but not all) of the protections afforded by the Bill of Rights apply to the states through the 14th Amendment Due Process Clause. The following sections provide a brief overview of those rights that come into play when the government investigates, prosecutes, and sentences people for crimes, limiting police officers, prosecutors, and judges who conduct criminal investigations and prosecutions.

REMEMBER

In examining the various protections in the following sections, you may be surprised to see that in many cases, these criminal-procedure protections not only fail to advance the judiciary's truth-seeking function, they seem to undermine it! This is by design, consistent with the core constitutional theme that true justice is achieved by honoring individual rights, even if it comes at a cost to the government's interest in enforcing the law. The Bill of Rights offers protections to people at every stage of a criminal case (which you can read about in Part 5).

Ensuring that searches, seizures, and interrogations are reasonable

The 4th and 5th Amendments are the primary sources of individual rights when law-enforcement agents are gathering evidence during investigations. Both provisions limit permissible investigative activities and punish the government when it breaks the rules:

>> **The 4th Amendment:** Prohibits unreasonable searches and seizures, requiring police to obtain search warrants based on probable cause before searching property or arresting individuals. But it also takes into consideration the government's duty to protect public safety by allowing exceptions to the probable cause and warrant requirements for emergencies and other specific circumstances.

>> **The 5th Amendment:** Grants individuals a privilege against self-incrimination. During investigations, this privilege requires police to advise in-custody suspects of their Miranda rights (discussed in Chapter 19) before questioning them. The 5th Amendment also requires federal prosecutors to obtain grand-jury indictments. (State prosecutors have other options to initiate criminal cases because the grand-jury requirement is one of the few Bill of Rights provisions that doesn't apply to the states.)

When the government obtains evidence through unconstitutional means (such as an unlawful search, seizure, or interrogation), the evidence is *suppressed* (the legal term for excluded) from the criminal trial. This *exclusionary rule* is a remedy intended to deter law enforcement agents from using improper investigative methods.

Providing a wide array of rights for defendants during prosecution and sentencing

The 5th and 6th Amendments offer protection for individuals who are charged with crimes and while they proceed through the criminal process:

>> **The 5th Amendment:** Its Due Process Clause ensures that prosecutions are fundamentally fair. It also prohibits double jeopardy, ensuring that the government can't repeatedly put someone on trial for the same offense.

>> **The 6th Amendment:** Provides a robust set of protections designed to ensure that defendants get a fair trial. A defendant has a right to

- A speedy trial

- A public trial

- A jury trial

- Be informed of the charges against them

- Confront and cross-examine witnesses

- Subpoena witnesses and present a defense (called *compulsory process*)

- The assistance of counsel

>> **The 8th Amendment:** Prohibits cruel and unusual punishment.

Chapter **4**

Interpreting the Constitution

Pick up a copy of the Constitution, read any section, and you may think that it's pretty straightforward. But after you start thinking about how to apply the language to different situations, you may not think the meaning is as clear as you first thought.

You might turn to your own experience and viewpoints (maybe even your biases?) to come up with an interpretation. But most people agree that they want judges and other decision makers to follow guidelines that move them beyond their particular biases. They want principled and consistent decisions about how the Constitution applies to high-stakes questions of government and rights. Not surprisingly, courts, advocates, and scholars have developed broad frames of reference about the proper way to conduct constitutional interpretation. Courts then apply more specific doctrines and tests that seek to yield more coherent constitutional applications over time and over a range of disputes.

This chapter discusses key issues that arise when anyone (whether judges or others) tries to interpret the Constitution and apply it to a current controversy and looks at the full range of people — including a lot of people who aren't judges — who interpret the Constitution. We trace major differences between two main interpretive approaches used to pin down the Constitution's meaning. You can also read about how constitutional interpreters use a variety of doctrines and tests as tools to guide their work.

Seeing Who Interprets the Constitution

Students of the Constitution (including us!) often get so focused on how judges (and especially Supreme Court justices) interpret the Constitution that they may forget that a lot of other non-judicial interpreters are out there.

REMEMBER

For the sake of simplicity, this book typically refers to constitutional interpretations made by courts (rather than regularly adding cumbersome qualifiers such as "or other non-judicial interpreters"). But the job of interpreting America's supreme document doesn't belong exclusively to those who wear black robes.

Federal branches of government

The federal branches of government equal to the Supreme Court — the President, members of Congress, and appointed federal officials (or at least the staff members who advise them) — regularly need to engage in constitutional interpretation. Many of the programs that these officials want to adopt into law raise serious constitutional questions.

Hopefully, federal officials take seriously their oath of office to follow the Constitution. And, even if they don't, they need to decide whether their desired programs can face constitutional objections when they initially propose them or in later challenges in court. For the same reason, a broad range of outside advocates who seek to persuade officials and their staffs to support or oppose various courses of action also need to engage in constitutional analysis.

State government representatives

State governors and legislators, mayors and councilpersons, school-board members, and many other officials — as well as those who advise or advocate before them — need to interpret the Constitution.

Many of these interpretations never get tested in court. And even when someone files a legal challenge, various judicial-restraint doctrines may prevent or delay judicial review of the constitutional interpretations that their non-judicial colleagues relied on. (We cover the most important judicial-restraint doctrines in Chapter 7.)

Practical restraints on the volume (large) and speed (slow) of judicial decisions mean that, for better or worse, the constitutional interpretations of non-judicial officials can stand unchallenged for significant periods of time.

We the people

Citizens of the United States need to interpret the Constitution when they engage in a wide range of civic activities. Political leaders make competing claims about what the Constitution means. Other supporters and opponents of governmental policies dispute the Constitution's import. When Americans decide how to react to these positions — including how to vote on candidates and issues — they do their own constitutional interpretation.

State judges

Not only *federal* judges do the interpretive lifting when it comes to constitutional issues (see the following section for talk about the federal courts). In the Article VI Supremacy Clause of the Constitution (which you can read more about in Chapter 1), the Framers specifically bound state judges to enforce the Constitution in the regular course of their duties.

Typical state civil and criminal proceedings raise constitutional issues; for example, state judges may have to rule during a criminal prosecution whether the police obtained evidence through a search valid under the Constitution (which we discuss in Chapter 19).

And a state supreme court may well interpret the Constitution differently than the highest court in another state.

The special federal judicial (and Supreme Court) role

Inevitably, the constitutional interpretations of federal judges — and, especially, the justices of the U.S. Supreme Court — receive the most attention.

Federal judges have life tenure and other protections that make them less vulnerable to political pressures than their state judicial counterparts, who are subject to initial election or re-election. So, when constitutional-rights advocates can go to either state or federal court, they often choose the life-tenured federal judges. (They may also gravitate to federal court for more practical reasons, such as more favorable procedural rules.)

Law reformers sometimes prefer starting with state courts. State judges have led the way to some important (even landmark) decisions. For example, the first Supreme Court to recognize same-sex *marriage equality* was the Hawaii Supreme Court. In the 1993 decision in *Baehr v. Lewin*, the Aloha State's highest court held that refusal to recognize same-sex marriage violated the Hawaii constitution's right-to-privacy provision. The decision in *Baehr* helped to influence the legislators and state and federal courts when they addressed issues of equality in the United States.

Standing at the top of the judicial hierarchy, the United States Supreme Court is the only court that can adopt constitutional interpretations applicable throughout the nation. Until the U.S. Supreme Court — commonly referred to as *the Court* — nationalizes its take on the Constitution, an interpretation from a particular circuit court applies only to federal courts in the states within that circuit (for example, the U.S. Court of Appeals for the 2nd Circuit applies only in Connecticut, New York, and Vermont); a different Circuit is free to (and often does) adopt a contrary constitutional interpretation binding on federal courts in the states within its jurisdiction. And a state supreme court may well interpret the Constitution differently than the highest court in another state.

Because of its unique ability to render nationwide decisions, the U.S. Supreme Court holds the greatest power among judicial interpreters — even though it decides only several dozen constitutional cases per year.

Facing Difficulty and Uncertainty in Interpretation

Interpreting the U.S. Constitution is a difficult and uncertain enterprise. Lack of an agreed-upon interpretive approach adds to the difficulties. The Constitution has, as has any legal document, ambiguities (words usually have multiple meanings), and the drafters may not be able to foresee future issues or clarify how they intend the document to resolve ambiguities.

Appreciating what makes the task so difficult

Three factors make the U.S. Constitution especially difficult to interpret:

>> **Most U.S. Constitution provisions are very brief and general.** Compared to many more modern state and foreign constitutions, the U.S. Constitution mainly speaks in generalities. In granting powers (such as the presidential power to "faithfully execute the Laws of the United States") and when

imposing limits (such as the First Amendment prohibition on "abridging the Freedom of Speech") the Constitution speaks in especially brief and general language, making it subject to multiple interpretations.

A few constitutional provisions, by contrast, are unusually precise. Elected presidents must be at least 35 years old. And Article I (in Section 7, Clause 2) offers a pocket-veto provision that allows a bill passed by Congress to become law without the president's signature (or veto) if the president doesn't either sign or veto the bill within ten days (Sundays excepted). No one has any big disputes about how to interpret these specific requirements.

» **The Constitution doesn't specify how to interpret it.** Compared to many federal and state statutes, which include guidance about to how to interpret them, the Constitution lacks any such provision.

» **Decades of constitutional decisions reveal ongoing disputes about the proper interpretive method.** Without a clear constitutional signal, many constitutional interpreters have proposed various frames of reference (meaning approaches) to give direction to their task. When it comes to the Constitution, interpretation needs to involve more than just the sum total of individual biases; it should involve a structured process, one that's governed by theories, methodologies, and rules.

The different interpretive approaches seek to produce more coherent interpretations, but they can also point to different results. Many methods have their strong supporters and detractors. For example:

- *Strict construction:* In the name of minimizing the Constitution's intrusion on state authority and private freedom, only those powers and rights that can be found "within the four corners" of the document should be recognized.

- *Representation reinforcement:* In case of doubt, interpreters should choose the constitutional understanding that makes governments more representative of the people's will.

- *Original intent:* What the Framers meant at the time they wrote Constitution, as gleaned from historical records of the time.

- *Evolving Constitution:* Considers changes in society; has led to the expansion of some rights. For example, the Court found a right to abortion as part of an evolving Constitution interpretation in the *Roe v. Wade* decision in 1974. The Court later, in *Dobbs v. Jackson Women's Health Organization* (2022), contracted the right back to the original intent that the Constitution contained no right to abortion.

You can read more about originalism and evolving constitutionalism in the section "Evaluating uncertainty in interpretation approaches," later in this chapter.

Facing uncertainties from a common starting point

All sound constitutional interpretive methods share an obvious starting point: the text of the Constitution. (You can't interpret a document without looking at its words!)

But very few constitutional provisions provide one clear meaning. In the face of uncertain constitutional language, then, any valid interpretive method looks next at whether the framers of the constitutional language at issue left behind specific indicators about how they wanted lawmakers and others to read the text.

TECHNICAL STUFF

Which framers to turn to depends on the when the text under review entered the Constitution:

>> **First constitutional articles:** The Framers of the first seven constitutional articles, ratified in 1789, attended the Constitutional Convention of two years earlier or otherwise influenced the drafting of these specific articles. (We refer to these Framers by using a capital F.)

>> **Bill of Rights:** The framers of the Bill of Rights (the first ten amendments added to the Constitution in 1791) included James Madison and other influential members of Congress.

>> **Civil War–era amendments:** The framers of the 13th, 14th, and 15th Amendments, influential members of Congress, crafted these provisions during the War and in its immediate aftermath.

Other specific amendments had their own distinct framers.

But available sources of specific framer intent often don't provide clear answers either. The framer history may not address the disputed questions in detail. Or the framers may give conflicting signals about their specific intent. For example, the Framers who proposed the Constitution in 1787 expressed varying views in the Federalist Papers about the president's role, in general, and the commander-in-chief power, in particular. Modern justices cite these varying views to support differing answers to presidential-power disputes.

Evaluating uncertainty in interpretation approaches

Interpreters don't have a single agreed-upon approach to constitutional interpretation. That alone creates uncertainty. But to further complicate matters, the two main approaches that contend for dominance in the modern era have very different methods and, often, very different outcomes.

The following sections discuss three key differences between the original-intent approach (called *originalism*) and the evolving-Constitution approach (known as *evolving constitutionalism*), concepts we introduce in the section "Appreciating what makes the task so difficult," earlier in this chapter. Table 4-1 offers a summary of these differences.

TABLE 4-1 **Comparing Originalism and Evolving Constitutionalism**

Approach	Focus	Source(s) Used	View of Constitution's Purpose
Originalism	Framers' original conceptions	Legal and social traditions of the framers' era	Protecting the original intention against majority change
Evolving Constitutionalism	Constitutional provision meaning in the current era	Expanded knowledge related to the subject and current societal consensus on the subject	Keeping the Constitution applicable to societal needs

Defining the interpreter's job

The original-intent and evolving-Constitution approaches define the role of the interpreter differently:

>> **Original intent:** Assumes that the essential job of the interpreter is to identify common framer-era conceptions about governmental powers and individual rights, and then apply those conceptions to the specific constitutional question at hand.

An interpreter who uses the original-intent approach doesn't look for whether the framers anticipated specific technological or social developments. For example, the framers' conceptions about unreasonable searches don't have to predict current technology in order to apply to a police search of a suspect's laptop. Instead, an original-intent interpreter applies how the 1791 concepts about reasonable searches should apply in the specific context of computers.

Evolving Constitution: Rejects the idea that the framers of disputed constitutional language mean to limit interpretation to those framers' original understandings of constitutional powers and limits. The original Framers lived in the Enlightenment era and believed in steady progress in learning and social conditions (which you can read more about in Chapter 1). That fact, along with how the Framers wrote constitutional guarantees in very brief and general terms, leads evolving constitutionalists to conclude that the essential job of the interpreter is to update the framers' intention so that the meaning of constitutional provisions is relevant to the modern era.

For an example of the difference in interpretation approach, flip to the sidebar "Examining the juvenile death-penalty dispute," in this chapter.

Viewing the Constitution's purpose

Originalists and evolving constitutionalists have different perspectives on the role of the Constitution in current government:

>> **Original intent:** Assumes that the basic purpose of the Constitution is to lock in core understandings about governmental powers and individual rights by protecting those powers and rights from change by means short of constitutional amendment.

As we explained in Chapter 1, changing constitutional meaning through constitutional amendment is a difficult process that usually requires super-majority support in the legislature over a substantial period of time.

>> **Evolving Constitution:** Assumes that the Constitution's basic purpose is to establish a framework of powers and rights that future interpreters can continue to update in light of the changing societal consensus and needs. For this reason, some people call evolving constitutionalism the *living constitution method.*

Consulting different sources

When interpreters can't find conclusive text and specific-intent indicators, these two groups turn to different sources to make their determinations:

>> **Original intent:** Historical evidence about the legal and social tradition of the framing era. In part, this approach reflects an assumption that, unless they say otherwise, drafters naturally use language consistent with the traditions in which they lived.

>> **Evolving Constitution:** Current sources that provide insights from expanded knowledge related to the subject (such as data or new discoveries) and the evolving consensus in current society about powers and rights.

EXAMINING THE JUVENILE-DEATH-PENALTY DISPUTE

The U.S. Supreme Court's 2005 decision in *Roper v. Simmons* illustrates the face-off between the original-intent and evolving-Constitution interpretation approaches. *Roper* posed the question of whether the 8th Amendment prohibition on cruel and unusual punishment forbids the execution of a *juvenile offender* (meaning a person who committed their crimes while under the age of 18).

The words "cruel and unusual" that appear in the 8th Amendment of the Constitution are subject to multiple interpretations. As applied to the death penalty, the text could prohibit cruel methods of punishment. Or it could forbid imposing the death penalty on defendants who can't fully appreciate the consequences of their actions — arguably making it cruel to put them to death. A number of different meanings are plausible, and no evidence of specific framer intent exists to help.

To determine the intent of the framers who wrote the Bill of Rights in 1791, the originalists would look to the legal and social traditions about capital punishment in

(continued)

(continued)

that era, which saw a broadly administered death penalty that didn't generally exempt kinds of offenders or worry much about the fairness and proportionality of the death penalty. Applying this tradition to the question in *Roper*, the originalist would find executing juveniles constitutional.

By contrast, the evolving constitutionalist would credit what modern brain science and psychology reveal about the limited moral development and impulse control of juveniles. The approach would also consult what an earlier decision called "the evolving standards of decency" that befit a maturing society.

The result suggested that the evolving-Constitution approach won out in *Roper* — but just barely. By a 5-4 margin, the Supreme Court justices declared the juvenile death penalty unconstitutional.

Still, the dominant approach in other decisions (including the 2nd Amendment gun-rights decisions that we discuss in Chapter 16) searches for and applies the history and tradition of the framing era.

WARNING

Although the original-intent approach more typically correlates with politically conservative outcomes and the evolving-Constitution approach more typically correlates with liberal outcomes, neither method is inherently political. For example, former associate Supreme Court justice Antonin Scalia, a leading proponent of originalism, wrote an important 2005 opinion that favored defendants (generally associated with a liberal outcome) based on the original intent of the 6th Amendment drafters to broadly protect jury-trial rights.

Using Doctrines and Tests to Aid Interpretation

Discussions of constitutional powers and rights reference various tools used to interpret the Constitution, including *doctrines* (meaning a broad framework or set of assumptions to use when faced with a controversy) and *tests* (analytical standards). In the following sections, we explain how some of these doctrines and tests might reduce the uncertainty in constitutional interpretation.

Referring to doctrines of deference

In Chapter 3, we discuss a core assumption of majoritarian democracy — that decision makers who adopt important laws and policies should be politically accountable or trace their authority back to politically accountable officials. Less politically accountable judges (especially life-tenured federal judges who don't face re-election pressures) should refrain from substituting their policy views for those of non-judicial officials; judges should countermand the laws and policy decisions of non-judicial officials only when the Constitution requires that ruling.

Out of this core assumption emerge two kinds of *doctrines of deference:*

>> **General presumption of regularity:** This simple but important principle gives decision makers the benefit of the doubt from the start. This principle requires courts to presume that the laws and policies that decision makers develop are valid, unless specific objections to the contrary persuade them otherwise.

>> **Special deference in particular policy areas:** Special deference doctrines apply in certain policy areas over which the Constitution seems to give officials more than the usual freedom of movement. For example, courts generally give Congress greater slack when it regulates immigration and naturalization. And when presidents act in matters of national security and foreign affairs, special deference norms kick in.

For example, in *Hawaii v. Trump* — an important 2018 presidential-power decision by the Supreme Court that we cover in Chapter 6 — the Court cited this deference doctrine to suggest that President Trump didn't have to face a searching inquiry into the factual bases for his ban on entry into the United States for residents of seven specified countries.

Guiding interpretation with constitutional tests

The U.S. Supreme Court has developed a variety of tests to help answer particular constitutional questions. The following sections discuss the different kinds of tests and how they may help reduce — although certainly not eliminate — interpretive uncertainty.

These tests don't eliminate uncertainty or personal bias. Whenever you use subjective descriptors — for example, *compelling* interests for strict scrutiny versus *important* interests for intermediate scrutiny — reasonable minds (judicial or otherwise) can disagree. But by focusing the relevant inquiry, the guidance that these tests provide can hopefully reduce the unpredictability of constitutional interpretation.

Categorical tests

Some of the tests that the Court developed for specific tasks of constitutional interpretation create two or more categories into which they can place a governmental law or policy. We talk about examples in other chapters, such as distinguishing protected from unprotected speech (discussed in Chapter 10).

Varying levels of scrutiny

Some tests in the constitutional-interpretation tool kit vary the extent to which government must justify its laws or regulations. Classic examples include

» Subjecting government line-drawing to strict scrutiny (for race and national-origin discrimination), intermediate scrutiny (for gender discrimination), and rational-basis review (for all other distinctions); flip to Chapter 12 for more on this test method.

» Subjecting fundamental implied-privacy rights to strict scrutiny and non-fundamental implied-privacy rights to rational-basis review (see Chapter 14 for a dive into implied rights).

Situation-specific and fact-based tests

Other areas of constitutional interpretation use tests that vary depending on the specific facts at issue. For example

» Determining whether the local economic activities that Congress regulates have a substantial effect on interstate commerce (discussed in Chapter 8)

» Using a test that weighs the totality of the circumstances related to the specific facts surrounding a police search to see whether the police based that search on reasonable suspicion (Chapter 19 covers this test)

2

Setting Up (and Limiting) National Government Powers

Understand how the Constitution creates a powerful (but limited) national legislature.

See the role the Constitution created for an executive branch of government.

Evaluate the powers that the Constitution gave to the judicial branch, including the Supreme Court.

Observe the three federal branches cooperating (and competing!) to set national policy.

Dive deep into how the Constitution balances national and state power.

IN THIS CHAPTER

» Setting up the two houses
of Congress

» Giving Congress the power
to legislate

» Limiting what Congress can do

» Protecting Congress against
other branches

Chapter **5**

Constituting the Legislative Branch

This chapter explores the important ways in which the Constitution (mainly through Article I) establishes, empowers, limits, and protects the national legislative branch. You can find out how the Constitution implements the Framers' decision to divide the national legislative authority into two legislative chambers that reflect different constituencies and dynamics — called *bicameralism*. We outline how the Constitution gives this bicameral Congress its powers to enact legislation and summarize the ways by which Article I limits congressional powers. We also briefly identify how the Framers sought to preserve congressional independence from encroachment by the other branches of government.

Setting Up a Bicameral Congress

A key moment in the writing and adopting of the Constitution was when the Framers brokered the Great Compromise. While the Convention attendees debated various contentious issues in the summer of 1787, one key sticking point was how to allocate seats in the national legislature. Two starkly different proposals for legislative representation competed for adoption in the Constitutional Convention:

>> **Virginia Plan:** Not surprisingly, the more populous states supported the Virginia Plan because it would apportion legislative representation based on population. States that had more residents would have more votes and therefore an advantage.

>> **New Jersey Plan:** The competing New Jersey Plan would have given each state equal legislative representation, thereby denying the populous-state advantage.

The Great Compromise created a bicameral system, avoiding a potentially fatal logjam by dividing the legislative power among two chambers — one based on population (the House of Representatives) and one based on equal representation for each state (the Senate).

REMEMBER

Delegates from slave-owning states sought to inflate their power in the House of Representatives by fully counting slaves for purposes of determining House seats. In the face of opposition from non-slave-holding states, the Convention delegates agreed to count slaves as three-fifths of a person for House representation and taxation. This Three-Fifths Compromise, even if a practical necessity at the time to secure ratification, is reprehensible to modern eyes.

The first five Sections of Article I of the Constitution establish the framework by which each legislative chamber functions:

>> **Section 1:** Gives legislative power to the two legislative chambers.

>> **Sections 2 and 3:** Define some important aspects relating to House and Senate organization, including

- Establishing an initial state-by-state allocation of House and Senate seats

- Providing for how changing population patterns adjust the number of House members each state has

- Establishing different terms of office for House members (two years) and Senators (six years)

- Stating procedures for filling vacancies

- Delineating how House and Senate members choose their leaders

>> **Section 4:** Provides for the election of House and Senate members by giving the legislature of each state initial control over the times, places, and manner of federal elections — subject to congressional alteration.

Section 4 also obligates the House and Senate to meet at least once a year and sets the date for convening the new legislative session.

>> **Section 5:** Regulates several aspects of how each house does business:

- Defines what constitutes a *quorum* to do business, usually a majority.

- Gives each house the power to judge its members' qualifications, discipline wayward members, and establish its own rules of procedure.

- Prevents either house from adjourning for more than three days without the consent of the other.

Don't assume that because voters now elect senators, that's how senators always got their positions. Before the 17th Amendment ratification in 1913, state legislators chose senators, consistent with both the Framers' intent that the Senate reflect state interests and their distrust of direct democracy. (The Constitution doesn't contain any process of legislating through a people's referendum, and it specifies that state electors decide the election of the president, rather than electing a president by tallying the votes of individual voters. You can read more about the electoral college in Chapter 17.)

Empowering Congress to Legislate

After establishing a bicameral Congress and stating each chamber's responsibilities and interconnection, Article I of the Constitution goes on to empower Congress in three main ways. Article I

>> Defines the procedures by which Congress legislates.

>> Enumerates most (although not all) of the subjects about which Congress is authorized to legislate.

>> Reveals an overall structure and Framer intent that led to a landmark 1819 Supreme Court decision giving Congress a generous range of implied means for achieving its *enumerated* (specifically listed) powers. In other words, this judicial green light for Congress to use all "appropriate and plainly adapted" means for achieving its enumerated powers laid the crucial foundation for the powerful federal government that Americans experience today.

Defining legislative procedures

In the 1970s, ABC television aired a Saturday morning children's program called *Schoolhouse Rock!* that included a song titled "I'm Just a Bill," which outlined a congressional bill lifecycle. (Do an internet search for "I'm Just a Bill" to find this cartoon tune on YouTube.) This song memorably captured the seemingly straight-forward steps for enacting legislation, as laid out in the Constitution's Article I, Section 7:

1. **A majority in both the House and the Senate must enact the identical version of a proposed bill.**

   In general, either body can act first to approve the bill and send it on to the other body — except that "all bills for raising revenue shall originate in the House of Representatives," according to the Constitution's Origination Clause of Article I, Section 7.

2. **After the bill passes both houses, Congress presents the bill to the president.**

3. **The president makes a decision about that bill.**

   The president can either

   - Sign the bill into law.

   - Take no action. If the president doesn't take action for ten days after receiving the bill when Congress is in session, the bill automatically becomes law.

   - *Veto* the bill by returning it to Congress with objections.

4. **After a presidential veto, the bill can still become law if a two-thirds supermajority in both houses supports it.**

FOLLOWING THE PROCEDURES OF SECTION 7

In 1982, the legislative procedures of the Constitution's Article I, Section 7, became the basis for *INS v. Chadha,* an important Supreme Court decision that invalidated several hundred provisions that allowed for legislative vetoes.

Legislative veto provisions allowed one or both houses of Congress (or, in some cases, even congressional committees) to reverse regulatory decisions of non-legislative officials. The Supreme Court held that Congress needed to present vetoes to the president for approval or over-ride. Because none of the vetoes incorporated such a presidential role, the Court declared them all unconstitutional. This Supreme Court decision significantly adjusted the legislative/executive balance of power in many important domestic and foreign-policy areas.

In practical reality, adopting legislation involves numerous political dynamics and complications not found among the Constitution's simple, barebones outline. Prominent real-world complications include

- The conference committee procedures by which House and Senate negotiators work to iron-out compromise legislation to reconcile the differing versions passed by each house.

- The Senate's filibuster rules, which prevent many important legislative proposals from coming to a floor vote unless a supermajority of 60 Senators agrees.

- The formal and informal consultations by which members of Congress and their staffers communicate with the presidential administration to avoid hard-to-override presidential vetoes.

Enumerating the subjects for federal government legislation

The primary source of Congress's power is the Constitution's Article I, Section 8, as discussed in the following section. Other sources of legislative authority are scattered throughout the Constitution, which we talk about in the section "Deriving legislative authority from other provisions," later in this chapter.

Cataloging Section 8's array of legislative powers

Article I, Section 8, of the Constitution is mainly a laundry list of 17 enumerated powers that Congress can exercise. Grouped by major subject area and order of listing in the Constitution, Section 8 grants Congress authority to exercise the following powers:

>> Economic and financial (Clauses 1–5 and 8)

- Tax and spend

- Borrow money

- Regulate interstate and foreign commerce

- Establish uniform bankruptcy laws

- Coin money and regulate its value

- Adopt patent and copyright laws

» Military and foreign affairs (Clauses 11–16)

- Declare war and make other wartime rules

- Raise, support, and make rules for land and naval forces

- Provide for organizing, training and calling forth the militia to "Suppress Insurrections and repel Invasions"

» Crime prevention (Clauses 6 and 10)

- Punish the counterfeiting of U.S. securities and money (Clause 6)

- Punish piracy and felonies at sea and "Offenses against the Law of Nations" (Clause 10)

» Organizational (Clauses 4, 7, 9, and 17)

- Make uniform rules for immigration and naturalization

- Establish post offices and roads

- Set up lower federal courts

- Set up and govern the District of Columbia

REMEMBER

As we talk about in Chapter 2, many of the enumerated powers in the preceding list reflect the Framers' dissatisfaction with the weaker national entity that attempted to govern under the Articles of Confederation before adoption of the 1789 Constitution.

Clause 18, named the Necessary and Proper Clause, gives Congress the authority "To make all Laws which shall be necessary and proper for carrying into Execution the foregoing Powers, and all other Powers vested by this Constitution in the Government of the United States, or in any Department or Officer thereof." This so-called *Elastic Clause* ensures that Congress — and any other national-government official who exercises congressionally delegated authority — can achieve enumerated powers.

Deriving legislative authority from other provisions

Beyond Article I, Section 8 of the Constitution (see the preceding section), other parts of Article I, other constitutional articles, and even constitutional amendments provide Congress with additional important powers

>> To consent to any public official receiving an otherwise prohibited "present, Emolument, Office, or Title, of any kind whatever, from any King, Prince, or foreign State" (Article I, Section 9).

>> To consent to deviations from some of the limitations otherwise imposed by Article I, Section 10, on state authority.

>> To alter certain procedures for electing the president and members of Congress initially set by state legislatures (Article I, Section 4 and Article II, Section 1).

>> To provide for appointment of lower-level executive officials through means other than presidential appointment with Senate confirmation (Article II, Section 2).

>> To "dispose of and make all needful Rules and Regulations respecting the Territory or other Property belonging to the United States" (Article IV, Section 3). This provision grants authority over a vast network of military bases, federal offices, national parks, and wilderness areas.

>> To determine whether state legislatures or state conventions will do State ratification of constitutional amendments (Article V).

>> To "enforce by appropriate legislation" the guarantees of various constitutional amendments.

Allowing Congress to use implied powers

In the landmark 1819 case of *McCulloch v. Maryland*, the Supreme Court made a crucial contribution to congressional empowerment by justifying an expansive view of implied powers. The context and stakes of this case, as well as the Court's holding and reasoning underline the broader impact on our modern understanding of legislative power.

Examining the *McCulloch v. Maryland* dispute

The Supreme Court case of *McCulloch v. Maryland* involved a question about national authority that may seem quaint to modern eyes, but was a highly controversial flashpoint in early debates over the scope of federal power. *McCulloch* posed the question whether Congress could constitutionally establish a national bank, even though the Constitution granted no enumerated power to do that — or to charter any institution, for that matter.

Specifically, the *McCulloch* dispute arose when the State of Maryland, whose government was in the hands of a states-rights faction that opposed the national bank as an example of federal oppression, taxed the recently established national bank. The question of whether one level of government could tax the institutions of another reached the Supreme Court, and the Court said no, in a portion of *McCulloch* that created an important inter-governmental tax immunity principle that endures to this day. But the Court first had to decide whether the federal government could constitutionally create a bank in the first place.

Without explicit authorization for the bank, the Court inquired whether bank establishment was justified by implication from the enumerated powers that the Framers gave. At this point in the dispute, the Court confronted two very different views about how broad a range of implied means the Constitution afforded to Congress:

>> **The Jeffersonian-Republicans (led by Thomas Jefferson):** Favored a more modest national government and emphasized states' rights. They thought that Congress could only adopt implied means that were essential (meaning that without these implied means, Congress couldn't achieve the important objectives behind its enumerated powers).

>> **The Hamiltonian-Federalists (led by Alexander Hamilton):** Supported a stronger central government, arguing for a broader range of implied measures.

As you can read about in the following section, the Supreme Court essentially sided with the Hamilton-Federalists' generous interpretation of implied powers.

REMEMBER

Neither side in *McCulloch* disputed whether the Constitution envisioned some implied congressional actions not explicitly specified. The question was about how narrow or broad the range of implied means was.

Understanding *McCulloch's* holding and reasoning

Beyond the specific national-bank fight in *McCulloch*, the decision's broader significance stems from the reasoning that the Court used to find the bank constitutional, despite the lack of any enumerated bank-creation power. In one of the most-quoted judicial opinion passages, the Court held that the Framers meant to give Congress the authority to employ all "appropriate and plainly adapted" means for achieving its enumerated powers that were not otherwise prohibited by the Constitution.

McCulloch relied on two major reasoning steps. The Court noted that

>> To make their Constitution understandable, the Framers had to speak in broad strokes about governmental powers; they could mark only the "great outlines" and "important objects" of legislative power. This need left "the

minor ingredients which compose those objects [to] be deduced from the nature of the objects themselves."

>> The Framers gave the Congress broad and significant enumerated responsibilities "on the due execution of which the happiness and prosperity of the nation so vitally depends." Given that, John Marshall, the Chief Justice of the Supreme Court at the time, asked rhetorically (and answered with a decisive no!), "Is that construction of the Constitution to be preferred which would render these operations difficult, hazardous and expensive?"

Having adopted a generous implied-power standard, the Court concluded that having a national bank to facilitate money collecting and expending would be an "appropriate and plainly adapted" implied means of fulfilling several enumerated powers.

WARNING

Although many people have the common misconception that *McCulloch* relies primarily on the Necessary and Proper Clause (discussed in the section "Cataloging Section 8's array of legislative powers," earlier in this chapter) for its generous view of implied means, *McCulloch* focuses first and foremost on general implications from the broad, general language of the Constitution and the Framers' intention that the federal government succeed in its crucial objectives.

Taking the broad view of implied means

The Supreme Court's ruling in *McCulloch* — which chose the broader, rather than the narrower, version of federal implied powers — had an incredibly significant impact on how the federal government operates. The size of the federal government and its workforce, and the vast array of policies it pursues, are a legacy of the Court's holding.

In light of the many weighty matters of economics, public safety, and national security on which Congress can exercise generous implied powers, you can easily see why *McCulloch v. Maryland* of is a pivotal Supreme Court decision.

WARNING

The federal government's broad implied powers don't give the national government carte blanche to do whatever it wants. Under *McCulloch's* formulation, the government must tie any congressional enactment to one or more enumerated powers, and the enactment must not violate any other constitutional limitation.

Limiting Congress

The Constitution reflects the adage that "with power comes responsibility" by imposing many limits on the congressional authority that it grants.

As a starting point, many of the power grants identified in the section "Empowering Congress to Legislate," earlier in this chapter, have built-in limits that the Supreme Court has interpreted. Here are a couple of examples:

>> **Patent limits:** The Constitution's Article I, Section 8, gives Congress the power to grant patents and copyrights only "for limited Times." In the 2002 *Eldred v. Ashcroft* decision, the Supreme Court held that a congressional extension of the copyright term to 70 years after the author's death was still sufficiently "limited" to meet constitutional requirements.

>> **Amendment restrictions:** The Constitution also limits Congress's power to enforce the restrictions that the 14th and 15th Amendments impose on state and local governments to "appropriate legislation." In the 1997 Supreme Court decision in *City of Boerne v. Flores* (explained more fully in Chapter 9), the Court significantly narrowed Congress's 14th Amendment enforcement options.

Beyond built-in limits on power grants, Article I, Section 9, specifically states things Congress can't do. Among the more important of these limits, Congress

>> May not generally suspend the *writ of habeas corpus* (which, as we discuss further in Chapter 21, allows an incarcerated person to force the government to either charge or release them)

>> May not enact a *bill of attainder* (meaning it can't make conduct retroactively illegal)

>> Must authorize public expenditures by passing regular appropriations laws

Even outside Section 9, the Constitution contains scattered sections that limit congressional power. For example, Article III, Section 3, grants Congress some authority over treason prosecutions; but the constitutional language locks in a definition of treason and limits the range of punishments that Congress may adopt.

All congressional power assertions must comply with the procedures for adopting legislation. Congress can't exercise any of the power grants through legislation that lack the required majorities of each house. And tax and revenue-raising bills have to originate in the House (although this isn't a simple requirement to enforce). The Supreme Court and lower courts have wrestled with defining just what falls into the tax/revenue category; the Affordable Care Act (commonly called Obamacare) generated controversies about the Origination Clause (Article I, Section 7, Clause 1) in the early 2010s.

Finally, of course, all assertions of congressional power — whether direct exercises of enumerated powers themselves (for example, establishing a post office) or adoption of implied means that appropriately further an enumerated power (for example, selling commemorative stamps at that post office) must comply with the limits that generally restrict all governmental officials. Throughout this book, we provide examples of courts ruling that a congressional enactment runs afoul of constitutional government-power and individual-liberties restrictions.

Protecting Congress Against Other National Officials

Consistent with their commitment to make each federal branch independent of reprisals from officials in other branches, the Framers granted important protections to members of Congress. These protections include provisions that specifically rule out abusive practices dating back to earlier times, when English kings and Parliamentary majorities would intimidate dissenting members of Parliament.

Article I, Section 6 (which guarantees that Senators and Representatives are paid a salary "ascertained by law" out of the U.S. Treasury) also provides two important safeguards against retaliation by executive-branch law enforcers and prosecutors:

>> Members of Congress can't be arrested (except for cases of "Treason, Felony and Breach of the Peace") while attending or traveling to and from legislative sessions, per Clause 2.

>> The Speech or Debate Clause (Clause 1) insulates House and Senate members from civil or criminal liability for anything they might say (even if defamatory) on the House or Senate floor.

As interpreted by the modern Supreme Court, this protection extends significantly beyond actual floor speeches and debates. For example, liability extends to a range of legislative acts, including statements made at committee hearings and during committee investigations. However, the Speech or Debate Clause doesn't extend to non-legislative political activities and communications, such as statements made in a constituent newsletter.

This clause can complicate legitimate criminal prosecution of members of Congress accused of bribery and other law violations; tough questions can arise about which actions can be entered into evidence.

Finally, many of the other constitutional procedures by which Congress interacts with executive and judicial branch officials provide implicit means for Congress to protect its prerogatives and resist usurpations. Here are some examples of leverage that legislatures can use to check and resist challenges from the President, the rest of the executive branch, and the courts:

>> Congress may override a presidential veto.

>> The Senate must confirm key presidential nominees.

>> Congress may alter Supreme Court rulings through legislation or constitutional amendment.

>> Congress must appropriate funds for the executive and judicial branches.

Chapter **6**

Constituting the Executive Branch

This chapter explores the important ways in which the Constitution establishes, empowers, limits, and protects the national executive branch, primarily through Article II. A large mandate for an Article that contains only 13 paragraphs!

We explain how the Constitution accomplishes the Framers' decision to vest executive power in a single official by expressly creating the office of president and recognizing that subordinate officials will implement many presidential initiatives. You can also get an outline of how the Constitution — as written and as interpreted by the Supreme Court — gives the president important powers and also limits executive powers, as well as seeking to protect executive-branch independence from encroachment by the other branches. This chapter also goes into the continuing uncertainty over the boundaries of executive power by cataloging some major issues still unresolved at the time of writing.

Setting Up the Presidency and Vice Presidency

In the same way that Article I of the Constitution vests legislative power in Congress (flip back to Chapter 5 for the lowdown on the legislative branch), Article II of the Constitution opens by entrusting the executive power to a president of the United States. Article II also indicates that the president can have the services of a vice president in wielding the executive powers but leaves any other details unspecified. Officials had to work out in practice and through legislation what is today a large and complicated federal executive branch.

After this initial power vesting, Article II, section 1 primarily focuses on presidential qualifications, terms, and electoral processes. It sets the presidential term of office at four years. (The 22nd Amendment, adopted in 1951, prevents any person from being elected to the office of president for more than two four-year terms.) To be eligible to be president, a person must be at least 35 years old, a *natural born citizen* (meaning that the person was, to quote the Bruce Springsteen song, "Born in the USA"), and a U.S. resident for at least 14 years (so no long sojourns overseas!).

These seemingly straightforward requirements can fuel major controversies. Opponents argued that presidential candidate John McCain was ineligible because he was born in the Panama Canal Zone, a U.S.-controlled strip of land that wasn't part of any particular U.S. state. And Donald Trump and others drew headlines for questioning whether former President Barack Obama was really born in Hawaii.

Article II, Section 1 also devotes a considerable number of words in complicated clauses to setting forth how the president and vice president get elected. Revisions from several constitutional amendments further complicate these provisions. Although we could write an entire *For Dummies* book on this electoral process, Chapter 17 talks about how the electoral college works.

Section 1 concludes by setting forth the oath or affirmation that the President must take before entering office.

Empowering the President and Subordinates

Sections 2 and 3 of Article II enumerate more than a dozen powers, varying in scope and magnitude, that presidents can exercise alone or with Congress. A landmark 1952 Supreme Court decision, *Youngstown Sheet & Tube v. Sawyer*, recognized these Article II powers as one of two main sources of presidential authority.

Enumerating presidential powers

In Chapter 5, we talk about one very important power given to the President — Article I, Section 7 gives to the president the ability to sign, acquiescence in, or veto bills passed by both houses of Congress.

But Article II, Sections 2 and 3 give presidents the bulk of their authority. These sections allow presidents to exercise the following powers:

>> **Military command:** Besides being the commander-in-chief of the Armed Forces, the president also can command state militias "when called into the actual Service of the United States" (such as with the National Guard).

>> **Foreign affairs:** The president can make treaties, if two-thirds of the Senate ratifies them. appoint U.S. ambassadors and "other public Ministers and Consuls," if the Senate consents. And they *receive* foreign ambassadors (meaning officially recognize a foreign ambassador).

>> **Criminal justice:** The president can "Grant Reprieves and Pardons for Offences against the United States, except in Cases of Impeachment."

A *reprieve* temporarily delays a sentence, pending further action. A *pardon* permanently and completely cancels a defendant's guilt and punishment.

>> **Governmental/organizational:** Require written opinions from principal department officials, "upon any Subject relating to the Duties of their respective Offices."

The president also appoints "Judges of the Supreme Court, and all other Officers of the United States," including lower federal-court judges, if the Senate approves. The president can fill vacancies during Senate recesses through *recess appointments* that last through the end of a legislative session.

>> **Interactions with Congress:** Give Congress information on the State of the Union. Recommend to Congress legislative measures that the president "shall judge necessary and expedient." They can also "on extraordinary Occasions,

convene both Houses, or either of them." For example, such extraordinary occasions might happen in time of war or other national crisis.

The president can also adjourn the houses of Congress "to such Time as [the President] shall think proper, if the houses themselves disagree about adjournment."

>> **Executing the law:** Last, but certainly not least, a brief but comprehensive power near the end of Article II, Section 3's catalog is the clause obligating the president to "take Care that the Laws be faithfully executed."

Enhancing executive powers through delegation

Congress often exercises its legislative powers in ways that, in turn, enhance the powers of the president and executive subordinates.

For almost 100 years, Court decisions have allowed Congress to fulfill its legislative powers by delegating authority to the president or subordinates so that they can fill in the important details. The Court maintains that a variety of factors justify broad delegation, including the

>> Sheer volume and complexity of regulatory problems confronting the federal government and the country

>> Inability of Congress to anticipate every challenge that will arise

>> Desirability of having executive-branch officials develop expertise about the many socially and technologically complicated issues that modern regulation poses

Critics of broad delegation to the executive branch regularly accuse Congress of shirking its primary policymaking responsibilities and giving too much power to less politically accountable bureaucrats. Nevertheless, a current relatively generous legal standard upholds delegation of legislative authority against constitutional attack if in the underlying legislation Congress has set forth a sufficiently *intelligible principle* (sufficient standard) to guide the executive officials who will implement legislative goals.

Don't overestimate the extent to which the intelligible-principle standard requires specific guidance. For example, the Court has upheld broad delegations that vaguely permit executive regulators to promote the "public convenience, interest, or necessity" or define and prevent "unfair methods of competition" (especially when other statutory provisions and evidence of congressional purposes arguably provide additional specifics).

Executive-branch officials end up filling in the details of how to implement legislative powers, acting through generous legislative delegations. The thousands of pages of rules, regulations, and other decisions issued each year by agencies as diverse as the Food and Drug Administration (FDA), the Environmental Protection Agency (EPA), and the Federal Trade Commission (FTC) attest to how delegated legislative powers add to executive authority.

Under a newly developed major questions doctrine, in cases such as *West Virginia v. EPA* (2022), the Court requires that Congress provide special clarity about the extent of the powers it delegates to administrative agencies when it comes to especially consequential economic, social, or technological regulatory issues.

Understanding how the modern Court views executive power

Understanding the constitutional scope of executive authority is especially difficult given the lack of a single measuring standard. Modern Supreme Courts have used several different approaches to defining limits; the approaches can at times justify different results. These approaches originate from the 1952 case of *Youngstown Sheet and Tube Co. v. Sawyer* (which you can read about in the following section). In fact, the Court quoted heavily from *Youngstown* and its approaches when it defined the limits of executive power in the 2024 decision in *Trump. v. U.S.* In this case, the Court considered for the first time the scope of presidential immunity from criminal prosecution for actions during the presidency.

Ruling on Executive Power

In the following sections, we explain the context and stakes of the 1952 *Youngstown Sheet and Tube Co. v. Sawyer* legal dispute, where then-President Harry Truman issued an executive order for the federal government to take control of U.S. steel companies, and examine the three different approaches used by the justices who agreed on the outcome. These different approaches can produce different results in some important types of executive-power disputes (discussed in the section "Getting different results with the three approaches," later in this chapter).

Seeing the stakes of the *Youngstown* dispute

The *Youngstown* dispute arose when, during military hostilities on the Korean Peninsula, America faced the possibility of a nationwide strike in American steel plants. Declaring the need to assure continued steel production to avoid harming

U.S. Armed Forces personnel and operations, President Harry Truman issued an executive order directing the U.S. Commerce Secretary to take control of the steel companies.

Steel companies challenged the legality of Truman's order. This presented the Supreme Court with a basic question about the extent of the president's power to act without a specific authorization from Congress. (Truman emphasized that he was acting temporarily to avert an emergency. He invited Congress to pass legislation to deal with the crisis, but Congress didn't accept the invitation.)

Understanding the three approaches of the majority justices

In *Youngstown Sheet and Tube Co. v. Sawyer*, by a 6-3 margin, the justices ruled that the Truman order exceeded presidential authority.

TECHNICAL STUFF

Because the Court invalidated the steel-seizure order on presidential-power grounds, it didn't have to rule on the challengers' alternative argument that even a temporary seizure of control over private property violated 5th Amendment guarantees against taking private property without just compensation.

Beyond the specific fight over Truman's steel seizure, *Youngstown*'s broader significance stems from the different approaches used by the individual justices agreeing that the executive order was unconstitutional. The following sections discuss the three different approaches, which remain relevant because analysts continue to emphasize all three to varying degrees in deciding important presidential-power controversies. The three approaches see presidential power through distinctly different lenses.

These approaches fall broadly into two categories:

>> **Formalistic:** A view that follows clearly defined forms, rules, and conventions

>> **Pragmatic:** A practical perspective that focuses on the details of a specific situation

Justice Black's formalistic approach

Writing the lead *Youngstown* opinion, Justice Hugo Black took a *categorical* (meaning a formalistic) view of presidential power. His interpretation said that, to be constitutional, a presidential initiative needs to fall within one of two buckets:

>> **Exercise of delegated legislative authority:** The president needs to be exercising power delegated by Congress.

Justice Black rejected the administration's argument that previous congressional enactments in the labor-relations and property-seizure area expressly or impliedly delegated authority for a large-scale takeover of domestic industry.

>> **Exercise of Article II authority:** Without a congressional power delegation, the president can turn to those powers specifically listed in Article II of the Constitution.

Justice Black also didn't find support in the powers that Article II grants to presidents:

- The president's commander-in-chief power didn't extend to controlling private domestic industries outside the Korean theater of war.

- The president's obligation to "faithfully execute" U.S. laws was of no avail because, according to Justice Black, the president made up his own policy and sought to implement it.

- Black rejected a more amorphous claim of inherent presidential authority to act in a crisis, stating that he found the claim profoundly at odds with the Framers' decision to "entrust the law-making power to the Congress alone in good and bad times."

Justice Jackson's three-scenario approach

Although he joined Justice Black's opinion, Justice Robert Jackson penned an influential concurring opinion that took a distinctly pragmatic approach. Although recognizing that "the Constitution diffuses power to better secure liberty," Jackson emphasized that the dispersed powers need to come together to achieve a workable government. Jackson wrote that "Presidential powers are not fixed but fluctuate," depending upon whether the president and Congress are on the same page:

>> **The congressional-approval scenario:** Jackson noted that presidential power is at its highest when the president's initiative falls within Congress's express or implied authorization.

>> **The congressional-disapproval scenario:** By contrast, Jackson noted that presidential power is at its lowest when "the President takes measures incompatible with the will of Congress."

> **The zone of twilight scenario:** Jackson's third scenario — one in which adventurous presidents often find themselves — involves what he described as a "zone of twilight" in which Congress hasn't expressed its will. In this scenario, the reaction to presidential action depends more on practical factors, such as the urgency of events, rather than legal niceties.

Justice Jackson found that relevant congressional deliberations showed that Congress disapproved of broad seizure authority. Therefore, Truman's order fell into the congressional-disapproval scenario and was unconstitutional.

Justice Frankfurter's gloss-through-past-practice approach

In his pragmatic opinion, Justice Felix Frankfurter emphasized the Constitution's creation of the separation of power and system of checks and balances. But the Constitution is a framework for a government whose separate parts must also interact: To clarify how the separation of powers should work, Frankfurter maintained the *pragmatic* (practical) position that "[d]eeply embedded traditional ways of conducting government cannot supplant the Constitution or legislation, but they give meaning to the words of a text."

Frankfurter focused on whether the history of congressional/presidential interactions show "a systematic, unbroken practice" long engaged in by presidents and known about, but never questioned by Congress, which adds a *gloss* (meaning a necessary, accepted expansion) to the scope of the president's Article II powers. According to Frankfurter, the past presidential practices need to be similar in "number, scope, duration, or contemporaneous legal justification" to the presidential-power exercise in dispute.

Because he could find just a few isolated examples of comparable presidential seizures, Frankfurter held that Truman's large-scale seizure was unprecedented and therefore ruled it unconstitutional.

Getting different results with the three approaches

As the *Youngstown* decision itself shows, sometimes justices who use different analytical approaches can arrive at the same conclusion about presidential power. (All three approaches pointed to unconstitutionality for different reasons, as discussed in the section "Understanding the three approaches of the majority justices," earlier in this chapter.)

TAKING *YOUNGSTOWN* TO *HAWAII*

A recent example of all three judicial approaches that we talk about in the section "Understanding the three approaches of the majority justices," in this chapter, is the Court's 2018 decision in *Hawaii v. Trump* — but this time, the opinions supported executive power, unlike in the *Youngstown* decision. The Trump administration issued an executive order that banned entry into the U.S. by residents of seven countries. All but one of these countries had majority-Muslim populations, leading challengers to argue that the so-called Muslim bans reflected anti-religious bias, which violated the 1st Amendment. A closely divided Court rejected this argument. The Supreme Court justices saw the bans as constitutional exercises of presidential power.

The lead *Hawaii v. Trump* opinion reflected an apparent Court consensus that every clause of the main statutory section in dispute gives discretion to the president to act. Looking further at the broader design of immigration and border-control statutes, the opinion concluded that Congress intended to provide broad presidential authority to exclude any persons from another country from admission into the country based on a finding that U.S. interests would be served thereby.

You can apply the three different *Youngstown* approaches to assess the constitutionality of President Trump's executive order:

- **Formalistic approach:** President Trump was acting as Congress's empowered delegate; alternatively, he was faithfully executing a clear congressional policy.

- **Three-scenario approach:** Points to the scenario in which the President's power is at its highest ebb because Congress had given its approval.

- **Gloss-through-past-practice approach:** Identifies a systematic, unbroken practice by other modern presidents; the Court specifically notes comparable practices by Presidents Reagan, Carter, Clinton, and Obama to which Congress didn't object.

REMEMBER

A legal precedent such as *Youngstown* can become *foundational*, meaning that other precedents build upon it. And when justices cite or quote those precedents, they implicitly cite the foundational case's principles.

In many executive-power controversies, however, the three *Youngstown* approaches can splinter — not just in analysis, but in outcome. Most important among these are executive-power assertions:

>> **When Congress hasn't been vigilant about asserting its authority:** Unfortunately, for a variety of reasons, legislators may not push back against creeping presidential power in many policy domains, especially in areas of

war, national security, and foreign policy, where a perceived sense of national crisis may temper congressional boldness. Even in important areas of domestic policies, Congress may not go on record with either support or opposition for presidential actions or agency regulations. In this circumstance, the *Youngstown* approaches might find different results:

- *Unconstitutional:* Justice Black's formalistic approach most likely sees insufficient congressional support (making the presidential action invalid).

- *Constitutional:* Justice Jackson's three-scenario approach counts Congress as missing in action, which supports the validity of the presidential action.

>> **When approaches serve opposite values.** For example, in the legislative-veto controversy in *INS v. Chadha*, which you can read about in Chapter 5, the legislative vetoes in question were designed to overturn executive-agency actions and rein in the power of the executive branch. But the Court found them unconstitutional because they bypassed the involvement of both houses of Congress and the president in the veto process. The Court decision reflects a clear formalist-versus-pragmatist pattern:

- *Formalistic:* The justices in the *Chadha* majority who invalidated hundreds of legislative vetoes saw them as inconsistent with the procedures that the Constitution provides for passing legislation — that is, passage in both Houses before being presented to the president for approval or veto.

- *Pragmatic:* Dissenting Justice White alone argued that the legislative veto was a practical and constitutional accommodation to modern realities of the workings of the executive branch and that the Framers would have approved of it; after all, wrote White, "[T]he wisdom of the Framers was to anticipate that the nation would grow and new problems of governance would require different solutions."

The *Chadha* majority countered Justice White's position archly (and formalistically) that "the Framers valued other values higher than efficiency," such as the separation of power.

Limiting the President and Subordinates

Like with legislative power (which we talk about in Chapter 5), the Constitution applies the adage that "with power comes responsibility" to executive authority:

>> **Built-in limits:** Some of the executive-power grants identified in the section "Empowering the President and Subordinates," earlier in this chapter, have

built-in limits. For example, the broad presidential power to grant pardons and reprieves excludes cases of impeachment.

>> **Limits for all officials:** Additionally, assertions of executive power must comply with the constitutional limits that restrict all governmental officials.

For example: in the 2004 decision in *Hamdi v. Rumsfeld,* the Court upheld the administration's authority to indefinitely detain an American citizen thought to be an enemy combatant — but only if the government provided adequate notice to the detainee and a meaningful right to disprove the allegation; the Court required these procedures to avoid denying Hamdi his right to due process under the 5th Amendment.

>> **Non-constitutional limits:** Broadly applicable non-constitutional limits also constrain executive officials who exercise delegated authority from Congress. For instance, the Administrative Procedure Act (APA) of 1946 (which we talk about in the sidebar "The power of procedure," in this chapter), the Freedom of Information Act (FOIA) of 1967, and many more — restrain the procedures that agencies can use to conduct important government business.

THE POWER OF PROCEDURE

The Administrative Procedure Act (APA) and other seemingly ho-hum laws about proper process can provide challengers with the crucial leverage they need to sideline highly controversial policies. For example, in the following two cases, the Supreme Court used the APA to stall two hot-button immigration-control initiatives from the first Trump administration:

- The Court used the APA in 2019 as the basis for rejecting a Census Bureau plan to include a controversial question about citizenship and documented status of families surveyed for the 2020 Census. Groups of plaintiffs sued, alleging that the threat of being outed to federal enforcers would cause families who had undocumented relatives to avoid the census, leading to undercounting that would seriously impact social services and voting rights in ethnically diverse parts of the country. The Court held that Census authorities failed to explain their reasoning and ignored uncontested data, thus violating the APA requirements of non-arbitrary decision-making.

- In 2020, the Court invalidated a Department of Justice memorandum rescinding the Deferred Action for Childhood Arrivals (DACA) policy, established in the Obama administration as a process by which *Dreamers* — undocumented residents brought to America as young children and who grew up in the U.S. — could receive renewable suspension of deportation. The Court held that the administration violated APA requirements for reasoned decision making by failing to adequately consider less onerous alternatives.

>> **Impeachment:** The Constitution offers at least theoretical protection against executive officials violating the law through impeachment. As established in Article II, Section 4, this process allows a House majority to indict and a two-thirds Senate majority to convict and remove any executive official, including the president, for "High Crimes and Misdemeanors."

Based on the record of modern impeachment attempts, you may doubt the impeachment process's future ability to meaningfully deter executive overreach. The threat of impeachment and conviction apparently convinced Richard Nixon to resign the presidency in 1974. But putting aside their merits, the three impeachments since — President Clinton's 1998 impeachment and President Trump's two separate impeachments in 2019 and 2021 — all resulted in acquittals when the Senate fell significantly short of the required two-thirds vote to convict. Unanswered questions remain about what misconduct qualifies as "High Crimes and Misdemeanors" and whether a challenge by a convicted president about the grounds of their impeachment and removal actually would be subject to legal review.

Protecting the President and Subordinates

Consistent with their commitment to make each federal branch independent of reprisals from officials in other branches, the Framers granted explicit protections for the president and, at times, executive subordinates. Modern Supreme Court decisions have also granted some implicit protections. The Constitution and the Court have decided the following executive protections:

>> **Salary:** Article II, Section 1 of the Constitution protects the President's salary in the same way that it protects legislative salaries, by requiring that the president be compensated and that presidential pay can't change (whether decreased or increased) during the president's term of office.

>> **Immunity:** The Supreme Court (or, in one instance, the Justice Department) determined that the presidential independence the Framers intended requires the following immunities from legal process:

- *Civil liability for presidential duties:* Absolute immunity from civil liability, while in office and after, for any claims based on acts *within the outer perimeter* of presidential duties (meaning the broad extent of presidential powers) recognized in the 1982 Supreme Court decision of *Nixon v. Fitzgerald*.

- *While in office:* Absolute immunity from criminal indictment or prosecution while in office (stemming from a long-standing Justice Department policy based on the design of Article II)

- *For utilizing core constitutional powers:* Absolute immunity, after leaving office, from criminal indictment and prosecution for any actions while president in furtherance of the president's *core constitutional powers* (exclusive and preclusive powers that the president doesn't share with Congress), as recognized in the 2024 Supreme Court decision in *Trump v. U.S.*

- *Criminal liability for presidential duties:* Presumptive immunity, after leaving office, from criminal indictment and prosecution for any actions that arguably fall within the outer perimeter of the president's official powers (also recognized in the 2024 decision in *Trump v. U.S*). These include powers the President shares with Congress in the "zone of twilight" recognized by Justice Jackson in his *Youngstown* opinion (which you can read about in the section "Justice Jackson's three-scenario approach," earlier in this chapter).

>> **Prerogatives:** Many of the constitutional procedures by which presidents interact with officials in the legislative and judicial branches provide implicit means for presidents and subordinates to protect their prerogatives and resist usurpations. Presidents may use certain types of leverage to check and balance the legislative and judicial branches. For example, presidents may block legislation by vetoes that Congress usually sustain, and presidents may pardon convicted defendants.

Looking at the protections afforded to subordinates, as well as the president, lower courts have recognized that subordinates may need to assert an implied executive privilege to protect the confidentiality of presidential policy discussions. The exact contours of such communication protections — including the extent to which executive-branch communications can be withheld from Congress and its committees — have yet to be clarified by the Supreme Court at the time of writing.

However, in *United States v. Nixon* (1974), the Court unanimously ordered President Nixon to turn over tape recordings of Oval Office conversations to high-ranking Nixon staff members defending themselves against criminal charges related to the Watergate scandal. Holding that a broad, generalized claim of executive privilege must bow to the needs of criminal defendants for relevant evidence, the Court's *Nixon* decision leaves other important executive-privilege questions unresolved.

Considering Unresolved Executive-Power Disputes

Pundits often describe disputes about the extent of executive power as *pushing the envelope*, suggesting that presidents are pushing the limits of their constitutional powers. For example, the number of executive orders has increased dramatically in the last several decades, as compared to in earlier presidencies.

REMEMBER

Many societal pressures try to push more and more power into the executive branch. Presidents want to pursue their agendas quickly as promised in their campaigns. The 24-hour news cycle and social media demand rapid change and results. A President may feel that furthering their agenda is like trying to turn a huge ship quickly. But these pressures aren't new: As Justice Frankfurter wrote in *Youngstown*, "A scheme of government like ours no doubt at times feels the lack of power to act with complete, all-embracing, swiftly moving authority. No doubt, a government with distributed authority, subject to be challenged in the courts of law . . . , labors under restrictions from which other governments are free."

Areas of unresolved power issues include

>> **Firing agency heads:** The authority of presidents to fire the heads of independent agencies without cause (as President Franklin Roosevelt tried, but the Court denied in *Humphrey's Executor v. United States* in 1935).

>> **Applying the Emoluments Clause to presidents:** This clause — Article I, Section 9, Clause 8 — prohibits all federal officeholders from accepting, among other things, financial benefits from foreign governments.

>> **Imposing tariffs:** The extent to which Congress has delegated power to presidents to impose tariffs on imported goods.

>> **Overlapping war powers:** The constitutional overlap between the president and Congress on war powers. In simple terms, Congress declares war, but the executive runs foreign policy, heads the armed forces, and can commit troops overseas.

>> **Using a shadow docket:** The Supreme Court issuing orders after accepting cases involving presidential authority on an expedited basis without full briefing (called a *shadow docket*). The effect of these orders as case precedents is unclear because the opinions are preliminary without substantial explanation.

>> **Making unorthodox appointments:** Unresolved issues involve when presidents make *recess appointments* (which we talk about in the section "Enumerating presidential powers," earlier in this chapter) or name officials as "acting." Questions exist about the constitutionality of these types of appointments when officials continue in their positions without the required advice and consent of Congress.

Chapter **7**

Constituting the Judicial Branch

In this chapter, we explore how the Constitution (mainly through Article III) establishes, empowers, limits, and protects the national judicial branch of the government. The Framers decided to insert a new national judicial authority into an existing system of state courts through the Constitution, in which they outlined a definition of the legal authority of federal courts. Also, key Constitution features paved the way for *Marbury v. Madison*, an early landmark Supreme Court decision in 1803 that claimed a decisive judicial review power. This chapter also talks about how judicial power comes with constitutional limits, as well as protections to preserve judicial independence from encroachment by the other branches.

Setting Up the Federal Judiciary

The Framers of the Constitution knew that they wanted to set up a separate federal judicial branch that had sufficient independence and authority to render neutral justice and protect the rule of law, which would help realize an important part of their general commitment to separation of powers and checks and balance.

The Framers knew about the drawbacks of more politically subservient judging in England and the colonies. The Framers also realized that they would have to insert the new federal judicial power into an existing framework of state courts.

Still, the Framers gave less thought to the structuring and empowering of the judicial branch than the other two national branches, as evidenced by the fact that the main constitutional article dealing with the judiciary (Article III) is half the size of the article covering the executive branch (Article II; see Chapter 6) and about a quarter of the size of the legislative-branch counterpart (Article I; discussed in Chapter 5).

Structuring the judicial branch

The constitutional plan for the federal judicial branch outlined in Article III, Section 1 specifies the following elements:

>> One Supreme Court

>> Congress-established "inferior Courts" (in this context, *inferior* means lower courts — the Constitution wasn't commenting on quality!)

Current legislation authorizes 677 district-court positions allocated among 94 judicial districts, and it divides 179 intermediate appellate slots among 13 circuit courts of appeal. Judicial retirements and deaths — and, especially, presidential and senatorial politics — ensure that some federal judicial positions remain unfilled at any given time.

Keeping the federal courts independent

To enhance their independence, Supreme Court justices and lower federal judges have life tenure (as the Constitution puts it, they "hold their Offices during good Behaviour" — raising a question that we discuss in the section "Limitations expressly stated in the Constitution," later in this chapter). After they receive their position in a very political process (the same presidential nomination and Senate confirmation that other key federal officials go through), federal justices and judges have the luxury of not having to submit to re-election.

By the way, this life appointment distinguishes federal judges from their state counterparts, who face elections and re-elections, or other retention and reappointment processes, which can subject them to political pressures.

As further protection for judicial independence, Article III, Section 1 requires that federal justices and judges must receive compensation at a level that "shall not be diminished" while they serve.

Obligating state judges

Not to be left out, state judges play an important role in promoting the supremacy of the Constitution and federal law. Especially nowadays, during typical state criminal and civil proceedings, issues arise when state judges apply constitutional-rights protections and the provisions of federal laws to criminal defendants and civil litigants. For that reason, the Article VI Supremacy Clause specifically obligates judges in every state to enforce the Constitution and valid federal law over "any Thing in the Constitution or laws of any State to the Contrary."

Comparing article provisions

The barebones nature of Article III's provisions on judicial structure and qualifications are as follows:

>> **Age:** The Constitution imposes no minimum age or citizenship/naturalization requirements on federal judges.

>> **Number:** Article III doesn't specify a number of Supreme Court justices, nor does it define the number or size of jurisdictional areas for lower federal courts.

Of course, the lack of explicit standards for federal judges — most notably, the lack of any requirement that judges have legal training! — doesn't mean the jobs don't have relevant qualifications as a practical matter. Graduation from a top law school and service in public or private legal circles is a must for any Supreme Court nominee to have a chance at confirmation. Although nothing in the Constitution prevents a president from nominating to the Supreme Court a young-adult foreigner who has no legal training, political realities make that sort of nomination highly unlikely.

Giving the Federal Judiciary Jurisdiction

Article III lists specific categories of cases to which "the Judicial Power shall extend." Just as with legislative and presidential powers (which we talk about in Chapters 5 and 6), enumeration limits the judicial branch from claiming a general free-wheeling judging power.

To be fully accurate — Article III lists categories of cases to which the judicial power might potentially extend. Supreme Court decisions indicate that Congress needs to make federal-court jurisdiction real through laws specifying how courts can exercise these powers in the courtroom.

The federal courts have jurisdiction over the following categories of cases in which, in varying ways, the national government has a special interest:

>> **Federal questions:** By far the most important category, it brings within the federal judicial arena all cases arising under the Constitution, the laws of the United States, and federal courts use this jurisdictional authority to decide a broad range of constitutional and nonconstitutional issues — and promote constitutional and national supremacy in the bargain.

>> **Foreign representatives:** "[A]ll Cases affecting Ambassadors, other public Ministers and Consuls." These cases, brought by or against these officials in their official capacity, can affect U.S. foreign relations.

>> **Maritime:** This grant covers a more limited but important subject, admiralty and maritime Jurisdiction. This power reflects the national government's predominant interest in navigational waters inside the United States, as well as in coastal and international waters.

>> **Jurisdiction based on parties:** These grants hand out jurisdiction based on the identity of the parties involved and the nature of what they're fighting about:

- *Involving foreign parties:* Foreign representatives are affected.

- *Involving the federal government:* In a case to which the United States government is a party.

- *Between states:* When "Controversies" exist between two or more states.

- *Between a state and non-local citizen:* If a state and a citizen of another state, are arguing a legal question.

>> **Citizens of different states:** If individuals from different states are locked in a legal dispute. This *diversity jurisdiction* is the power to hear civil cases not involving federal law when the parties reside in different states. It reflects an understandable Framer desire to avoid the appearance of favoritism if the case is decided in the state of one of the parties. Having the case heard in federal court is designed to reduce the risk of biased judgments because federal judges have life tenure and greater independence from state politics.

>> **Land claims:** In which citizens of the same state claim lands under different state land grants.

>> **Domestic v. foreign:** A U.S. state or its citizens are suing foreign governments or foreign individuals.

Diversity jurisdiction differs from the other case-and-controversy categories because federal judges who exercise diversity jurisdiction essentially get to play state judge. For example, a federal district judge deciding whether to award civil damages for a catastrophic traffic accident involving California Driver A and Illinois Driver B would apply the relevant state-law rules of liability. (Complicated choice-of-law criteria determine which state rules apply.) Diversity jurisdiction also shows how Congress can limit federal-court jurisdiction by setting a threshold amount-in-controversy, a minimum that reduces the risk that federal courts get overrun by a flood of small lawsuits.

Article III, Section 2 contains a wrinkle in how it divvies up court jurisdiction for the Supreme Court:

>> **Original jurisdiction:** Clause 2 of Section 2 provides that, for two case categories — lawsuits that affect foreign officials and cases that have states as parties — the Supreme Court has *original Jurisdiction,* which means that the Court can serve as the *trial court* (the initial court of decision), rather than waiting for cases to come to it on appeal.

>> **Appellate jurisdiction:** Legal fights that fall into the other federal-jurisdiction categories (besides those involving foreign officials or that have states as parties) start out in lower federal and state courts and go to the Supreme Court through the appeals process, known as *appellate jurisdiction.* As we explain in the following section, this technical division forms a crucial reasoning step in the Court's momentous claim of judicial review.

Paving the Way for Judicial Review

The Constitution never explains exactly how the federal courts should exercise the power of *judicial review* — the term for judges deciding the validity of challenged actions and declaring whether they're valid.

Judicial review is a commonplace and crucial part of the constitutional order. But how did this come about in the absence of clear, express constitutional guidance? The answer is the landmark 1803 decision in the Supreme Court case

Marbury v. Madison. The following sections examine this case and its role in shaping U.S. judiciary review.

Seeing the context and stakes in the *Marbury* dispute

At the turn of the 19th century, William Marbury was a Federalist party loyalist on his way to becoming a justice of the peace for the District of Columbia. President John Adams and his Federalist party lost the presidency and its majority in Congress in the 1800 elections. But before he left office, Adams managed to nominate Marbury and others for justice-of-the-peace positions, have the outgoing Federalist-controlled Senate confirm the nominations, and get official commissions of appointment signed and sealed.

Then there was a hitch: No one delivered the commissions before Thomas Jefferson, the leader of the rival political party, was elected president. Seeing no reason to reward Federalists, Jefferson instructed that the commissions stay undelivered.

Marbury and colleagues responded by suing James Madison, Jefferson's new Secretary of State, requesting that the Supreme Court order Madison (through a *writ of mandamus*, a court order requiring an official to perform a specific act) to deliver the commissions. Marbury started his lawsuit at the Supreme Court, as authorized by an obscure clause in the first Judiciary Act, which Congress enacted to provide further specifics about responsibilities and procedures for the judiciary under the new Constitution.

The Supreme Court and its Chief Justice, John Marshall, faced a dangerous dilemma where the Court would look weak whatever it did:

>> **Issuing the order:** If a new and relatively untested Supreme Court ordered Madison to act against Jefferson's wishes, Madison might refuse to comply (to avoid being fired). Because the Court at the time lacked (as it does to this day) its own independent power to enforce its orders, executive defiance would demonstrate judicial weakness.

>> **Not issuing the order:** On the other hand, if the Court shrunk back from remedying a presidential directive it clearly found invalid, it looked similarly feeble.

Understanding *Marbury's* holding and reasoning

Chief Justice Marshall sidestepped the dangerous ruling dilemma (see the preceding section) by simply avoiding Marbury's request. The Court held that it couldn't exercise the Act's original-jurisdiction authority (which you can read about in the section "Giving the Federal Judiciary Jurisdiction," earlier in this chapter), and so it lacked power to issue the commission-delivery order that *Marbury* requested.

Key to *Marbury's* importance is the Court's reasoning about why it couldn't order delivery of the commission. The Court explained that deciding William Marbury's case would be akin to exercising "original jurisdiction." As we note in the section "Giving the Federal Judiciary Jurisdiction," earlier in this chapter, Article III, Section 2, Clause 2 says that original actions shall include cases

>> Affecting foreign officials (both William Marbury and Secretary Madison were domestic)

>> To which a state is a party (since, clearly, neither Marbury nor Madison qualified as a state)

Reading the original-jurisdiction language as exclusive, the Court viewed Congress as illegitimately adding a third category (writs of mandamus against domestic federal officials), thus violating the Constitution.

REMEMBER

The Court claimed the power of judicial review with respect to its powerful co-equals (the Congress that passed the Judiciary Act and the president who signed it). And the Court cleverly established its judicial-review authority in a case that didn't need anyone outside of the judicial branch to agree or implement its decision.

What was the basis of the *Marbury* Court's conclusion that it could review and declare invalid an act of Congress? In authoring the opinion for a unanimous Court, Chief Justice Marshall found it "only necessary to recognize certain principles, supposed to have been long and well established." These three principles were primary:

>> **The Constitution established "certain limits not to be transcended" by Congress and the presidents.** Generations of skeptics see this undoubtedly correct statement of constitutional supremacy as beside the point. The issue in *Marbury* wasn't whether Congress has to follow the Constitution, but whether the federal courts should be part of the institutional forces making Congress do so.

> » **"It is emphatically the province and duty of the judicial department to say what the law is."** This famous phrase answers the question why the judiciary should be involved in reviewing the constitutionality of legislation. It's consistent with their role, as assumed by the Framers.
>
> » **Invalid legislation can't "bind the courts and oblige them to give it effect."** The opinion stated that such a position would be "an absurdity too gross to be insisted on."

Underscoring the enduring significance of *Marbury*

Marbury's judicial-review holding has enduring importance. Early in the nation's history, *Marbury* confirmed that the relatively independent and less politically sensitive national judicial branch has an important role to play in protecting constitutional values and the rule of law.

Of course, nothing in *Marbury* guarantees that federal courts will resist short-term political pressures; the Supreme Court notably has failed this mission at times. Most historians would cite *Korematsu v. United States*, decided in 1944, which in the shadow of World War II upheld the internment of Americans of Japanese ancestry, many of whom were citizens. And people regularly debate whether particular Supreme Court decisions serve or undermine constitutional values.

Still, if the Court hadn't seized on the unusual facts of *Marbury* to establish judicial review, legislative and executive officials might control the fate of constitutional values.

As important as *Marbury* is, the opinion doesn't necessarily intend to claim that federal judges have a special — much less the ultimate — role in interpreting the Constitution. Arguably, *Marbury* claimed for judges the same power that Congress and the President have — to act in their own arenas based on their interpretations of the Constitution and the law.

It took a much later Court, in the 1958 *Cooper v. Aaron* opinion, to claim that *Marbury* "declared the basic principle that the federal judiciary is supreme in its exposition of the law of the Constitution." The *Cooper* case specifically involved the Court's power over state officials; so the *Cooper* opinion held that state officials had to follow Supreme Court interpretations because, like constitutional text, these interpretations are "the supreme law of the land." Some scholars believe that this statement implies that Congress and the President also must immediately follow judicial constitutional interpretations as supreme law — rather than continuing to act on their contrary reading of the Constitution.

Limiting Federal Judicial Power

The Constitution places three types of limits on the powers of the judiciary:

>> Express limitations on courts

>> Limitations that are a byproduct of powers and responsibilities given to nonjudicial officials

>> Constraints that the Court has itself developed out of a concern for judicial self-restraint

Limitations expressly stated in the Constitution

Beyond limiting the federal judiciary to the jurisdictional categories enumerated in Article III (which we talk about in the section "Giving the Federal Judiciary Jurisdiction," earlier in this chapter) — an initial important constraint — the Constitution imposes several express limitations on judicial power:

>> **Impeachment:** Justices and judges, as "civil Officers of the United States," can face impeachment, conviction, and removal from office for "Treason, Bribery, or other High Crimes and Misdemeanors" (which appears in Article II, Section 4).

The language in Article III, Section 1 provides life tenure for federal judges on their "good Behaviour." The Framers left it unclear to what extent this behavior requires conduct higher than not committing impeachable offenses.

>> **Amendments:** The various constitutional limits on how legal proceedings can be conducted limit the actions of judges. For example, the 5th and 6th Amendments include prohibitions on depriving criminal defendants of due process or meaningful right to counsel (which we explain in Chapters 19 and 20), which control judicial behavior.

>> **Trial limits:** Article III itself specifies limits on trials, including requirements about where they can be conducted (Section 2, Clause 3) and, for treason as defined by the Constitution, the number and kinds of witnesses (two who saw "the same overt Act") needed to convict (Section 3, Clause 1).

>> **Rights:** Federal judges are subject to the many general limitations in the constitutional articles and amendments. For example, when judges impose *gag orders* that forbid trial participants from talking to the press or when they close judicial proceedings to avoid prejudicial pretrial publicity, they must take into account the guarantees of the 1st Amendment to free speech and free press, and the 6th Amendment right to a public trial.

Byproduct limits from congressional and executive authority

A key constitutional pillar is the ability of the three national branches to check and balance each other. Therefore, the Constitution gives Congress and the president a variety of powers that the two nonjudicial branches can use — for better or worse — to influence and even retaliate against the federal courts. These powers raise unresolved and unsettling questions about judicial independence and the rule of law.

All the powers that Congress and the president hold over the courts can rein in a rogue federal judiciary. On the other hand, Congress or the executive branch might abuse these powers to undermine judicial independence and the rule of law.

Exercising congressional and presidential powers over the courts

The Constitution provides the legislative branch explicit powers relating to court establishment and operation. Legislation

>> Defines the number and rank of lower-court judges, the geographic reach of their authority, and the specifics of how they exercise their jurisdiction.

>> Appropriates budgetary funds for the federal courts.

Sometimes public officials become so disenchanted with federal-court rulings that they threaten to take court-operation powers to unprecedented lengths, such as abolishing lower federal courts entirely or slashing court appropriations to the bone. The constitutional limits on such sweeping measures remain unclear.

>> Can make exceptions and regulations to the Supreme Court's appellate jurisdiction.

Both the president and Congress hold powers relating to judicial selection and personnel:

>> The president nominates, and the Senate confirms, Supreme Court justices and lower court judges.

>> Legislation sets the salary levels of Supreme Court justices and lower federal judges.

>> A variety of statutes and rules authorized by legislation set forth ethical and good-conduct standards that govern lower federal judges (and, at times, Supreme Court justices).

Powers relating to overriding judicial decisions exist for both the legislative and executive branches:

>> In response to judicial interpretations of laws enacted by Congress and regulations adopted by executive officials, legislators can vote to revise statutes, and executive officials can issue revised regulations.

>> The legislature can deem erroneous constitutional interpretations that the judicial branch issues and seek to overturn them by constitutional amendment.

Potentially dangerous Supreme Court expansion

The Constitution doesn't provide a set number of justices for the Court. An 1869 statute set the size to nine justices. But no branch of government has yet resolved whether officials can *pack* (meaning expand) the number of justices on the Supreme Court (as President Franklin Roosevelt proposed to do in 1937) to alter the Court's ideological balance and change the likely direction of its rulings.

Many think that such a change is constitutional. They note the lack of any limiting language in the constitutional text that authorizes nomination and confirmation of justices. Plus, history before 1869 shows that Congress periodically changed the number of justices, often to serve short-term political ends.

Still, others argue that the appointment power must align with the Framers' core commitment to a sufficiently independent Court that can promote constitutional values. They say the Framers wouldn't have intended Congress and the president to (mis)use their appointment power to fundamentally shift the direction of constitutional interpretation.

Congressional exceptions to jurisdiction

Article III expressly gives Congress the power to make exceptions and regulations. In other words, Congress has the power to define the Supreme Court's appellate jurisdiction (which is the source of almost all the modern Court's cases). And Congress's extensive authority over the structure and procedures of the lower federal courts that it created allows it to shape lower-court jurisdiction.

To what extent can the legislative branch use these jurisdiction-altering powers to influence the direction of court rulings? For example, suppose members of Congress or the president feared that future courts would dilute — or, instead, double down on — the controversial 2024 decision in *Trump v. United States,* which significantly immunizes former presidents from criminal indictment for executive actions. Could so-called *court stripping* legislation, which removes a court's jurisdiction over a particular type of case, prevent that court ruling on any new case involving presidential immunity?

Like with Court expansion (see the preceding section), those who find nothing unconstitutional about court-stripping say that it falls comfortably within Congress's express and implied power over federal-court jurisdiction. But contrarians doubt that isolated clauses in the Constitution mean to undermine the ultimate independence of the judiciary to, as the landmark *Marbury v. Madison* opinion put it, "say what the law is." (Flip back to the section "Paving the Way for Judicial Review," earlier in this chapter, for discussion of the groundbreaking case.)

Judicially imposed restraints

Nonelected federal judges have an awkward position in a majoritarian democracy. Potential dangers to the reputation and public perception of judges arise when they make rulings that countermand policies of elected or politically appointed officials. Recognizing this, and for a range of other reasons, Supreme Court justices have themselves developed several self-restraint doctrines that seek to minimize these pressures.

These *justiciability* doctrines seek to ensure that a court handles only cases or controversies within its jurisdiction, as outlined in Article III. Court cases have fleshed out these justiciability doctrines over time. A court can't issue advisory opinions or act on cases requesting resolution before an actual controversy exists or after the issue has disappeared. Beyond that, these doctrines aim to minimize unnecessary potential conflicts with political officials, yield specific fact patterns that promote good judging, and avoid the perception that jurists have inappropriate involvement in politics and policymaking.

Because the justiciability doctrines are rooted in Article III, which only constrains federal judges, they don't formally bind state judges. To honor similar judicial-restraint policies in their state constitutions, many states follow the doctrines exactly or with variations. But state courts may act in ways not in line with these doctrines — for example, providing their legislatures with judicial advice about the validity of proposed bills (discussed in the following section).

Aversion to advisory opinions

Federal judges decline to give advice on legal matters to political officials while those officials formulate policy. This justiciability doctrine goes back to the 1790s, when the Supreme Court declined to give constitutional advice on two important questions under consideration by the administration of President George Washington. Federal judges also won't decide *friendly lawsuits*, those disputes between parties who don't need a judge to resolve their adverse positions.

Mootness and timeliness

According to justiciability doctrines, litigants must continue to be in an *adverse position* (meaning in opposition to each other on the point of the case) throughout a lawsuit. An originally adverse dispute becomes *moot* (meaning it loses its practical significance) for various reasons, including

>> The plaintiff no longer claims injury.

>> The defendant rescinds a challenged policy.

A case isn't yet timely (and therefore not justiciable because it's *unripe*) when more needs to happen to clarify exactly what the parties are disputing.

Maximal application of the mootness doctrine would unacceptably zone entire rights out of federal court. For example, pregnancy-rights litigation would never survive the judicial timeline because women are pregnant for only about nine months.

To take a very prominent and controversial example of application of the mootness doctrine, *Roe v. Wade* (1973) involved the injury that a pregnant woman claimed from not being able to choose to have an abortion because of Texas's strict ban. Roe was no longer pregnant when the Court heard oral arguments. But the Court overlooked mootness under a two-part exception:

>> The plaintiff could again suffer the injury (that is, Roe herself was capable of getting pregnant again).

>> The same timing issues would again evade review in a future instance of injury.

The role of standing

Standing, the most frequently invoked and practically important justiciability doctrine, screens out legal challengers who assert only an abstract objection to governmental policy that any citizen or taxpayer could make. To meet this requirement, challengers bringing a case before a federal court must

>> Allege an injury that's distinct, actual or imminent, and concrete (not speculative).

» Allege injuries caused by the government defendant (and not by the acts or omissions of other parties not before the court).

» Courts must have a means to redress the challenger's injuries through appropriate relief.

The Court has also defined when a court decision may be constitutional but not *prudent* (meaning advisable) for courts to decide. For example, federal courts in general don't take cases in which challengers seek to represent the rights of others (third parties) rather than their own rights. But, like with mootness (see the preceding section), courts make exceptions. For example, in *Singleton v. Wulff* (1976) a court allowed a doctor to assert the rights of patients on whose behalf the physician is ethically obligated to act.

Inappropriately political questions

The justiciability doctrine, known as the political question doctrine, provides especially strong medicine because it precludes a federal court from ever deciding entire issues, regardless of timing or challenger. The political question doctrine directly reflects the core concern that federal courts must avoid disputes that would undermine the perception that they're exercising appropriately judicial, not political, judgment. For instance, because the Senate has the sole power to try impeachments under Article I, Section 3, a court can't second-guess its procedures for an impeachment trial.

The political question doctrine doesn't require that federal courts stay out of all issues *about* politics. Federal judges decide many disputes related to the right of candidates to speak, candidate ballot access, and voting rights. As long as the political issues raised in such litigation don't run afoul of the specialized political question doctrine, the judicial agenda can include politics.

A good example of what a judge can or can't decide under this political question justiciability doctrine is the 2019 decision in *Rucho v. Common Cause*. The Supreme Court held that *political gerrymandering* (when a state legislature's majority political party draws election districts to exaggerate its influence) requires judgment appropriate for politicians and political scientists, not judges. Therefore, the legislature can more appropriately address political gerrymandering rather than federal courts.

Chapter 17, which talks about election law, discusses whether the Court should have avoided deciding *Bush v. Gore* — and ultimately deciding which candidate won the 2000 presidential election — on grounds that it was the ultimate political question.

Protecting Federal Judges from Other National Officials

We note in the section "Keeping the federal courts independent," earlier in this chapter, that the Constitution protects federal judges by granting them life tenure and bans Congress from diminishing their salaries as punishment. Another protection involves the standards for removing a judge from their position.

If you strictly interpret the "high Crimes and Misdemeanors" standard for impeachment and removal (which appears in Article I, Section 3), this standard protects federal judges from petty or politically motivated retaliation. The history of judicial impeachments and removals appears to bear that protection out:

>> Lower federal court judges have been removed from office for actual crimes, such as bribery and tax evasion.

>> No judge or justice has been removed for unpopular views. For example, in 1804, the House impeached but the Senate didn't convict Supreme Court Justice Samuel Chase. Most observers see the basis for Chase's impeachment as states-rights-based ire at his pro-national-government leanings. When the Senate votes to convict him fell short of the requirement, it set a practical precedent against politically motivated use of impeachment and removal of judicial officials.

Chapter **8**

Seeing How the Government Branches Interact

hapters 5, 6, and 7 explain how the Constitution sets up, empowers, limits, and protects the three branches of the U.S. federal government: the legislative, executive, and judicial branches.

This chapter focuses on how the three branches use their powers in action and in relation to each other. For example, Congress (with the president's approval, acquiescence, or unsuccessful veto attempt) can develop major national policies and impose far-reaching regulations — subject to judicial review to enforce constitutional limits. The different federal branches must work together for issues such as national taxing and spending, and to regulate commerce.

We also discuss in this chapter what the Constitution has to say — and what it doesn't clarify — about several key issues of war, national security, and foreign policy.

Unpacking the Power Template
of *McCulloch v. Maryland*

In Chapter 5, we dive deep into the 1819 landmark Supreme Court decision in *McCulloch v. Maryland*. *McCulloch* upheld a law that chartered a national bank by using a generous standard for when Congress can use implied means to further enumerated ends. This decision provided the template still used today for determining when the federal government is acting within constitutional limits. The Court wrote in its opinion: "Let the end be legitimate, let it be within the scope of the Constitution, and all means which are appropriate, which are plainly adapted to that end, which are not prohibited, but consist with the letter and spirit of the Constitution, are constitutional."

To unpack that statement, *McCulloch* requires that legislation meet one of the requirements in the following sections.

Exercising an enumerated power

Congress might directly exercise one of the powers that the Constitution explicitly provides. To pick just one of many possible examples, assume that Congress enacts a law responding to growing concern about international piracy by increasing criminal penalties for certain already-defined piracy offenses. This action would be a direct and literal exercise of the Constitution's Article I, Section 8, Clause 10 congressional power to "punish Piracies and Felonies committed on the high Seas."

Using implied means to achieve an enumerated power

If the congressional action in question doesn't directly exercise an express power (which we discuss in the preceding section), *McCulloch* requires that the enactment be "appropriate and plainly adapted" to fulfilling an enumerated power.

To stick with the piracy example started in the preceding section, suppose that under statutory authority delegated by Congress, a federal agency requires the crew of any U.S.-registered ship regularly sailing in international waters to take a two-week mandatory course on the laws of piracy and how to deal with pirate threats.

This law doesn't literally define or punish piracy, as the Constitution allows, so the enumerated piracy power doesn't justify the law. But under the generous

McCulloch standards of whether an implied means is useful, helpful, conducive, and so on, you can argue that a well-trained and law-savvy crew is certainly helpful to bringing brigands to justice. *McCulloch* satisfied!

Acting in accord with constitutional restraints

McCulloch recognizes the bedrock rule of constitutional supremacy (discussed in Chapter 1). Any congressional-power exercise — or any act or omission by a government official — must follow the Constitution. To pick a (hopefully absurd) example, if male (but not female) crew members of U.S.-registered ships had to take mandatory anti-piracy training, that would violate the Constitution's Equal Protection ban on gender discrimination (detailed in Chapter 12).

Taxing and Spending

Federal taxing and spending policies have big impacts on all Americans. The *McCulloch* federal-power template applies to these bread-and-butter matters through analyzing the constitutionality of the various ways Congress raises revenue and the public programs and services on which it spends. These functions are often the subjects of political controversy.

The enumerated power to tax (and spend)

Article I, Section 8, Clause 1 of the Constitution enumerates the power "To lay and collect Taxes, Duties, Imposts and Excises, to pay the Debts and provide for the common Defense and general Welfare of the United States."

Technically, the express constitutional language doesn't include a power to spend. But the power to spend is a commonly understood element of the taxing power. After all, the only way to pay debts, defend the country, and promote its general welfare through taxation is to spend tax revenues. (They don't do any good stockpiled in the Treasury Department basement!)

When Congress raises and spends trillions of tax dollars, it simply exercises its enumerated power. And, with a couple of exceptions noted in the section "Constitutional restrictions to taxing," later in this chapter, Congress faces few legal (as opposed to political) constraints on its taxing and spending power.

Modern courts have gotten out of the business of judicially reviewing whether a particular tax levy or expenditure really serves "the general Welfare" or promotes "the common Defense." Modern courts leave these judgments to Congress and the president, as well as the constituents and special interests that loudly weigh in on the merits of particular tax and spend programs.

Identifying tax-related implied means

As any taxpayer knows, federal taxation requires you to file numerous forms and keep many backup records. These required filings don't directly generate taxes, but they qualify as "appropriate and plainly adapted" means to fulfill revenue raising. For example, a taxpayer who wants to claim a deduction for business use of their personal car must record dates, destinations, and miles traveled in case the Internal Revenue Service (IRS) audits their tax return.

Implied means also apply for federal spending. Requirements that student loan and government grant recipients keep records and undergo independent audits fall into "appropriate and plainly adapted" to ensure that the federal government can achieve its spending goals.

Constitutional restrictions to taxing

Despite the generally free hand Congress has with taxing and spending, courts enforce a few constitutional constraints:

>> **Congress can't impose a tax that's really a disguised penalty.** A tax qualifies as a penalty only when Congress imposes the tax "as punishment for an unlawful act or omission."

 An illustration: Many Americans who don't have health insurance felt the Affordable Care Act's individual mandate to buy insurance to meet federal standards or pay a tax was a penalty. But in upholding the mandate in a closely divided 2012 decision, the Court noted that the Act did "not attach negative consequences to not buying health insurance, beyond requiring a payment to the IRS." That the mandate "clearly aim[ed] to induce the purchase of health insurance" did not rule it out as a valid tax; and "taxes that seek to influence conduct are nothing new." (A statement that taxpayers paying steep cigarette excise taxes or getting tax breaks for buying electric cars know!)

>> **Congress can't violate other individual rights or protections when it taxes and spends.** For example, a 1968 decision, *Marchetti v United States,* held that the 5th Amendment prohibition on self-incrimination protected a professional gambler from the dilemma of either not reporting their income as any other taxpayer must (thus being guilty of tax evasion) or having their

self-reported illegal gambling become known to state law enforcers. Similarly, requirements that federal-fund recipients restrict their free speech could run afoul of the 1st Amendment.

When Congress imposes conditions on or arguably coerces state and local officials to whom they give federal grants, special limits kick in (which we talk about in Chapter 9).

Regulating Interstate Commerce

Article I, Section 8, Clause 4 grants the federal government authority to "Regulate Commerce . . . among the several States." These few simple words provide broad-ranging authority for thousands of laws (and hundreds of thousands of pages of federal rules and other agency actions) that regulate a broad array of economic, social, and health–and–safety issues:

>> **Enumerated power:** Modern legislators can assert strong regulatory control just by using the enumerated Interstate Commerce power itself; this involves passing legislation that controls (or delegates to executive regulators the power to control) commerce that crosses state borders or involves the *instrumentalities* (facilities and conduits) of interstate commerce (such as the internet).

>> **Implied means:** Congress can extend its commerce power into individual states by regulating local activities that substantially effect the national economy; this holding is a specialized application of *McCulloch's* permission for Congress to legislate "appropriate and plainly adapted" implied means.

>> **Restrictions:** Several recent Court decisions limit the far-reaching Interstate Commerce power in order to preserve the federal/state power balance, as we discuss in the following section.

Regulating interstate commerce itself

In the modern American economy, goods, services, and even people often cross state lines. Whenever they do, Congress can regulate interstate commerce (including illegal commerce) by using its enumerated powers in any of the follow-ing three ways:

>> **Ban the commerce.** The strongest form of commerce regulation is when Congress prescribes federal criminal or civil penalties for engaging in actions

across state lines. Obvious examples include federal laws that criminalize the interstate shipment of illegal drugs or the transportation across state lines of persons for sex trafficking.

>> **Allow but restrict the commerce.** Short of an outright ban, Congress can allow goods, services, or people to cross state lines but impose restriction on that crossing. For example, federal laws allow hazardous materials to travel across state lines but require driver qualifications and training, imposing limits on the number of hours any driver can work, and so on.

>> **Promote the commerce.** Congress can interpret the constitutional term *regulate* expansively to promote a national market, such as regulating railroad rates to prevent a state from enacting a trade barrier.

Sometimes, Interstate Commerce regulation seems to fit more than one of the categories in the preceding list. For example, a bipartisan majority in 2024 enacted the Protecting Americans From Foreign Adversary Controlled Applications Act. (Catchy name, we know.) Reflecting concerns about data security and privacy, the Act

>> Banned U.S. companies from facilitating the popular social-media app TikTok after January 18, 2025, if a Chinese-owned company still controlled it.

>> Allowed TikTok to continue its U.S. presence if specified restrictions on ownership and operation achieved what the Act called a "qualified divestiture."

>> Promoted national commercial activity while seeking to defuse security concerns, given TikTok's popularity and profitability with hundreds of millions of U.S. users.

This TikTok example illustrates *McCulloch's* three approaches at once: The Supreme Court considered, but rejected, arguments that the Act violated 1st Amendment free-speech guarantees.

In addition to regulating how commerce is conducted across state borders, the modern Supreme Court, in a long series of cases, broadened the reach of the enumerated Interstate Commerce power to include authority to regulate activities within a single state that are nevertheless closely related to the "means or instrumentalities" of interstate commerce. So, based on this opinion, Congress can regulate what happens aboard interstate bus, railroad, and air travel corridors; on interstate highways; and through interstate communication platforms — even if the person or entity regulated never crosses a state line.

In short, by directly regulating commerce across state lines and in interstate instrumentalities, Congress can make a significant mark on a wide swath of economic activity.

Regulating local economic activity through implied means

Congress needs to use implied means to its enumerated Interstate Commerce power in order to have influence on a lot of truly local economic activity. For example, Congress can't use its enumerated Interstate Commerce power (as described in the preceding section) to justify any of the following laws:

>> A labor law that prevented employers from firing employees who tried to organize a union affiliate for workers in a particular steel plant (*NLRB v. Jones & Laughlin Steel Corp.*, 1937)

>> A farm-price-stabilization law that restricted the size of the crop that individual farmers could produce (*Wickard v. Filburn*, 1942)

>> A law that criminalized *loan sharking* (extortion through onerous loans, used by organized crime to subvert legitimate businesses; *Perez v. United States*, 1971)

None of these local activities crossed state lines or connected to interstate instrumentalities. Yet the Court upheld these federal laws — and has greenlit many others — under the theory that the cumulative "substantial effect" of the local activities made their regulation an appropriate and plainly adapted means for fulfilling the congressional power to protect the national interstate economy.

Under current doctrines, Congress can ban, regulate, or promote local commerce over which it doesn't have express regulatory power when Congress can satisfy all three of these requirements:

>> A rational basis for its proposed legislation

>> Evidence that it developed itself (in hearings and reports) or borrowed from other sources (such as state legislatures)

>> Showing that the cumulative effect of all the local activities being regulated would have a substantial effect on the national economy

If Congress can show the elements in the preceding list, its actual motivation doesn't have to relate to cumulative economic effects. For example, even if Congress is really concerned about the adverse health and safety effects of malfunctioning nuclear-power plants, legislators can justify regulation through the economic ripple effects caused by impaired health and safety.

APPLYING COMMERCE REGULATION DOCTRINES FOR CIVIL RIGHTS

The Commerce Regulation doctrines allowed Congress to pass the immensely conse-quential Civil Rights Act of 1964. The Act eliminated segregation practices that denied African-Americans equal access to restaurants and other public accommodations. Concluding that its 14th Amendment authority to remedy governmental inequality (as discussed in Chapter 10) didn't reach private racial discrimination, Congress turned instead to its Interstate Commerce power. But because most private discriminatory practices didn't involve the crossing of state lines or the *instrumentalities* (facilities and conduits) of interstate commerce, Congress's plenary enumerated power fell short. Instead, Congress turned to its implied power to regulate local activities based on their economic effects.

The Supreme Court upheld the Act because the legislative record was "replete with evidence of the burdens that discrimination by race or color places on interstate commerce." The Court noted that, in addition to diminishing overall commercial activity, segregation suppressed African-American travel.

The Court held that Congress didn't have to provide an especially strong justification for its economic theory, beyond showing a "rational basis for finding that racial discrimination in restaurants had a direct and adverse effect on the free flow of interstate commerce." (As we explain in Chapter 12, a law can pass the rational basis test much more easily than, say, the evidentiary burden for civil litigation [more likely than not] or criminal conviction [beyond a reasonable doubt].)

The Court also rejected the argument that the Act was unconstitutional because Congress was using the negative economic effects of segregation as a pretext to regulate a moral and social issue. As you can read in the section "Regulating local economic activity as implied means," in this chapter, the relevant question is whether Congress illustrated the economic effects as plausible, not whether those effects are the real motivator.

Putting judicial brakes on regulation of local activities

The Court recognizes that expansive modern Interstate Commerce doctrines pose a major risk to the role that state and local governments traditionally play as prime regulators of their residents' economic and social life. In 1995's opinion for *U.S. v. Lopez*, the Court expressed concern that federal officials could "pile infer-ence upon inference" to show that almost all criminal activity, health and safety impairment, and environmental degradation eventually has downstream economic impacts. Such a showing seems especially easy, given that many activities, insubstantial in themselves, can be combined. Because Congress needs to meet only the low rational-basis standard, it could relatively easily undercut the state and local role.

A federal regulatory presence in many areas of daily life would, at a minimum, add complexities to state and local efforts; and because Congress can preempt state and local laws (which we discuss in Chapter 9), national legislators could significantly displace the state and local role on certain matters. To preserve traditional state commercial regulation roles, the modern Court places two potentially significant restrictions on Congress's power to regulate local activities, discussed in the following sections.

No power to force into a market

In the much-watched 2012 *NFIB v. Sebelius* case, the Court considered the constitutionality of the Affordable Care Act's individual-mandate requirement that most Americans who didn't have health insurance had to either buy minimally adequate coverage or pay a penalty. Rejecting the Obama administration's argument based on the billions of dollars uninsured Americans cost the healthcare system, a closely divided Court ruled that the Interstate Commerce power didn't stretch that far. The Court wrote that the Framers never envisioned that Congress's power to regulate existing commercial activity permitted Congress to "regulate individuals precisely because they are doing nothing."

As you can read about in the section "Constitutional restrictions to taxing," earlier in this chapter, the Court ultimately upheld the individual mandate under an alternative Taxing Power theory.

No power over non-economic local activities

In the *Lopez* decision, the Court states that Congress can't use its power to regulate local activities based on their cumulative "substantial effect" on the national economy if Congress isn't regulating activities that the Court defines as commerce or "any sort of economic enterprise."

Congress can still regulate non-economic activities to avoid undercutting federal economic regulation. Just to make things more complicated, ten years after imposing the limitation in *Lopez*, the Court held that federal drug-enforcement officials could apply the federal law that criminalizes illegal drug transactions to individuals who grow and consume marijuana as a state-approved method for dealing with chronic painful disease. Although the patients didn't seem to be engaged in any commerce or economic activity with respect to their home-grown and -consumed marijuana, the Court noted that medical marijuana looked identical to illegal marijuana and had a high street value, which, it argued, created strong incentives to divert it into illegal drug channels. The Court established a *Lopez* exception that allows federal regulation of non-economic local activity when that regulation is essential to avoid undercutting "a larger regulation of economic activity" (such as federal anti-drug laws).

WARNING

Don't confuse characterizing an activity as economic with the activity having economic *effects*. For example, the local activity deemed beyond the federal Interstate Commerce power in the 1995 *Lopez* case, transporting guns within 1,000 feet of school property, can have tragic results with large economic costs. But the substantial economic *effects* of gun transportation leading to school crimes or shootings didn't save the law in question. The Court saw transportation of a gun as not an inherently economic (as opposed to physical) activity, and the law wasn't limited to gun toting for commercial reasons.

Balancing War, National Security, and Foreign Policy Powers

In Chapters 5 and 6, we talk about several war, national security, and foreign policy powers that the Constitution gives Congress and the president. Court decisions identify some clear boundaries for when the other branches can or can't exercise these powers. The Court established limits on presidential power to seize private property during a war (stemming from the *Youngstown Sheet & Tube Company v. Sawyer* decision that you can read about in Chapter 6).

Court decisions have also established that, as part of their general authority to conduct foreign policy and recognize the legitimate authorities of a foreign country, Presidents can

>> Exercise broad authority to compromise private claims against foreign governments.

>> Not hold an American citizen, even though accused of being an enemy combatant, in indefinite military-brig confinement without providing "modified due process" to give the accused a chance to show that the allegation is unwarranted.

And Congress can't close initial access to federal civilian courts for non-citizens accused of being enemy combatants; so those accused get to raise initial claims that their confinement is unlawful, and the federal judiciary remains part of the process.

>> Cite border-security concerns to justify preventing entry into the country of all foreign nationals from specific countries. (This holding stems from the 2018 Supreme Court decision in *Trump v. Hawaii,* which relied on the broad discretion that federal law grants to presidents to control border entry.)

Yet, many important presidential power questions remain unresolved, including

>> **Whether presidents can nullify without Senate approval a treaty that requires initial Senate ratification.** In the 1979 Court decision in *Goldwater v. Carter,* which arose out of President Carter's revocation of a Taiwan defense treaty, five justices avoided deciding the matter, citing political-question and ripeness grounds (as discussed in Chapter 7). As a result, the revocation of the treaty stood, thus furthering the president's aim to foster relationships with China.

>> **The extent to which presidents can deploy U.S. Armed Forces or weapons in a foreign country without Congress declaring war or specifically approving.** In the aftermath of opposition to executive-branch escalation of the undeclared war in Vietnam, Congress passed (over President Nixon's veto) the War Powers Act of 1973. The Act requires presidents to consult with Congress and give timely notice of deployments; they're limited to 90 days unless Congress passes a joint resolution ordering an earlier end.

Although the Act would appear to resolve substantial uncertainties, successive presidents have claimed that the Act unconstitutionally usurps their Article II powers. The Court hasn't resolved the Act's constitutional merits, and several of the *justiciability barriers* (obstacles to reaching the legal merits raised in a case) we talk about in Chapter 7 could pose substantial hurdles to the Court ever doing so.

>> Whether presidents can decline to spend funds that Congress appropriates for military and foreign aid. This issue poses an especially difficult version of a more general uncertainty about the scope of presidential *impoundment powers,* meaning declining to spend funds already appropriated.

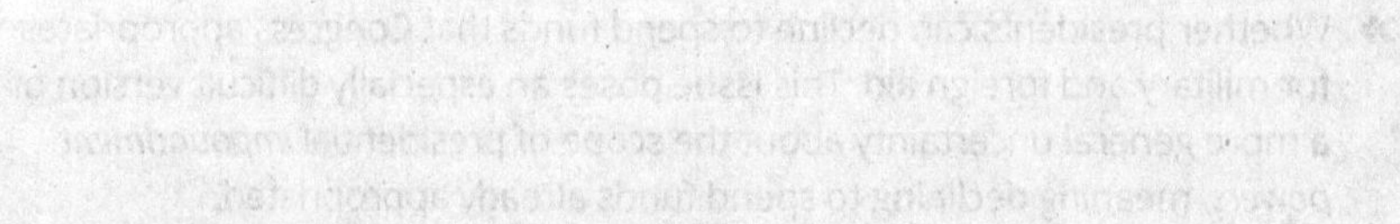

Chapter **9**

Dividing Power between National and State Officials

The Constitution's Framers inserted a new federal government into an existing scheme in which states already exercised significant authority. Both to recognize political reality and because they thought that powerful and independent states would provide a crucial hedge against abusive federal authority, the Framers tried to balance the federal and non-federal roles.

This chapter highlights the importance of states in the constitutional scheme and explains three specific limits that the Supreme Court has imposed on federal officials in the name of protecting state sovereignty. Then we turn the tables to explore two doctrines created by the Supreme Court aimed at preventing states from taking actions that would undermine the supremacy of federal law and the commerce-protecting policies behind the Interstate Commerce power (Article I, Section 8).

Checking Federal Power through the States

The Constitution's Framers intended for state governments and officials to have substantial independence and authority so that they could serve as one key defense against national-government overreach.

Evidence of the Framers' intention to encourage a substantial state presence begins with the powerful role they gave state officials in the workings of the national political process:

>> Each state chooses its presidential electors.

>> Each state has initial control over the "Time, Place, and Manner" of electing members of Congress (Article I Section 4, Clause 1).

>> State legislatures draw House districts, which can certainly affect the electoral chances of incumbent members.

>> States establish an election/re-election process that encourages Senators to reflect the interests of their states and House members to reflect the wishes of their districts.

REMEMBER

Under the original Constitution (Article I, Section 3), state legislatures chose Senators, which provided another way for the Constitution to reinforce incentives for Senators to respond to state needs. (In 1913, the 17th Amendment replaced state–legislative appointment with direct election, which you can read about in Chapter 2.)

The 10th Amendment, adopted soon after the Constitution's adoption, promotes respect for state authority by "reserving to the States" powers not specifically delegated to the national government.

Protecting State Sovereignty through the Constitution

In narrowly interpreting the scope of certain federal powers, Supreme Court justices seek to preserve a sufficient state role (which we talk about in Chapter 8). Beyond that, the modern Court has developed three constitutional limitations on the power of Congress when it seeks to directly control state and local governments.

Limiting coercive legislation

Whenever Congress directs its legislative powers at state and local governments, it faces an *anti-commandeering limit* as developed by the Court. In other words, Congress can encourage state officials (and local officials authorized to exercise state power) in order to further national legislative goals. But Congress can't *coerce* (compel through force or threats) state and local officials to do their bidding, such as to administer a federal program.

The key to distinguishing encouragement from coercion involves identifying whether the state or local target of federal legislation can choose to act or not. If state and local officials can say no to federal entreaties, federal authorities aren't coercing them. If the state officials must act or face, for example, loss of federal funds, that qualifies as coercion.

Court decisions in relation to coercion establish these dividing lines. Congress can't compel states to adopt or change their laws or regulations.

An example is the 1992 decision that articulated the anti-commandeering limit for the first time, in *New York v. United States.* The Court invalidated one provision in a law regulating low-level radioactive waste (such as that generated by medical tests and some manufacturing processes). The rejected provision seemed at first glance to offer the states a choice, but the choices required action either way. States could regulate low-level wastes under congressional instructions or *take title* of the wastes, becoming the owners of those wastes, which they then would have to deal with. The Court concluded that "[a] choice between two unconstitutionally coercive regulatory techniques is no choice at all."

Congress also can't compel state and local officials to execute federal law. In 1997, the Court decided in *Printz v. United States* that Congress couldn't require state and local officials to implement a federal policy conditioning gun permits on applicant background checks.

In the *New York v. United States* opinion, the Court explained that Congress may, as part of imposing a nationwide regulatory scheme, allow states to create an alternative law (meeting federal standards, of course!) that applies to their state residents, instead of federal law. This opt-out method, a key feature of several federal laws, including an environmental law upheld in *Hodel v. Virginia Surface Mining & Reclamation Association* (1981), allows states to deal with national problems in a way that better fits specialized state needs. In contrast to the restrictions on federal power discussed in the preceding list, these opt-outs provide states with a real choice about whether to spend the public's money and bureaucrats' time to develop and implement their own regulatory program. They can decide to do so or can decline, so this falls on the non-coercion side of the ledger.

The *New York v. United States* opinion also underlined two constitutional policies behind the anti-commandeering principle:

>> **State and local governments are sovereigns.** States having a degree of independence from federal control creates a special relationship and status (plus 10th Amendment protection, which you can read about in Chapter 2). A sovereign can claim more delicate treatment when it comes to regulatory controls than, say, private individuals and companies can.

>> **Anti-coercion principles promote political accountability.** If state and local officials make the decision whether to act, voters legitimately hold them responsible at elections or otherwise. But voters misdirecting their ire at state and local officials, when the feds really call the shots, which doesn't serve accountability.

Limiting conditions on federal grants

Chapter 8 discusses how Congress can use its spending power to dispense federal grants and then impose paperwork and other conditions on recipients. Congress can also place standard implementation conditions (such as audit requirements) on state and local grant recipients. But when Congress tries to use federal financial leverage to prompt state and local recipients to change their laws, regulations, or enforcement processes, a specialized set of limitations kicks in.

In its 1987 decision in *South Dakota v. Dole*, the Court laid out this four-part test for determining the constitutionality of federal grant programs:

>> **The spending program must be "in pursuit of the general welfare."** Given the great discretion courts afford to Congress's political judgments, Congress can easily meet this test.

>> **The law must "unambiguously" state the condition imposed as the price of getting federal dollars.** Again, Congress can easily meet this test as long as a clear law alerts recipients to the conditions of the grant.

>> **The condition must be related "to the federal interest in particular national projects or programs."** This requirement limits the scope of Congress's ability to get state and local governments to do its bidding by dangling financial carrots.

If Congress could seize on any spending program to require any unrelated condition — say, require states to reform their welfare laws in order to receive federal anti-pollution grants — the Congress could too easily use its spending power to extort through federal funding what it can't directly coerce.

> **» The condition must not violate any other constitutional limit.** This limitation includes the general anti-coercion principle discussed in the preceding section.

WHY THE ACA MEDICAID-EXPANSION CONDITION WAS UNCONSTITUTIONAL

A coalition of states led by Florida challenged the Affordable Care Act's Medicaid-expansion feature in 2012 in *NFIB v. Sebelius.* This feature offered states billions of dollars in new federal funding; to accept, states had to raise Medicaid eligibility limits from 100 percent of the poverty level to 133 percent.

In its *NFIB v. Sebelius* opinion, Court analysis of the Medicaid-expansion feature is a textbook example of applying the four-part *South Dakota v. Dole* template (see the section "Limiting conditions on federal grants," in this chapter):

- Congress easily concluded that giving poor people access to good healthcare serves the general welfare of the country by promoting individual and societal health.

- The litigating states certainly had clear notice that enhanced Medicaid funding came with a condition; that's why they sued!

- Significantly expanding the Medicaid ranks obviously related to the federal interest in quality healthcare for poor Americans.

But the Medicaid-expansion condition transgressed the fourth requirement by violating the unconstitutional-coercion limit because a state that didn't agree to the condition not only forfeited all new Medicaid money, but also lost 100 percent of the existing federal funds it received. Faced with a choice to expand Medicaid despite the financial risk or lose billions of dollars that they needed to support years of healthcare infrastructure, states faced what Chief Justice Roberts described in his majority opinion as a "gun to the head." States had no choice at all.

This coercive setup contrasted dramatically with what states stood to lose in the law upheld in *South Dakota v. Dole* — 5 percent of their existing federal interstate-highway construction funds. Even if highway-dependent states would beg to differ, the Court saw the 5 percent loss as "a relatively mild encouragement" to follow the federal lead and raise their drinking age to 21.

The Court hasn't clarified the dividing line between "encouragement" and "coercion," nor answered Justice Ruth Bader Ginsburg's rhetorical questions in her dissenting opinion in *Sebelius,* "[H]ow will litigants and judges assess whether 'a state has a legitimate choice?' Are courts to measure the number of dollars the Federal Government might withhold? The portion of the State's budget at stake?"

Limiting 14th Amendment enforcement

A limit arises when Congress uses its power under Section 5 of the 14th Amendment "to enforce, by appropriate legislation, [the amendment's] provisions." The 14th Amendment comes into play anytime the protections of the Bill of Rights apply to the states; the amendment imposes important restrictions on how state governments (and the local governments acting under state authority) treat persons subject to their legal authority; notably, states can't deny "equal protection of the laws" or deprive persons of "life, liberty, or property" without "due process of law."

Especially because almost all of the rights protected in the Bill of Rights have been incorporated into the liberty that states can't deprive, Section 5 gives Congress potentially broad power to pass laws that restrict the authority of state and local governments and their officials, as well as imposing additional compliance costs on those governments.

In its 1997 decision in *City of Boerne v. Flores*, the Court developed two limitations to protect state authority against inappropriate congressional control:

>> **Section 5 allows Congress to remedy only existing legal rights, not define new ones.** Congress can't use its power to enforce rights not yet identified by the Court. The *Boerne* Court invalidated the 1993 Religious Freedom Restoration Act (RFRA), to the extent that it would have forced courts to replace an easily met *reasonableness standard* (similar to the rational-basis test, this standard analyzes whether a rational person would agree with government's justification) with a much more rigorous *strict standard* (as explained in Chapters 10 and 12) when deciding whether state or local actions violate the Free Exercise of religion.

The *Boerne* Court viewed Congress as illegitimately going beyond its role of remedying *existing* constitutional understandings. Instead, Congress invalidly attempted to "decree the substance of the 14th Amendment's restrictions" by changing what rights the Amendment protects.

>> **Any Section 5 remedy must fit the injury.** The opinion states that you need "a congruence and proportionality between the injury to be prevented or remedied and the means adopted to that end." As applied in *Boerne* and later cases, this protection against excessive remedies essentially requires

- Reviewing the record of past state and local rights violations to determine how much evidence exists to show a pattern of illegality

- Assessing whether the remedy will impose broad-ranging compliance costs or is "narrowly targeted" and limited by safeguards

Protecting Federal Supremacy

Article VI, Clause 2 of the Constitution succinctly but powerfully states that "This Constitution, and the Laws of the United States which shall be made in Pursuance thereof . . . shall be the supreme Law of the Land." Constitutional and federal-government supremacy provides a crucial (and much litigated) constraint on the ability of state and local officials to pass laws and adopt policies that they would otherwise have authority to do under their state constitutions.

In expressly prioritizing the laws of the United States, the Supremacy Clause applies to more than congressional enactments. Federal regulations can preempt conflicting state and local laws, as can executive orders that validly implement the president's Article II authority.

Here's how the modern standards work to determine whether a particular state law is inconsistent with a particular federal law:

>> **Presumption against preemption:** Reflecting the Constitution's division of governmental power among federal and state governments, federal and state law should coexist. Those asserting that a state law is invalid because the federal law preempts it bear the burden of showing inconsistency.

>> **Express preemption:** Congress can include *preemption provisions* in laws that it passes, which identify the extent to which federal law does or doesn't oust state law.

>> **Implied field preemption:** Even if Congress doesn't make its preemption wishes known when legislating, courts can infer that Congress intended to preempt a particular field of legislation when

- The federal statutory scheme is so pervasive that state laws can't interfere.

- The scheme reflects a dominant federal interest.

- A single, uniform approach seems necessary.

For example, in 2012, in *Arizona v. United States*, the Court invalidated a provision of an Arizona law that made violating federal alien-registration requirements a state misdemeanor. The Court saw the comprehensiveness of federal law as a strong indicator that Congress wanted to leave states out of the alien-registration field — even if the states wanted to support or enhance federal law.

>> **Implied conflict preemption:** Courts can infer a congressional intent to preempt laws that conflict with federal law when

- Those subject to the law can't comply with both federal and state dictates.

- The state law or policy "stands as an obstacle" to fulfilling "the full purposes and objectives of Congress."

For example, in the same 2012 decision, the Court struck down two other Arizona-law provisions, not because these provisions occupied a preempted field, but because they would be an obstacle to federal immigration-law enforcement.

In 2012, the Supreme Court put off making a final decision on the most controversial section of Arizona's immigration law, which required law-enforcement officers in some circumstances to verify a person's immigration status during a stop, detention, or arrest. Noting that the law had written safeguards against racial profiling and civil-rights violations, the Court held that it was premature to invalidate the disputed section before state courts had construed it and without recorded evidence of abuses in practice. (In 2016, Arizona announced that it no longer engaged in the disputed practice.)

The Preemption doctrine requires courts to make difficult judgments. Determining the meaning behind express preemption provisions requires courts to consider multiple plausible interpretations of statutory language and apply it in situations the legislature may not have anticipated. And defining and prioritizing the purposes behind federal laws, deciding what qualifies as "full achievement" of the purposes, and making real-world policy judgments about state laws' impact on federal objectives appear to some critics as calling more for political judgments than for judicial analysis.

FEDERAL POWER + PREEMPTION = CONTROVERSY!

By empowering broad-ranging national legislation and then allowing federal law to preempt state and local laws to the contrary, the Constitution creates a prescription for ongoing political controversy. For example, as we explain in Chapter 14, the 2022 decision in *Dobbs v. Jackson Women's Health Org.* overturns 50 years of precedents that gave special constitutional protection to the right of adult women to choose abortion; *Dobbs* returns power to regulate abortion to the political process free of special constitutional restraint.

Dobbs is widely understood as returning power to state regulators — and many state legislatures enacted laws significantly restricting abortion access after *Dobbs*. But the decision also frees up Congress to pass national abortion legislation. (The Interstate Commerce power, detailed in Chapter 8, would directly allow a national enactment both

Preventing States from Undermining Economic Integration

The modern Court has declared in hundreds of cases that the Interstate Commerce power (Article I, Section 8, Clause 3 of the Constitution) performs an additional important duty, beyond empowering federal regulation (as we detail in Chapter 8). The Interstate Commerce Clause also reflects the Framers' commitment to a nationally integrated economy free of the trade barriers that states erected in pre-Constitution days to benefit their own businesses and residents. Through the so-called Dormant Commerce Clause doctrine (inferred by Chief Justice John Marshall, who served from 1801 to 1835, from the Commerce Clause), courts invalidate state and local policies that inappropriately interfere with the smooth flow of commerce among the states.

REMEMBER

Courts can't easily apply the Dormant Commerce Clause doctrine because, even if a state or local government doesn't try to impose illegitimate barriers, out-of-state businesses may face natural disadvantages in competing with in-state businesses. It may just cost more for out-of-state businesses to comply from a distance with legitimate health, safety, and environmental regulations — especially when they face multiple and potentially conflicting rules from the several states in which they compete for business.

To help courts distinguish between the burdens that out-of-state businesses naturally face and those erected by illegitimate trade barriers, they use the following presumptions to decide Dormant Commerce Clause cases:

>> **Discriminatory laws are presumed invalid.** The courts presume that laws or policies that a state adopts for the purpose or effect of discriminating against out-of-state commerce are unconstitutional unless the state shows

that its laws or policies are the only practical means for achieving legitimate economic, social, or health-and-safety benefits for the state's residents.

» **Non-discriminatory laws are presumed valid.** The court presumes that not-clearly-discriminatory laws or policies are constitutional, unless they impose substantial burdens on out-of-state commerce that are "clearly excessive" in light of the legitimate benefits achieved in-state.

Applying these guideposts requires difficult but important judgments, including:

» **Determining whether a law that doesn't appear discriminatory is discriminatory in effect:** Some challenged laws are clearly discriminatory on their face; they draw explicit in-state vs. out-of-state distinctions. For example, a New Jersey law addressed environmental concerns by letting only in-state residents and businesses access its landfills.

But sometimes a law that applies equally to in-state and out-of-state businesses can nevertheless have such lopsided burdens on the out-of-state businesses to deserve the dread discriminatory label. For example, a North Carolina law forbade any retailer, whether in-state or out-of-state, from marketing apples in the state by using any standard other than the U.S. Department of Agriculture (USDA) baseline grade. The Court found that North Carolina's law discriminated in effect against Washington State apple growers, who had developed marketing advantages by advertising that Washington-grown apples were of a superior quality.

» **Finding the rare case in which the state must discriminate:** Most of the time, a state can achieve any legitimate goals sought through a discriminatory law or policy in a less- or non-discriminatory way. For example, New Jersey could have solved its landfill problems by limiting the amount of landfill access equally for both in-state and out-of-state businesses. But the Court found in one unusual case that completely banning out-of-state, but not in-state, baitfish was the only practical way to protect Maine's fishing industry, because the risk to the industry came only from out-of-state baitfish.

» **Weighing the burdens and benefits of non-discriminatory laws:** Deciding whether the benefit/burden tradeoff is "clearly excessive" involves difficult policy tradeoffs that some deem inappropriate for judges to make because they could appear to be stepping into the shoes of legislators and other officials who make policy.

WHERE'S THE PORK?

A Dormant Commerce Clause decision in *National Pork Producers Council v. Ross,* in 2023, greenlit Proposition 12, California's voter-passed law to promote more humane pork production. In a fractured decision splintering into more than a half-dozen different opinions, the Supreme Court justices signaled potentially important shifts in their analytical approach.

The Proposition 12 case highlights the central importance of finding that a challenged state law is discriminatory. Although Proposition 12 applied equally to in-state and out-of-state pork producers, out-of-state producers felt the brunt of the burden because they provide almost all pork sold in California. The challengers asserted that even a non-discriminatory state law is unconstitutional if has the "practical effect of controlling commerce outside the State."

The various opinions in the Proposition 12 challenge showed significant internal divisions about the legitimacy of weighing a non-discriminatory law's burdens against its benefits. A majority supported considering this balance as an independent basis for attacking state and local laws. But the justices disagreed on how to engage in the analysis. And three justices openly called it a task inappropriate in "a functioning democracy, [where] policy choices . . . usually belong to the people and their elected representatives."

3

Broadly Protecting Civil Liberties

Appreciate the breadth of 1st Amendment protections that cover freedom of speech, as well as freedom of and from religion.

Scrutinize how the Constitution monitors government line-drawing to ensure people are treated equally.

Explore the power of due process to protect against the arbitrary deprivation of property or liberty by requiring fair processes and government accountability.

See how the Due Process Clause forces state governments to honor most individual protections in the Bill of Rights.

Chapter **10**

Assuring Freedom of Speech

The 1st Amendment to the U.S. Constitution boldly declares that "Congress shall make no law. . . abridging the freedom of speech." In this chapter, we focus on key aspects of constitutional protection for free speech. You can compare today's relatively robust safeguards with the more limited protection that speech received throughout most of the history of the U.S.

This chapter also examines one of the two basic questions that guide modern free-speech protection — does the speech in question fall into one of several narrow categories of unprotected speech, as outlined by the Supreme Court? The second basic question surrounding protected speech includes two essential dimensions: How much protection does speech deserve (in terms of why and where government can regulate)? To offer some examples, we examine different speech situations in which modern free-speech precedents deviate from the standard analysis, by giving either more or less protection to speech.

THE 1ST AMENDMENT'S OTHER PROTECTIONS

TECHNICAL STUFF

The 1st Amendment protects freedom of the press and rights of assembly. In general, however, these rights become interwoven with free-speech rights; many important free-speech cases involve the rights of journalists to publish or protesting crowds to assemble. In Chapter 20, we discuss how the 1st Amendment fits into the criteria used to assess the constitutionality of closing judicial proceedings to protect defendants' fair-trial rights at the expense of journalists' rights to observe and report.

Developing Modern Free-Speech Safeguards

REMEMBER

Many commentators think that the guarantees of free expression have a preferred position among constitutional rights (and not just because they're among the first rights that the Bill of Rights mentions!). Not only are free-speech rights crucial to the ability of Americans to speak truth to power, the right of people to speak and receive wide-ranging communications about political, social, spiritual, and artistic matters essentially links to the right to vote intelligently and to pursue a meaningful professional and personal life.

You live in an era in which the courts have given the 1st Amendment a very broad and robust free-speech protection. You might think that this protection has always been that generous — but it hasn't. Most of the speech protections covered in this chapter come from modern Court decisions that elevate protections for many, though not all, kinds of speech.

A HISTORY OF SPEECH SUPPRESSION

Here are a few historical free-speech low points that constitutional restraints didn't meaningfully limit:

- **The Alien and Sedition Acts:** A Federalist-party-dominated Congress passed these acts in 1798, in the same decade in which Americans ratified the 1st Amendment. As part of a broader restriction on immigrants and foreigners, it imposed serious criminal penalties for false, scandalous, or malicious writing about the government.

Although the text of the 1st Amendment literally addresses only speech abridgment by Congress, modern cases protect speech rights from attack by all federal officials, from the president down to the lowest-level employee. As you can read about in Chapter 3, in 1925, the Court applied the Free Speech Clause to all state and local officials through the Due Process Clause (meaning the Free Speech Clause was *incorporated* into the Due Process Clause). In fact, American constitutional law attaches such importance to the Free Speech Clause in part because the clause was one of the first provisions selectively incorporated.

Identifying Unprotected Speech

The first step in standard free-speech analysis involves determining whether case precedent classifies the speech in question as protected or unprotected. Basically, the default rule is that any speech not explicitly identified as unprotected is protected. So, the standard approach involves determining whether the speech being regulated falls into any of the narrowly defined unprotected-speech categories; if not, the speech emerges unscathed and is protected.

Defamation

Essentially, *defamation* is a written statement (*libel*) or verbal expression (*slander*) that injures a person's reputation in the community by spreading a disparaging falsehood. One nuance in defamation law is that when a *public figure* sues for damages for alleged defamation, a higher *actual malice* standard applies (which includes reckless disregard of the statement's falsity); the Court developed this additional protection to give media and other critics of public officials and other prominent figures additional breathing room.

Obscenity

By following a three-part test, developed in 1973 the *Miller v. California*, an especially hardcore swath of sexual speech (such as highly vivid sex scenes in books, magazines, and movies) unprotected if, analyzed as a whole, the speech

>> Appeals to a "prurient interest in sex," according to the *Miller* Court (meaning that which incites lasciviousness or lust)

>> Depicts sexual conduct in a patently offensive way

>> Lacks serious literary, political, or scientific value

For the first two elements of the obscenity test, judges or jurors in each community apply their *contemporary standards* (the benchmarks a community uses to assess whether to consider a work obscene). So, what people in one locality might consider sufficiently prurient or patently offensive to earn a defendant serious prison time, another locality's people might not.

The third element, however, protects against overzealous local prosecutions by judging value from a national perspective. Consider the 1974 case *Jenkins v. Georgia*, involving the sexually edgy but mainstream movie *Carnal Knowledge*. Although it included nudity, the film featured major Hollywood actors and a screenplay by a nationally known social satirist making serious points about gender relations. The Supreme Court overturned the Georgia jury's conclusion, finding serious value by using a national lens.

Speech in furtherance of a crime

Speech used in the planning or execution of a crime doesn't insulate the crime from punishment. A counterfeiter can't claim protection because their crime includes speech. ("Hey, want to buy this watch? It's a genuine Rolex!") And speech used to plan a crime can support charges for criminal conspiracy.

Subversive speech

The following sections discuss categories of unprotected speech that relate to *subversive speech* (speech that advocates the use of force or unlawful action and is likely to incite or produce such force or action). In each category, the Court seeks to reconcile the right of speakers to criticize government policies and officials (and groups within society) with the government's core responsibility to protect public safety and, ultimately, the survival of the Republic.

Incitement

After the landmark 1969 decision in *Brandenburg v. Ohio*, the Supreme Court established that speakers may underline the strength of their opposition to government policies by advocating, teaching the inevitability of, or expressing sympathy for violence or other violations of law (such as resisting being drafted into the military) — so long as their advocacy falls short of incitement. Per the *Brandenburg* opinion, subversive advocacy becomes unprotected only when it's "directed to inciting or producing imminent lawless action and is likely to incite or produce such action." It must contain all the following elements:

>> The speaker intends to cause violence.

>> That violence is happening now or in the near future.

>> The speaker is encouraging illegal activity.

>> People will likely act on this speech.

REMEMBER

When speakers fervently urge a crowd to fight for their rights, an observer might wonder why the legal system doesn't charge the fight-urgers with incitement to riot or similar crimes. Prosecutors might legitimately wonder in these circumstances whether they can convince a jury that the situation includes all four *Brandenburg* elements beyond a reasonable doubt. Especially if speakers mix in suggestions to seek peaceful resolution of grievances by legal means, a jury might question intent, imminence, and lawlessness.

The hostile audience situation

The *Brandenburg* incitement standard (discussed in the preceding section) deals with a speaker who encourages those who sympathize with their views to take immediate illegal action. By contrast, the hostile-audience situation arises when a speaker, whether intentionally or not, utters such emotionally charged rhetoric that opponents come to the point of rioting.

TECHNICAL STUFF

Unlike in *Brandenburg*, the Court hasn't clearly defined the elements for distinguishing between a speaker who simply arouses strong feelings and a situation so dangerous that it justifies shutting down a speaker. But analysts deduce from the facts and statements in different cases a two-part standard in which authorities face

>> A clear and present danger of immediate violence

>> Violence that can't suppressed by reasonable police measures (including restraining the aroused crowd)

Fighting words

The 1st Amendment doesn't protect a speaker who directs speech to an individual or identifiable group that would cause the average addressee to immediately fight back. (The *average addressee* is a hypothetical typical recipient of provocation who's neither abnormally tolerant nor especially short-fused.)

True threats

As the Court explained in the 2003 decision *Virginia v. Black*, the 1st Amendment doesn't allow a speaker "to communicate a serious expression of an intent to commit an act of unlawful violence to a particular individual or group of individuals."

Like fighting words (see the preceding section), unprotected true threats can arise outside of the subversive-speech context — for example, if a criminal extorts money by threatening violence if not paid — but they present gnarly free-speech problems when a provocative speaker entwines threats of violence with their otherwise protected political speech.

For example, in 1982's *NAACP v. Claiborne Hardware Co.*, the Court reviewed a Mississippi conviction for a speech given by an official of the NAACP, which was supporting an economic boycott of local White-owned stores accused of racial discrimination. With one small phrase in a long, vigorous, but peaceful speech, the official warned any listener who broke ranks that "we'll break your neck." The Court overturned the official's conviction because listeners would understand the isolated threat as *hyperbole* (spirited exaggeration) in the context of an otherwise peaceful call for concerted action.

ONLINE INCITEMENT

Even staunch advocates of civil liberties express concern that the *Brandenburg* test (discussed in the section "Incitement," in this chapter) fails to give governments sufficient leeway to counter the dangers of extremist social-media postings. Critics specifically worry that online messages that incite violence would be protected by the *Brandenburg* limit that the inciter must call for imminent violence. A message that urges violence might not call for viewers to take immediate action; even if it did, supporters might not immediately act on it (if, for example, the target isn't near that group or individual at that moment). Instead, the message might be preserved online until a later time, when an especially impressionable viewer takes up the call. At the time of writing, the Supreme Court hasn't officially responded to these concerns.

The True Threat doctrine raises other perplexing questions, including whose perspective counts. Can a court convict the speaker because threat recipients reasonably feared injury? Or must prosecutors show that the speaker intended the recipients to become fearful — or that they at least acted with reckless disregard to that happening? In a 2023 case, *Counterman v. Colorado*, the Court resolved years of uncertainty by holding that the speaker's intent is key to determining whether speech qualifies as a true threat.

Protecting Objectionable Speech

A lot of speech falls into the category of protected speech (because it doesn't fall into any unprotected-speech categories, as discussed in the section "Identifying Unprotected Speech," earlier in this chapter). But all kinds of speech fall into the protected category:

>> Just because speech is protected doesn't necessarily mean that it's important or likely to contribute to civic discourse.

>> Much highly objectionable and very uncivil speech ends up protected because it doesn't fall into any of the unprotected-speech categories.

In the *Terminello v. City of Chicago* decision of 1949, the Court asserted that free speech "may indeed best serve its high purpose when it induces a condition of unrest, creates dissatisfaction with conditions as they are, or even stirs people to anger." Here are a few of the many examples of offensive protected speech:

>> **Hate speech:** A speaker is protected when using highly objectionable racist, sexist, homophobic, or any other bigoted slurs. Such speech loses its 1st Amendment protection only when it's so provocative as to likely start an immediate fight, cause an immediate riot, incite immediate violence, and so on.

>> **False political speech:** The false statements that bedevil current political discourse are broadly protected. Modern speech doctrines place the burden of detecting and censoring untrue messages not on the government, but instead on the public through the marketplace of ideas.

>> **Pornography/indecency:** The multi-billion-dollar pornography industry's products don't fall within the government's narrow definition of obscenity because they don't meet the criteria that we discuss in the section "Obscenity," earlier in this chapter.

Determining How Protected to Make Speech

If speech is protected (which the section "Identifying Unprotected Speech," earlier in this chapter, analyzes), an important question arises: How much protection does it get?

The amount of protection due to protected speech varies, depending upon two major factors:

>> On what basis is government regulating speech? (Is the regulation based on the content of the speech?)

>> If government regulates speech in a specific location, does that location qualify as a public forum, to which stronger protection generally applies?

Varying protection based on why government is regulating

REMEMBER

Free-speech doctrines are on special alert when governments censor speech because the government — or a group that they serve — object to the message of that speech (which makes it *content-based* regulation). Concern lessens significantly, but not completely, when governments suppress speech for reasons other than reaction to the message (called *content-neutral* regulation). These different levels of concern lead to very different hoops that government must jump through to establish the constitutionality of its regulation.

Content-based regulation

You can break down content-based regulation into two types:

>> **Viewpoint regulation:** Targets only certain positions about a subject.

   For example, if a law prohibits the federal government from approving "immoral or scandalous" product trademarks, this content-based regulation is a viewpoint regulation. Authorities who apply the prohibition must examine the message of a proposed trademark and prohibit only certain types of product identifications.

>> **Subject-matter regulation:** Declares speech about a certain subject off limits, regardless of the speaker's point of view.

   Say that a municipally owned bus company refuses to allow political advertisements on the paid-advertising message boards on its buses. This content-based regulation involves the type of message of a proposed ad and determines whether it can be posted, but the point of view of that ad doesn't matter. This is subject-matter regulation.

A content-specific regulation requires *strict* scrutiny. The government must show that it needs to impose content-based regulation to fulfill a compelling government interest — highest-order concerns, such as protecting the country, preventing deaths and serious injury, or stopping counterfeiters from undermining the currency system. And the government must achieve its compelling interest through a *narrowly drawn* (meaning least restrictive yet practical) law.

To meet the narrowly-drawn requirement, government must show that the law isn't

>> **Over-inclusive:** A fancy term for going further than necessary to achieve the compelling interest. Given the 1st Amendment's strong aversion to message censorship, it makes sense to prevent government from regulating more speech than it has to.

>> **Under-inclusive:** Because it fails to regulate kinds of speech whose suppression would achieve the government's interest.

Content-neutral regulation

Content-neutral regulation deals with regulation of speech unrelated to (*neutral* about) the speech's content:

>> **Time, place, and manner:** This type of regulation affects speech based on when, where, and how that speech occurs — regardless of its message.

   After anti-abortion-rights protestors caused disturbances at clinics, state law made it unlawful for any person within 100 feet of any healthcare facility to approach another person within 8 feet without that person's consent to pass out a leaflet, display a sign, or engage in oral protest, education, or counseling with that person. Although the state adopted the law in response to a group that has a particular viewpoint, because the law applied equally to any protester who attempts to have an unwanted conversation about any subject near a healthcare facility, the ordinance is location-and-manner based and therefore content-neutral.

>> **Speaker status:** Who the speaker is and their role can influence a content-neutral regulation.

In the section "Seeing the different standards in action," later in this chapter, we unpack a content-neutral decision that upheld a school's policy about regulation of communication by unions with teachers. The Court found that the distinction between the group that was allowed to communicate and the group that wasn't depended on their differences in status, not subject; the official union had been chosen in an election by teachers.

Content-neutral regulation must pass intermediate scrutiny (as compared to content-specific regulation, discussed in the preceding section, which must face strict scrutiny). Government can more easily justify regulation of content-neutral protected speech because it faces this lower level of scrutiny. The government only needs

>> **A significant interest:** Although a *significant* interest is heightened, it's not a *compelling* interest (for which the government must show the strongest justification for regulating speech), which strict scrutiny requires.

>> **To avoid regulating substantially more speech than necessary:** Instead of any over- or under-coverage dooming the law.

>> **To leave the speaker with ample alternative channels for communication:** This last requirement doesn't guarantee a speaker their most-desired communication method. The speech restriction just has to allow ample, if second-best, alternatives.

Determining protection based on location

The level-of-scrutiny analysis for free speech must take into consideration when governments regulate protected speech in particular locations (as opposed to speech regulations applying everywhere within a jurisdiction, such as a state law broadly prohibiting true threats, which you can read about in the section "True threats," earlier in this chapter, regardless of location).

- **» Traditional public forums:** A fixed category that includes only streets, sidewalks, and public parks. These locations, according to a 1939 Court decision, *Hague v. Committee for Industrial Organization,* "have immemorially been held in trust for use by the public" for "purposes of assembly, communicating thoughts between citizens, and discussing public questions."

- **» Non-traditional public forums:** Locations that a government has voluntarily opened for general public communication. A common example is when a state university opens an internal plaza on campus as a free-speech zone where student and outside groups can express positions on political and other matters. Decisions charting this concept look for an official policy or actual pattern of governmental encouragement of wide-ranging speech.

- **» Non-public forums:** Government hasn't broadly opened up its property (for example, sidewalks on post-office premises that allow postal patrons to get from the parking lot to the entrance) for general public speech.

A key factor in sorting non-traditional public forums and non-public forums involves whether general-public speech is compatible with the primary purpose and characteristics of the government property in question. The primary purpose of a university-designated free-speech zone is general-public exchange; the venue's qualities lend themselves to that. An internal post-office sidewalk's primary purpose is to get patrons safety and swiftly to and from a government service.

TECHNICAL STUFF

Not all sidewalks are created equal. The open-to-all-comers sidewalk that runs along the street in front of a post office is, like the street itself, a traditional public forum. (Patrons who protest postage-stamp price increases on that kind of sidewalk have full 1st Amendment protection.) But the internal sidewalk on postal property, which runs up to the post office door, falls into a non-public forum.

Applying different location standards

After you characterize the location where the government is regulating speech (see the preceding section), you can determine the applicable levels of scrutiny that government must meet:

- **» Public forums:** Regulation of protected speech in either a traditional public forum or a non-traditional public forum plays by the standards that you can find in the section "Varying protection based on why government is regulating," earlier in this chapter: Namely, content-based regulation gets strict scrutiny and content-neutral regulation gets intermediate scrutiny.

- **» Non-public forums:** The standards for judging regulation of speech in a non-public forum are much more generous and significantly easier to meet in a non-public forum than in a public forum. Subject-matter regulation needs

only be *reasonable* (meaning appropriate or fair), a standard more forgiving than the intermediate-scrutiny standard applied to public forums.

The leniency of non-public forum regulation has an important exception: Even in government venues not designated for general speech, content-based viewpoint regulation still draws strict scrutiny.

Seeing the different standards in action

To give you an example of how the public-forum wrinkle plays out in a Supreme Court case, we examine *Perry Education Association v. Perry Local Educators' Association*, an opinion from 1983 (mentioned in the section "Content-neutral regulation," earlier in this chapter). This case is a content-neutral decision that upheld a school's policy about regulation of communication by unions with teachers. The Court found that the distinction between the group that was allowed to communicate and the group that wasn't depended on their differences in status, not their viewpoint on labor issues. The Court upheld the school board's policy of allowing exclusive access to the mail slots by the union that the teachers had chosen in an election. The Court also looked at the following factors:

>> **Forum:** The Court ruled the mail slots were a non-public forum because, to qualify as a non-traditional public forum, the school would need a policy or practice of opening them up for general-public exchanges of ideas. At most, the school had a pattern of providing selective access to communications regarding outside events of interest to students; the primary purpose of the internal mail system was to efficiently facilitate communication among school staff (a use not lending itself to general public communication).

The forum characterization wouldn't have mattered if the Court had found that differential treatment of the official and rival unions was based on their viewpoints; that's the one kind of censorship not allowed even in a non-public forum.

>> **Type of regulation:** The Court found this type of regulation content-neutral, so it just had to be reasonable (versus strict or intermediate). (We talk about levels of scrutiny in the section "Varying protection based on why government is regulating," earlier in this chapter.) Even a low-level concern about message clutter sufficed because it qualified as legitimate, the interest level that reasonable scrutiny requires.

Protecting Speech in Special Situations

In some special situations, speech receives treatment that deviates from the standards. Some situations see unusually strong protection under free-speech doctrines, but other types of speech get less protection.

Providing unusually strong speech protection

Challengers to speech regulation can rely on several special tools that courts use to protect speech.

Prior restraint

An especially strong judicial skepticism to laws that seek to censor speech before it takes place honors the Framers' special concern with that form of censorship. Particularly when prior-restraint laws allow the suppression of disfavored messages, courts are inclined to apply an especially protective version of strict scrutiny.

For example, judges are quick to strike down laws that let officials reject licenses or permits for marches or other political gatherings without objective standards (such as crowd size and location logistics). Judges worry that, without objective limits, officials can deny permits merely because they object to the permit-seeker's message.

Vagueness

The Constitution's Due Process Clauses in the 5th and 14th Amendments prohibit vague criminal laws (laws that don't inform "a person of reasonable intelligence" as to their reach). Due Process regards vague laws as fundamentally unfair because they force people to guess whether conduct that they want to engage in can put them in criminal jeopardy. (Chapter 13 goes into detail about the Due Process Clauses.)

When vague criminal laws regulate speech, however, courts are especially likely to ride to the rescue, taking the position that vagueness leads to would-be speakers self-censoring to avoid the law's uncertain reach. Vague laws that punish speech also allow conviction based on a speaker's disfavored views.

Substantial overbreadth

Chapter 7 notes that the judicial-restraint rule of *standing* (when a challenger has a sufficient personal stake to be able to bring suit) generally frowns on one litigant asserting the rights of another. But a special concern for speech causes the Court to waive its general objection in one specialized speech context.

This Substantial Overbreadth doctrine allows a speaker who could be validly convicted under a narrow law to nevertheless escape conviction by showing that the law under which they were in fact convicted (or are being charged) also covers a substantial amount of protected speech. Essentially, the substantial-overbreadth doctrine rewards an unprotected speaker by reversing their conviction when they point out a law's tendency to negatively impact the rights of protected speakers.

For example, the 1972 decision in *Gooding v. Wilson* overturned a protester's conviction under a statute that made it a crime to utter "opprobrious words or abusive language" tending "to cause a breach of the peace." This statute covered a lot more than unprotected fighting words: Many words might strike hearers as abusive but still be protected because they wouldn't lead to an immediate fight. The Court therefore nullified the statute as substantially overbroad. The Court overturned Gooding's conviction without having to decide whether Gooding's provocative statements to police officers qualified as unprotected fighting words because the potential existed for using the statute under which he was convicted to regulate a lot of protected speech, as well.

The *Gooding* decision shows one downside of using the Substantial Overbreadth doctrine: A court doesn't have to pinpoint the dividing line between protected and unprotected speech.

Receiving less protection than the standard

In some situations, free-speech doctrines afford less protection than the standard rules provide. We talk about some of the more notable examples in the following sections.

Conduct that speaks (symbolic speech)

Some conduct is *expressive*, meaning that it seeks to physically convey a point of view. Flag burning and draft-card burning are obvious examples. In *United States v. O'Brien*, in 1968, the Court indicated that government faces an easier time in justifying *content-neutral* regulation of expressive conduct; *O'Brien* developed a different four-factor test for analyzing a federal law that punishes anyone who destroyed or mutilated a draft card for any reason. But in the later 1989 case *Texas v. Johnson*, the Court's opinion invalidated a conviction under Texas's anti-flag-burning law. In that case, the Court applied the standard strict-scrutiny analysis because the law was *content-based* because it reflected the state's aversion to a disrespectful message.

The Supreme Court at the time of writing takes a strict-scrutiny approach when governments regulate campaign spending. (You can read about the levels of scrutiny in the section "Varying protection based on why government is regulating," earlier in this chapter.) We discuss this position in Chapter 17, as part of our coverage of constitutional doctrines affecting voting and elections.

Speech involving students and institutionalized persons

The Court loftily declared in the *Tinker v. Des Moines* case in 1969 that "students do not shed their constitutional rights to free speech . . . at the schoolhouse gate." Nevertheless, because students are minors and school officials are charged with special supervisory and educational responsibilities, school officials can restrict student speech rights in ways adult speech rights can't be restricted. For example, those officials can censor student newspapers to promote educational goals. And school officials can punish student speakers at an assembly for speech that includes sexual double meanings, the kind of speech that appears on any late-night talk show.

SPEECH AND SOCIAL MEDIA AT SCHOOL

Social media create difficult free-speech puzzles — especially when the discussion involves school children. School officials generally have a freer hand to control student speech on campus (see the section "Speech involving students and institutionalized persons," in this chapter); this control includes student social-media access while on school grounds.

But what if a school-related communication occurs off campus? The Court confronted this question in the 2021 case of *Mahanoy Area School District v. B.L.*, which involved high-school administrators suspending a student from the cheer team after she posted a profanity-filled temporary Snapchat post. (Hurt by not being selected for the varsity cheer team, the student roundly vilified the school and her teammates.) The Court held that, because school officials failed to show that the student's off-campus social-media post "materially disrupted" the learning environment, the suspension violated the student's free-speech rights.

The Court has yet to work out clear rules and limits for schools attempting to deal with more ominous off-campus student communications, such as cyber-bullying.

Prison officials can restrict the rights of adult inmates to speak and receive litera-
ture in ways that non-incarcerated adults would find intolerable.

Speech that raises special child-welfare concerns

Sometimes — but not always — the Court bends free-speech rules when government has a special concern for child welfare. For example:

>> **Child pornography:** Although the Constitution protects non-obscene adult
pornography (as we talk about in the section "Protecting Objectionable
Speech," earlier in this chapter), it doesn't protect pornography involving
children.

>> **Media that has a child audience:** Offensive and profane speech is generally
constitutionally protected. But in the case of *FCC v. Pacifica Foundation* (1978),
when a radio station aired a comic monologue that contained profanity in the
middle of the afternoon, the Court found that the uniquely pervasive acces-
sibility of mass communications to children justified special limitations by
government regulators.

Commercial speech

Advertising and other speech related to commercial transactions started out as an
unprotected speech category. Speech proposing illegal transactions and false
advertising remain unprotected. But Court decisions since the 1970s developed
different standards for judging when governments can regulate *commercial
speech* (such as advertisements by lawyers and other professionals, product labeling, and price advertising). Recent developments enhance the level of free-speech
protection.

Professional regulation that incidentally suppresses speech

Because many professionals use speech to treat clients and patients, various
regulations imposed by governments at all levels can generate free-speech
controversies.

For example, *Chiles v. Salazar*, a case on the 2025–2026 Supreme Court docket, has
a therapist challenging a Colorado law that forbids licensed therapists from using
conversion therapy to treat patients under the age of 18. (The law in question
defines *conversion therapy* as "any practice or treatment . . . that attempts . . . to
change an individual's sexual orientation or gender identity.") How the Court
interprets the regulation type of the law determines the level of scrutiny it must
apply to the case:

>> **Strict scrutiny:** If the challenger persuades the Court to see the law as discrimination against a disfavored viewpoint — significantly, the law doesn't ban therapy that provides "acceptance, support, and understanding" for a patient's gender-identity exploration — Colorado will face the rigors of strict scrutiny.

>> **Rational-basis test:** If Colorado persuades the Court to treat this law as regulation of conduct that has only incidental effects on speech, Colorado needs to meet only the easily winnable rational-basis test (a reasonableness standard).

To see whether the Court has reached a decision in this case, go to the official website at www.supremecourt.gov.

Government-funded speech (and book bans)

Governments routinely spend public funds to speak about a wide array of issues, such as the dangers of smoking and illegal drugs. Governments also suppress the speech of persons who carry out government-funded programs; for example, federal law forbids doctors who provide care in federally funded family-planning programs from advocating abortion as a method of birth control.

REMEMBER

Governments generally have a freer hand in suppressing speech when they pick up the tab. But one very controversial intersection of government funding and speech is book banning. A 1982 Supreme Court opinion in *Island Trees School District v. Pico* failed to provide clear guidance for future cases facing these issues. Several justices did express the following benchmarks:

>> "[S]chool boards may not remove books from school library shelves simply because they dislike the ideas contained in those books and seek by their removal to 'prescribe what shall be orthodox in politics, nationalism, religion, or other matters of opinion.'"

>> But those same justices said that removal of books from a public-school library would be constitutional "if the removal decision was based solely upon the 'educational suitability' of the books in question," versus the unpopular ideas in the books themselves.

How the Constitution might relate to bans by public libraries that serve adult readers remains murky. Active litigation at the lower-court level may lead the Supreme Court to clarify.

THE RIGHT NOT TO SPEAK

Since 1943, the Court has identified a flip side of the 1st Amendment's right to speak. In that year, in *West Virginia Board of Education v. Barnette*, the Court invalidated a state law that required students to salute the American flag. When several students objected that their religion saw this act as idolatry, the Court held that free-speech guarantees include the right not to be forced to speak a government-crafted message. This Compelled Speech doctrine later led to a 1977 ruling in *Wooley v. Maynard* that New Hampshire couldn't punish a pacifist resident for covering up the State's "Live Free or Die" motto on their license plate.

In recent years, the Court has expanded the reach of the Compelled Speech doctrine. Among the notable cases are

- ***Janus v. American Federation of State, County, and Municipal Employees:*** A 2018 holding that public employees can't be required to pay union dues that could fund political activity with which they disagree

- ***National Institute of Family and Life Advocates v. Becerra:*** A 2018 ruling that a state may not force crisis-pregnancy centers, which oppose abortion on religious grounds, to post a state-written disclosure giving clients information about state-provided abortion services

- ***303 Creative LLC v. Elenis:*** A 2023 decision that a state's anti-discrimination law may not compel a wedding-website designer who objects on religious grounds to same-sex marriage to craft a webpage for same-sex couples

Although the Compelled Speech doctrine arises in the unusual context of a person *not* wanting to speak, the speech-protection standards are the same. Government requirements that reluctant speakers parrot government viewpoints or subjects must meet strict scrutiny.

Chapter **11**

Protecting Freedom from and of Religion

Religion plays an important (and controversial) role in modern America, including in the application of the 1st Amendment. In two separate clauses, the amendment prohibits any government official from favoring a particular religion ("respecting an establishment of religion") or disfavoring religion in general ("prohibiting the free exercise thereof").

This chapter explains how the Court has interpreted these two prohibitions in a variety of ways and examines the current doctrines for implementing the first prohibition, generally known as the Establishment Clause, and avoiding violation of the second limit, the Free Exercise Clause. You can also read arguments about whether the two clauses conflict or are complementary in this chapter.

Like all Bill of Rights provisions (which you can read about in Chapter 2), the 1st Amendment directly restricts only the federal government. But through the process of 14th Amendment selective incorporation (explained in Chapter 3), the 1st Amendment now constrains all state and local governments, as well.

Avoiding Religious Favoritism

At a minimum, the Framers of the Establishment Clause meant to reject England's establishment of an official church (The Church of England) and coercion of non-believers to support it financially and through required attendance. And, despite a diversity of religions in colonial America, some colonies also established official churches, such as Congregationalism (specifically, Puritanism) in parts of New England.

Modern Court interpretations of the Clause's anti-establishment principle go significantly beyond this barebones prohibition. To set the boundaries of anti-establishment protections, the Court must make sense of differing perspectives among the 1st Amendment's Framers about the proper interaction of church and state. The Establishment Clause doctrines apply to how government interacts with religion in several distinct ways.

Confronting the Framers' disagreements about church and state

Modern anti-Establishment Clause decisions reflect substantial disagreements among justices about which criteria to use to fulfill the 1st Amendment's meaning. This disagreement continues a tradition — the Framers themselves disagreed about what they wanted to accomplish.

Some Framers sought to erect a high wall of separation between church and state. These separationist Framers fell into two subgroups, depending on their goal:

>> **Protect religion:** Emphasized the need to protect religion against the corrupting influence of government; they worried that religions would dilute their doctrines to curry government favor.

>> **Protect government:** Worried more that religious believers would compromise governmental independence and social unity when they competed to bend laws and policies to their desires.

Either focus sought to keep religion and government in largely separate spheres.

Some people mistakenly think that the words "separation of church and state" appear in the Constitution itself. They don't, and the extent to which the 1st Amendment embraces the concept is debatable.

Constitutional Framers who didn't fall into the separationist camp favored a more religion friendly view that sometimes goes by the difficult-to-pronounce name of *non-preferentialism.* Under this view, as long as governments don't pick favorites among religions (preferring, say Lutherans over Catholics or Christians over non-Christians), they can recognize the special role of, and even foster, religion in general. One prominent example of the non-preferentialist approach is when then-President George Washington declared a "day of public thanksgiving and prayer" to acknowledge "the many and signal favors of Almighty God."

Limiting prayer and other religious practices in public schools

Establishment Clause controversies have prominently played out in the nation's public schools. Starting with the landmark 1962 case of *Engel v. Vitale,* the Court has consistently prohibited school officials from "officially prescribing a particular form of religious worship." However, this prohibition doesn't mean that religion has no place at public school.

Religious practices that the Court prohibits

Engel struck down a New York policy that required each public school day begin with an officially led prayer. ("Almighty God, we acknowledge our dependence upon Thee, and we beg Thy blessings upon us, our parents, our teachers, and our country.") In so doing, the Court set out the core principle that governments act unconstitutionally when they put their "power, prestige, and financial support behind a particular religious belief."

REMEMBER

Engel also established the important principle that a voluntary government-supported prayer is still unconstitutional. Even if students may remain silent or leave the classroom during the prayer, *Engel* found it "plain" that students from religious minorities or non-believers would feel "indirect coercive pressure . . . to conform to the prevailing officially approved religion."

Post-*Engel* decisions followed *Engel*'s logic to strike down the following forms of religious worship:

>> Prayers that school authorities borrow from religious texts such as the Lord's Prayer (*Murray v. Curlett,* 1963).

>> Prayers said at the opening of school functions outside of the normal school day and away from school grounds, such as graduation (*Lee v. Weisman,* 1992) and before the start of football games (*Santa Fe Independent School District v. Doe,* 2000).

But you can read about a case where the free-exercise right of a football coach who prayed at the end of the game won out in the section "Considering whether the Religion Clauses Conflict," later in this chapter.

>> Voluntary prayer when amended to a law as a favored use of a moment of silence at the beginning of a school day (*Wallace v. Jaffree*, 1985).

>> Bible verses (or other religious texts) read without comment (*Abington School District v. Schempp*, 1963). (See the following section for how religious texts can fit into public education.)

>> The Ten Commandments posted on schoolroom walls so that students "read, meditate upon, and perhaps to venerate and obey" its religious teachings (*Stone v. Graham*, 1980).

The Court's concern about religious teachings in public school also led it to strike down

>> A law banning the teaching of the scientific theory of evolution (*Epperson v. Arkansas*, 1968)

>> A law requiring a school to teach *creation science* (a pseudoscientific belief system) whenever it teaches evolution (*Edwards v. Aguillard*, 1987)

Religious practices that the Court allows

Engel emphasized that its ban on officially approved religion doesn't require a "hostility to religion." Backing up that sentiment, a year after *Engel*, the Court opined that the Bible and other religious texts or materials may be "presented objectively as part of a secular program of education" in *Abington School District v. Schempp*, The Court elaborated that education should include a study of "comparative religion or the history of religion and its relationship to the advancement of civilization," and therefore "the Bible is worthy of study for its literary and historic qualities." By extension

>> A curriculum can include religious art in a world-civilization or art-appreciation class.

>> School bands and choral groups can perform religiously-inspired music.

>> Officials can include religious songs and holiday decorations in holiday assembly programs to highlight their historical or social significance.

In determining whether the presence of religious materials in schools is valid, the Court examines whether government is using its power to prescribe religious worship and support religious beliefs. If not, schools can use religion as a legitimate part of an objective curriculum.

Finally, religiously motivated students are always free to offer their own prayers at any time during the school day — and they may pray publicly in cafeterias, on sports fields, or in other public spaces — as long as their prayers don't disrupt the educational environment. (And as the old joke goes, "As long as there are math tests, there will be prayer in school.")

Allowing prayer in the legislature

Outside of the public-school context (discussed in the section "Limiting prayer and other religious practices in public schools," earlier in this chapter), Establishment Clause doctrines are more tolerant of prayers at official proceedings.

A prime example is the 1983 *Marsh v. Chambers* Court decision upholding a state legislature's practice of starting each legislative-session day with a prayer by a publicly paid chaplain. The U.S. Congress follows a similar tradition. Although the Court hasn't ruled directly on this congressional practice, the logic of the 1983 decision — that the chaplain's prayers are intended to serve the spiritual needs of legislators and aren't addressed to the public observing the legislative sessions — would appear to greenlight Congress's chaplain practice.

A more recent 2014 decision extended the range of allowable prayers at legislative sessions. In *Town of Greece v. Galloway*, the Court upheld the practice of a local town council starting each monthly meeting with a prayer led by a randomly selected community volunteer. The volunteers were predominantly Christians, and many of their prayers overtly invoked Christian themes and holidays. Yet, the *Town of Greece* Court rejected a claim that this practice inappropriately associated government with religious rituals with the following arguments:

>> **Private sentiment:** Because town officials did not try to influence the content of the prayers, meeting attendees would understand that the prayers represented private, and not governmental, religious sentiments.

>> **No coercion:** The Court rejected the claim that attendees would feel coerced to participate (at least to the extent of remaining silent) in the prayers to avoid the disapproval of the town councilmembers.

>> **No disparagement:** Significantly, no pattern existed of the prayers at these meetings over time disparaging other believers.

The Court doesn't provide a clear explanation of the difference in treatment between public school and public legislative events in relation to religion. Perhaps

> » The limits on prayers in the public schools reflect a greater concern that impressionable children and teenagers are more likely to see governmental approval and sponsorship of a religion than the adult attendees and observers at legislative sessions.

> » The decisions represent a desire to allow traditional civic-ceremonial practices.

> » The different treatment for prayers in and out of public schools might reflect real differences in the context, method, or motivation of those who offer the prayers.

Whatever the motivation, current Establishment Clause doctrines prominently feature this difference in treatment.

Limiting government's financial support for religious private schools

In the section "Limiting prayer and other religious practices in public schools," earlier in this chapter, we discuss how the *Engel* Court expressed concern about government providing "financial support," in addition to lending its "power and prestige," to prayer and other religious practices in public schools.

Prevailing Supreme Court precedents indicate that the answer to whether government providing significant financial support to religious private schools is constitutional depends on whether government gives its aid directly or indirectly:

> » **Direct aid:** The government can give aid directly to religious private schools to support non-religious teaching and activities. But aid programs must have sufficient safeguards to ensure that the school doesn't divert more than a minimal amount of aid from secular teaching (such as math and science classes) to religious teaching (such as classes teaching the elements of a particular religious faith).
>
> These standards were specified in the 2000 decision *Mitchell v. Helms*, which allows state education agencies to lend computers, software, and library books to public and private schools, including private religious schools. (This case illustrates that aid can involve material aid, not just cash grants.)

> » **Indirect aid:** When government aid flows indirectly, public funds can support religious teaching and activities if the following requirements are met:

- The parents or students who opt to use government aid at religious private schools have a true private choice of the school.

- The government-aid program i must be *broadly available* (meaning that a broad class of students who attend non-religious and religious private schools must be offered this aid).

- The program must be *neutral* (meaning it must give aid on the same basis to students, whether they attend religious private schools or their non-religious counterparts).

Various critics on and off the Court have objected that the direct-versus-indirect distinction doesn't have a meaningful difference. But the distinction reflects the view that direct aid more clearly reflects a decision by government officials (and not private individuals whose conduct the Establishment Clause doesn't regulate) to favor religious teaching.

Indirect aid in Ohio education

The 2002 Court decision in *Zelman v. Simmons-Harris* provides an illustration of the precedents related to indirect aid. Susan Zelman, the superintendent of an Ohio school district, approved a voucher program that gave very-low-income parents a check to help fund education for each of their school-age children; the parents could sign those vouchers over to the school that their child attended. The voucher payment wasn't limited to the secular components of the school's education, so the vouchers supported religious education for those students who enrolled in a religious school (as well as religious services and rituals associated with attending a religious private school).

The Court's majority opinion in *Zelman* stated that the program checked off the three boxes required under the indirect-aid requirements:

>> **True private choice:** Private individuals (parents), not government officials, decided to what school they gave the public funds.

>> **Broadly available benefits:** Parents could apply voucher funding to attend any private school (religious or non-religious) or any public school that charged tuition (such as a magnet school that had a specialized program).

>> **Neutral treatment:** The voucher benefit amount was the same, whether the student attended a private religious school or another school. No special incentives or treatment encouraged religious private-school attendance.

The justices who dissented to the *Zelman* ruling saw a clear violation of the core Establishment Clause principle that taxpayers shouldn't be forced to support religious training or religious ceremonies.

The first indirect-aid Court decision

Compared to the extensive (and expensive) voucher plan in *Zelman* (see the preceding section), the indirect–aid line of decisions started out more modestly in the 1983 decision of *Mueller v. Allen*. The *Mueller* Court validated a Minnesota state law that gave parents of school–age children a \$500- to \$700–per–pupil annual tax deduction for tuition, textbook, and transportation expenses. In theory, the deduction could apply to expenses to send children to public or private schools; but because most public schools didn't charge tuition or make parents pay for textbooks or transportation, the deductions mainly benefited parents who sent their kids to private school. (And, in fact, 96 percent of the tax benefits went to parents whose children attended private religious schools.)

The Court upheld the program under the theory that the tax break ended up providing an indirect, marginal assist to private religious education only as "a result of numerous, private choices of individual parents."

Avoiding favoritism when associating with religious symbols and sentiments

Establishment Clause controversy exists when government associates in a more passive way with religious symbols and sentiments:

>> **Nativity scene:** For example, in the 1989 case *County of Allegheny v. American Civil Liberties Union,* the Court concluded that a county violated the Establishment Clause by displaying inside the courthouse during the holiday season a *crèche* (nativity scene) that portrayed Jesus Christ's birth.

Unlike the school- and legislative-prayer cases discussed in the sections "Limiting prayer and other religious practices in public schools" and "Allowing prayer in the legislature," earlier in this chapter, simply displaying the crèche didn't use government's power and prestige to support an active religious ritual. Nor did it expend substantial public funds. Rather, the Court opinion stated that just by associating with the crèche and the religious sentiments it reflected, government would send a message that it endorsed the Christian account of Jesus's divine origins.

>> **Menorah and Christmas tree:** The Court in *County of Allegheny v. American Civil Liberties Union* didn't categorically rule against all religious symbols in public spaces. In a companion decision handed down at the same time, the Court upheld the constitutionality of a holiday display outside a government office building that included a menorah (symbolizing the Jewish festival of Hanukkah) along with a Christmas tree, and a salute to liberty. The Court concluded that, given the broader context in which the menorah appeared, the display didn't send a message of endorsement of the Jewish faith.

The two different results illustrate the influence of the endorsement approach to deciding Establishment Clause controversies. This approach, as stated in an important concurring opinion in the 1984 case of *Lynch v Donnelly*, asks whether the symbolic association of government with religion sends a message to those who don't adhere to the beliefs represented that they're outsiders and "an accompanying message to [believers] that they are insiders, favored members of the political community." The approach focuses on the perceived message to a hypothetical reasonable observer who's "aware of the history and context of the community" and the place at which the symbol is displayed.

CEREMONIAL REFERENCES TO GOD

You probably know some examples of religious sentiments expressed at governmental proceedings and functions. Anyone who handles U.S. currency can see the national motto "In God We Trust" (signed into law in 1956) emblazoned on the back of various bills. Since the 1950s, the Pledge of Allegiance said at civic functions has included the phrase "One nation under God." And the Supreme Court opens public sessions with a marshal intoning a standard call to attention that ends, "God save the United States and this Honorable Court."

In 2004, the Court avoided deciding whether beginning the public-school day with student recitation of the Under-God version of the Pledge of Allegiance violates the

(continued)

(continued)

Establishment Clause. The Court held that the non-custodial father challenging the Pledge on behalf of his daughter didn't have *legal standing* (meaning a sufficient stake in the outcome) and so couldn't challenge the practice.

The Supreme Court hasn't directly ruled on the constitutionality of these and other ceremonial religious references. But statements in other opinions suggest that the Court sees them as a legitimate part of the Nation's social and political traditions, rather than attempts to support particular religious views.

Preventing the Disfavoring of Religion

A clause in the 1st Amendment outlaws government actions "prohibiting" Americans from engaging in "the Free Exercise" of their religion. The narrow purpose of the clause is to allow believers to attend the houses of worship of their choice and engage in religious rituals and practices consistent with those beliefs. Robust discussion and controversy on and off the Supreme Court have focused on how much further the clause extends.

Distinguishing between discrimination and incidental burden

Current Free Exercise doctrines are more skeptical of governmental laws or policies that discriminate against religion, as opposed to those that don't:

>> **Religious discrimination:** The Court presumes that a law or policy that discriminates against religion is unconstitutional unless it passes strict scrutiny. (You can read about the levels of legal scrutiny in Chapter 10.) As the name implies, *strict scrutiny* requires an especially strong showing from the government. The discriminatory law or policy must be the narrowest means for furthering a *compelling* (highest-order) interest. To narrowly draw a law or policy, it must not be

- *Over-inclusive:* It must not do more than the least necessary to further its interest.

- *Under-inclusive:* It must not leave out practices equally or more worthy of coverage.

>> **Non-discriminatory:** A neutral and *generally applicable* restriction (meaning one that applies equally, regardless of religious motivation) is valid even if it incidentally burdens some or all religious believers. Such a restriction is

constitutional if government's decision not to grant a religious-based exception reflects a *valid secular policy* (in other words, a legitimate, non-religious government interest).

To help you understand all the legalese in the preceding list, the following sections trace this distinction through two examples.

Special skepticism for discrimination against religion

The Court understands the Free Exercise Clause to provide special protection against a law or policy that "discriminates against some or all religious beliefs or regulates or prohibits conduct because it is undertaken for religious reasons." The quoted language comes from the 1993 decision in *Church of the Lukumi Babalu Aye v. City of Hialeah*. This decision invalidated a city ordinance in Hialeah, Florida adopted to quiet public controversy over plans to open a church, school, and cultural center for the practice of Santeria; this religion, brought from Africa to America through the Caribbean, regards animal sacrifices as central to the celebration of important rituals.

The disputed ordinance forbade "animal sacrifices" (defined in part as a ritual that "unnecessarily" killed an animal for a primary purpose other than "food consumption"). Finding that the purpose and effect of the ordinance was discriminatory against Santeria's religious practice, the Court subjected the law to strict scrutiny:

>> Assuming the importance of avoiding unsanitary conditions and preventing animal cruelty, the Court found that the ordinance wasn't narrowly drawn. It went further than necessary because it didn't restrict its prohibition to animal killings that were unsanitary or cruel.

>> It under-prohibited by failing to cover other animal killings that raised as much of a potential risk to public health or animal cruelty.

Therefore, the Court ruled that the ordinance was invalid.

TECHNICAL STUFF

The City's ordinance didn't specifically prohibit Santeria sacrifices. But the Court examined the ordinance's text, the background of its adoption, and its deliberate design to avoid prohibiting more typical non-religious animal killings (such as hunting for sport) or reaching other religiously oriented ritual killing (such as kosher butchering of food eaten by observant Jews). The Court found the ordinance discriminatory and prohibitive of certain religiously motivated conduct — namely, Santeria's.

Greater tolerance for incidental burdens

Free Exercise doctrines recognize that, even when government doesn't intend to discriminate against religious believers, the even-handed and general application of its laws or policies might *incidentally* (unintentionally) burden religious exercise.

For example, the 1990 decision of *Employment Division, Department of Health Resources of Oregon v. Smith* challenged how the State's anti-drug and unemployment-compensation laws worked together to burden two members of a Native American church. The members were fired from jobs as drug counselors when they used *peyote* (a hallucinogenic drug made from cactus) in a bona fide religious ceremony, even though that use violated Oregon's anti-drug laws. The church members were denied unemployment-compensation benefits under the State's general policy that employees who lose their jobs for violating state law don't receive benefits.

The Court concluded that Oregon wasn't deliberately trying to discriminate against religiously observant Native Americans. It was simply applying its anti-drug and employment-compensation laws equally to all Oregonians. But these laws had an incidental burden on believers who used illegal drugs in their rituals; no other Oregon residents were similarly burdened.

Retreating from a previous era in which even incidental burdens triggered strict scrutiny if they were substantial enough, the *Smith* Court held that governments don't normally need to exempt religious persons from neutral and generally applicable laws. (Oregon could legitimately decide that creating a peyote exception to its drug laws would undermine their enforcement.)

Reconsidering *Smith* with strict scrutiny

In recent years, several Supreme Court justices have expressed strong doubts about the *Smith* ruling (discussed in the preceding section). Along with other critics, these justices think that the framers of the Free Exercise Clause wanted to root out serious burdens on religious expression, whether intentionally discriminatory or not. And challengers have suggested in filings to the Court that it should overrule *Smith*. At the time of writing, the Court has so far declined to take that step, however.

Identifying an action as deserving strict scrutiny

In a consistent line of decisions over almost a decade, the Court made active use of several theories for bypassing *Smith* and preserving strict scrutiny. The Court has decided that a challenged governmental action is not neutral and generally applicable for the following reasons:

» If the government denies benefits based on the religious status or identity of potential beneficiaries

» If a religious person or institution would have to act against their religious beliefs to receive governmental benefits

» In dealing with a religious believer, if government officials showed anti-religious bias

» If a governmental official makes case-by-case exceptions from the challenged policy, thus making it not generally applicable

An example of the first two principles is the 2017 decision in *Trinity Lutheran Church of Columbia v. Comer*. The case concerned a state program that provided public funding to modernize playgrounds. The Trinity Lutheran Church school's application to use program funds scored well compared to competing applicants. But state officials ultimately denied public support, concluding that funding Trinity Lutheran would violate a state constitutional ban on public money directly or indirectly aiding any religious institution.

The Court found discrimination based on Trinity Lutheran school's status and identity as a religious school. The Court also emphasized past decisions that held that persons or institutions shouldn't have to choose between following their religious scruples or receiving governmental benefits on the same basis as other beneficiaries.

AVOIDING A BIGGER ISSUE

A noteworthy Free Exercise case is *Masterpiece Cakeshop v. Colorado Civil Rights Commission* (2018). The decision in *Masterpiece Cakeshop* reversed the Colorado state Commission's ruling against a baker who declined, based on religious beliefs, to bake a specialty cake for a same-sex couple who wanted to celebrate their marriage. (The Commission found that the baker violated state laws that forbid discrimination against customers.) Although ruling for the baker, the Court sidestepped the bigger issue of whose rights win out — the rights of believers who invoke the Free Exercise Clause or the rights of customers to equal treatment in the marketplace. Instead, the Court relied on unique facts that show that state officials ridiculed the baker's religious beliefs and ruled differently when the rights of other bakers who had objections to anti-gay non-religious messages were before them. (Thus, although the general anti-discrimination laws were neutral as written in theory, the Commission's application of them wasn't.)

(continued)

(continued)

The bigger question of Free Exercise versus Anti-Discrimination remains unresolved while we write this book. In a later 2023 case, *303 Creative LLC v. Elenis,* the Court ruled in favor of a website designer who claimed that Colorado officials couldn't sanction them if they refused, based on their religious beliefs, to design a wedding website for a same-sex marriage. But the decision turned on narrower 1st Amendment free-speech protections against compelled speech (as discussed in Chapter 10).

Using strict scrutiny with parenting questions

In a 2025 decision, the Court opened up a new front for imposing strict scrutiny, even if a government policy is neutral and generally applicable. *Mahmoud v. Taylor* applied strict scrutiny to the district's refusal to allow parents to opt out of LGBTQ-themed curricular materials that they found inconsistent with the religious views they wanted to instill in their children. The no-opt-out policy seemed neutral and generally applicable, in that it denied opt outs for any objecting parents, whether their objection was based on religious views or otherwise. Still, the Court said that a policy's neutrality and general applicability doesn't save it from strict scrutiny when government "substantially interfer[es]" with the right of parents to direct the "religious development" of their children.

REMEMBER

The future implications of this new route to strict scrutiny, both for public education and beyond, are unclear at the time of writing, yet they can have a potentially significant effect on schools and other institutions that serve children's development.

Considering whether the Religion Clauses Conflict

In theory, the 1st Amendment's prohibitions don't conflict — as long as governments treat religion neutrally (neither favoring nor disfavoring it). But many observers see this balance of neutrality as difficult to achieve.

A high-profile 2022 decision illustrates the potential collision between the Establishment and the Free Exercise clauses, even though the Court downplayed any conflict.

In *Kennedy v. Bremerton School District,* the Court invalidated the school district's firing of a controversial high-school football coach who made a point of praying on the football field's 50 yard line immediately after the end of games. The school district argued that this very visible prayer said by a school employee would send a message that the district "endorsed" the coach's religious practices.

But the Court accepted the argument that, in the specific time frame between the end of the game and the resumption of the coach's post-game duties, Kennedy was a private individual who had a Free Exercise-based right, under the district's policy on employee break time, to pray. The Court went on to find that the district's application of the break-time policy to Coach Kennedy discriminated against religious uses of breaks, compared to non-religious uses. The Court applied strict scrutiny and invalidated the disciplinary action.

This controversy puts the Establishment and Free Exercise Clauses seemingly at odds:

>> **Establishment:** Does tolerating the Coach's prayer violate the anti-establishment principle because it evidences government favoritism for religious rituals engaged in by persons seeming to represent government authority?

>> **Free Exercise:** Or must the prayer be tolerated to avoid disfavoring religious free exercise?

Notably, in reaching its result, the *Kennedy* Court

>> Downplayed the idea that the Establishment and Free Exercise Clauses could be at odds. The majority decision noted that (along with the Free Speech Clause), the religion clauses "appear in the same sentence of the same [1st] Amendment," suggesting that "the Clauses have 'complementary' purposes, not warring ones."

>> Added that harmony will flow from interpreting the Establishment Clause "by reference to historical practices and understandings" — and not by any message of religious endorsement sent by government's association with religion.

The Court's decisive turn away from the endorsement approach with the *Kennedy* decision could significantly alter the application of doctrines turning on the extent to which government appears to support religious beliefs.

Chapter **12**

Ensuring Equality When Government Makes Distinctions

Both the 5th and 14th Amendments prohibit federal, state, and local governments from denying to persons within their jurisdictions "the equal protection of the law."

These few words that set forth this equality concept have generated many thousands of words of interpretation and a network of varying doctrines designed to ensure that government acts fairly when it treats different people differently. This chapter examines how the Constitution protects individuals and groups from discriminatory government-imposed divisions, for example, in business regulation.

Understanding the Basic Rules for Government Divisions

The Equal Protection guarantees of the 5th and 14th Amendments apply whenever a government law or policy creates categories or divisions as part of pursuing its objectives. The methods in place to determine when and how government can apply distinctions reflects the political realities of government policymaking and the judicial role in monitoring this policymaking.

The 5th Amendment doesn't contain a clause that explicitly talks about equal protection comparable to the clause in the 14th Amendment. But both because the 5th Amendment was the model for key 14th Amendment provisions and because the federal government shouldn't act unequally in ways that the later amendment says states can't, modern decisions speak of an implicit 5th Amendment Equal Protection guarantee.

Why the government makes distinctions

In pursuing a wide range of social and economic objectives, government officials at all levels often make distinctions in the way that laws and policies treat different people or entities. Tax laws differentiate between large and small businesses. Environmental regulations distinguish among companies based on the types and quantities of chemicals that they produce.

For the most part, government draws appropriate — or, at least, well-intentioned — lines. These distinctions seek to concentrate governmental benefits or impose regulatory burdens where they can do the most good. But these divisions may produce seemingly arbitrary or unfair results. Worse, the way government draws lines may suggest an illegitimate desire to discriminate against a disfavored group.

How the judiciary reviews government divisions

The Equal Protection guarantees themselves actually inspire much line drawing when it comes to evaluating government distinctions: Current doctrines require different levels of review, depending upon the bases on which government makes distinctions.

Over time, courts have developed three levels of review when parties challenge the constitutionality of the distinctions that the government has drawn. These review levels vary in terms of their strictness, balancing the importance of the individual right and the government's interest. We will discuss each level of scrutiny (and exceptions) below. Table 12-1 outlines what kind of scrutiny the judiciary applies to government-imposed divisions and the reasons for each level of scrutiny.

TABLE 12-1 ## Scrutiny Levels for Government Distinctions

Level of Scrutiny	Type of Distinction	Government Interest	Distinction Focus	Allowed Inclusiveness
Strict	Race and national-origin	Compelling interest	Narrowly tailored	No over- or under-inclusiveness
Intermediate	Based on gender and parental-marital status	Important interest	Substantially related to the interest	Somewhat over- or under-inclusive
Rational basis	All other distinctions	Conceivable legitimate interest	Serve the interest to some extent	Very over- or under-inclusive

Under applicable Supreme Court precedents, Equal Protection requires that the government treat *similarly situated* people and entities (those who are equally worthy of government benefits [or equally deserving of having their conduct regulated]) similarly. The government can't treat them differently based on distinctions unrelated to their merits or relevant comparable circumstances.

Meeting the Rational-Basis Standard

Courts assess the basic fairness of most government distinctions through a rational-basis standard. As Table 12-1 shows, rational-basis government divisions are constitutional as long as government seeks to further a conceivable, legitimate interest and it's rational to conclude that the challenged distinction serves that interest in some way.

Government can easily meet this rational-basis standard by design. In giving substantial deference to the judgment of elected officials (and others who exercise authority granted by elected officials), the rational-basis test seeks to promote an appropriately restrained judicial role. Only when a truly arbitrary law clearly violates the core equal-protection fairness principle can courts step in and find it unconstitutional.

The rational–basis standard gets called *low level* for these reasons:

>> **"Legitimate" doesn't place a very high threshold.** Essentially, *legitimate* means that government's interest is (if you'll pardon the double negative) not illegitimate; it's not an objective forbidden by the Constitution or an interest that calls for heightened scrutiny as outlined in Table 12-1, in the preceding section.

>> **Justification doesn't have to match motivation.** The legitimate interest that justifies the applied distinction doesn't have to be the interest that actually motivated government. Courts can readily imagine what interests might have motivated government; usually lawyers who defend the government happily suggest what those interests could be during litigation.

>> **Officials can make incomplete or excessive distinctions.** If a rational analyst would conclude that the different treatment of persons or entities serves the government interest in some way, the challenged law or policy can leave out those equally deserving of benefits or burdens. These two distinctions use the following terms:

  - *Under-inclusion:* Government's line-drawing scheme leaves stuff out that would have been equally valid to include.

  - *Over-inclusion:* The line drawing distributes burdens or benefits much further than necessary to achieve the government interest.

>> **Whether government can achieve some of its objectives needs only be "at least debatable."** This phrase doesn't create a very high standard; most assertions about the effectiveness of laws and policies are at least arguable.

Road testing rational-basis review

In the decision from 1949 *Railway Express Agency, Inc. v. New York*, the Court faced an equal–protection challenge to a New York City ordinance forbidding any vehicle on city streets from advertising goods or services — except for business delivery vehicles that promoted the goods and services of the owner. Here's the analysis the Court undertook:

>> **Does this case present an equal-protection issue?** Yes, because the law doesn't treat all similarly situated vehicles similarly. Vehicles that advertise goods and services not associated with the vehicle owner face a burden that self-advertising vehicles don't.

>> **Does the city government have a conceivable legitimate interest?** Yes. In New York City traffic, reducing visual distraction can help reduce fender benders or worse.

> **Is it rational to think that the city's law will advance its interest in some way, even if incompletely and excessively?** Yes. The law will keep some visually distracting vehicles off the streets. You can make a basic "in some way" connection between what's prohibited and what the city presumably seeks.

> **Is it at least debatable that advertising can undermine safe driving?** Definitely! Anyone looking at this law can debate it — a court, a legislator, or someone just reading about the case.

After analyzing the case, the Court upheld the ordinance. (Constitutional doctrines define what governments may do, not what they're required to do.)

Reflecting political realities with rational-basis review

The rational–basis standard of scrutiny's low bar seeks to reflect realities about governmental policymaking:

>> Government officials rarely craft perfect laws or policies. To begin, a rational legislature might pursue a partial solution. Public-administration principles might suggest testing a limited pilot program before rolling out the full scheme.

>> Practical politics might reflect insufficient political support for the complete version of a policy; legislators may need to carve out groups or entities to grease the legislative skids.

>> Good-government imperatives or political pressures to "just do something" may lead legislators to cast the regulatory net much wider than strictly necessary.

>> Government officials may pass laws or adopt policies that don't seem of real importance or for which the government doesn't have a well-documented need.

Using Strict Scrutiny

When government draws lines based on race (or its close cousin, national origin), modern Equal Protection doctrines demand strict scrutiny in court review. (See Table 12-1, earlier in this chapter, for the breakdown of scrutiny levels based on type of divisions made.)

In the following sections, we unpack this strict-scrutiny standard and illustrate it through a prominent example, as well as examining how affirmative action fits into the strict-scrutiny picture.

Charting and illustrating strict scrutiny

As Table 12-1 illustrates, strict scrutiny presumes that government making race-based or national origin-based distinctions is unconstitutional unless the government can show that these distinctions

>> **Actually serve a compelling government interest:** Courts applying strict scrutiny aren't willing to imagine what the government's interest is; they must identify the actual interest the government is pursuing. And the interest must be a *compelling* (highest-order) interest, not just any old legitimate one.

>> **Are narrowly tailored to achieve that interest:** The distinction can't over- or under-include. With strict scrutiny, any over- or under-inclusion makes a law or policy unconstitutional.

Strict scrutiny's strictness

The 2005 decision in *Johnson v. California* provides a useful example of how applying strict scrutiny, and not rational-basis review, to race discrimination matters. In *Johnson*, a 7-justice majority invalidated a California Department of Corrections (DOC) policy to house new inmates for 60 days in cells with inmates of their same race. The DOC justified its race-based divisions as the narrowest practical way to avoid gang violence among inmates while it investigated the possible gang affiliations of the new inmates. The Court thought the DOC procedure violated the Constitution based on strict scrutiny:

>> Avoiding gang violence in prison is clearly a compelling interest, in the abstract. But the justices found the DOC's approach illogical and not narrowly drawn in actual practice.

>> Among other objections, the majority said that, contrary to the DOC's assumption, inmates of the same race were as likely or more likely to be rival gang members, compared to inmates of different races. Therefore, housing same-race inmates together wasn't likely to reduce the risk of gang violence.

Under rational-basis review, California would only have to show that a rational person could think that its temporary housing policy would prevent some violence among different-race inmates — a much easier sell.

Putting affirmative action under strict scrutiny

Unlike distinctions and divisions that hurt members of racial-minority groups, affirmative action draws racial lines in an (admittedly controversial) attempt to help members of racial-minority groups, primarily through promoting specific policies and opportunities in education and employment, in order to remedy the intergenerational ravages of slavery and post-slavery race discrimination. Affirmative action poses a special equal-protection puzzle:

>> Should the courts scrutinize affirmative action less strictly because it uses race with benign intentions and arguably in service of a core 14th Amendment remedial purpose?

>> Or does affirmative action merit the same strict scrutiny because it arguably serves a core 5th and 14th Amendment command that government policies be *color blind* (meaning to not take race into specific account)?

The Supreme Court's has responded to affirmative action in different ways at different times:

>> **Before 1989:** The Court used varying scrutiny levels or none at all to uphold some affirmative action programs and reject others.

>> **In 1989:** A majority of the Court held that affirmative-action programs had to survive strict scrutiny. In *City of Richmond v. Croson*, the justices invalidated an affirmative action *set-aside program,* a program designed to afford a certain percentage of contracts or opportunities for minority-owned subcontractors in public-works projects.

>> **Until 2022:** Affirmative action in undergraduate and graduate-school admission programs passed the Court's scrutiny. Specifically, a pair of 2003 cases (*Grutter v. Bollinger* and *Gratz v Bollinger*) established that these schools could have a compelling interest in achieving a racially diverse first-year class by using race as one factor in an "individualized" and "holistic" assessment of applicant qualifications; the Court ruled this practice was constitutional as long as race wasn't reflexively used to make admissions decisions.

>> **In 2022:** The Court decided a pair of cases that invalidated long-standing affirmative-action-in-admissions programs at Harvard and the University of North Carolina. Although the Court didn't formally overrule the 2003 precedents, most observers (including three strong dissenters on the Court) think that affirmative action in admissions is now a practical nullity.

JAPANESE INTERNMENT DURING WORLD WAR II

If national-origin discrimination gets strict scrutiny, how did six justices in the 1944 case of *Korematsu v. United States* uphold the World War II–era relocation of thousands of Americans of Japanese ancestry (most of whom were American citizens) to be interned in generally cramped and inhospitable relocation camps? The answer is both controversial and complicated.

Justice Hugo Black's lead *Korematsu* opinion anticipated the Court's more modern strict scrutiny by stating that, if the military's relocation order were based on racial or nationality prejudice, the Court would need to use the most rigid scrutiny. But the Court saw the internment program as instead based on concerns about the loyalty of some Japanese-ancestry residents; Black relied on the view of American military officials that, in the aftermath of the Pearl Harbor attack and declaration of war, internment was necessary to weed out potentially disloyal Japanese-ancestry residents on the West Coast who might assist the enemy.

Many people today regard *Korematsu* as one of the Court's biggest errors. In 1988, Congress enacted a law that provided reparations and letters of apology to surviving internees and their heirs.

Elevating Scrutiny for Gender-Based Distinctions

In 1976, in *Craig v. Boren*, a Supreme Court majority coalesced around an intermediate-scrutiny standard for reviewing gender distinctions. Intermediate scrutiny differs from rational-basis scrutiny and strict scrutiny (which you can read about in the sections "Meeting the Rational-Basis Standard" and "Using Strict Scrutiny," earlier in this chapter) — both in terms of the elements that the Court reviews and how the doctrinal difference can affect Court decision-making.

Finding a new level of scrutiny

No Supreme Court justice has ever explained the disparity in skepticism used between distinctions based on gender and those based on race and national origin. But some analysts suggest that treating gender-based line drawing as quasi-suspect (with the intermediate level of scrutiny) makes sense because gender discrimination bears some, but not all, of the attributes that merit full skepticism for race and national-origin discrimination.

Gender shares similar history or attributes with race and national origin because they all have been used as a basis for discrimination throughout history and have been stereotyped disparagingly.

But the two groups do have differences that cause race and national origin to receive a greater level of scrutiny:

>> **Minority status:** Because they make up a majority of the population, women are hard to characterize as a "discrete and insular minority," as an influential opinion footnote put it in arguing for heightened scrutiny for race discrimination.

>> **Association with slavery:** Remedying gender discrimination wasn't the primary purpose of the post-Civil War amendments. (Although the post-Civil War 15th Amendment sought to remedy racial discrimination in voting, the Constitution amenders continued to deny women the right to vote until passage of the 19th Amendment in 1920.)

Illustrating intermediate scrutiny

As Table 12-1 shows, intermediate scrutiny presumes that gender-based distinctions are unconstitutional unless the government can show that the distinction

>> **Actually serves an important government interest:** Unlike with rational-basis review, courts that apply intermediate scrutiny aren't willing to imagine what government's interest is; government must pursue that actual interest. For example, in the 1996 challenge to Virginia Military Institute's male-only admissions policy, *United States v. Virginia,* the state of Virginia invoked the tradition of single-sex higher education to argue that providing gender-diverse educational offerings was an important interest. The Court agreed in the abstract but said that Virginia didn't actually provide diverse single-sex offerings, just one male-only school.

>> **Through a focus of a means to a particular end that's substantially related to achieving that interest:** This facet intends to carve out a middle ground, in which the analysis focuses on finding a closer connection between government's interest and its use of gender distinctions than the rational-basis standard's "some connection," yet not as exacting as strict scrutiny's requirement of the closest-possible connection.

Intermediate scrutiny in action

The *Craig v. Boren* decision that established the intermediate-scrutiny standard for gender distinctions perfectly illustrates how heightening the scrutiny above rational basis makes a practical difference and protects against gender stereotypes and discrimination.

The *Craig* decision rejected an Oklahoma law denying 18-to-20-year-old males, but not their female counterparts, the right to buy low-alcohol beer.

Ultimately, the Court saw Oklahoma's law as lacking the required substantial relationship to show that this law prevented driving under the influence because the law

- » Prohibited only purchase, not consumption
- » Disproportionately prevented 100 percent of young adult males from purchasing low-alcohol beer to respond to a low percentage (less than 2 percent) of male drivers arrested for DUI

Heightening intermediate scrutiny

Gender-discrimination decisions following *Craig* (discussed in the preceding section) suggest that intermediate scrutiny may, as a practical matter, be moving toward strict scrutiny.

In *United States v. Virginia* (1996), the Court prominently noted that the justification for gender distinctions must be "exceedingly persuasive" when it

- » Is based on archaic stereotypes
- » Denies women important real-world opportunities

The *VMI* decision (which you can read more about in the section "Illustrating intermediate scrutiny," earlier in this chapter) edged closer to strict scrutiny also by holding that, even if most women wouldn't qualify for or want to attend the school, as long as some women did, denying them admission wasn't substantially related to valid educational goals. (As Table 12-1 shows, insubstantial under-inclusion is a problem only under strict scrutiny.)

Scrutinizing gender-based affirmative action

The only kind of gender discrimination that receives a relatively easier version of intermediate scrutiny involves the government treating women more favorably than men to compensate for past gender discrimination. For example, the Court upheld a U.S. Navy policy that gave women four additional years in service before their lack of promotion ran up against the Navy's *up or out policy* (where either you receive a promotion or must leave the Navy within a certain amount of time). Without requiring data and documentation or other searching scrutiny, the Court saw giving women extra time as a roughly proportional remedy for past restrictive Naval policies (such as not assigning women to submarine duty), which made it harder for women to get promoted.

Understanding Specialized Applications of Scrutiny

Although most Equal Protection decisions fall into the three-tiered scrutiny scheme outlined in Table 12-1 (see the section "How the judiciary reviews government divisions," earlier in this chapter), certain specialized applications may use non-standard scrutiny. The following sections examine two of these types of applications.

Heightening scrutiny based on animus

Even though a law or policy could otherwise pass rational-basis review, a court can invalidate it because that law or policy reflects *animus* (irrational prejudice) against a politically unpopular or disfavored group.

In three major decisions over three decades, the Court struck down laws that seemed to serve conceivable legitimate interests, but which the Court concluded reflected animus against certain groups:

>> The residents of hippie communes (*USDA v. Moreno,* 1973)

>> Developmentally disabled individuals living in a group home (*City of Cleburne v. Cleburne Living Center,* 1985)

>> Lesbian, gay, and bisexual (LGB) Coloradans excluded from protection through state and local civil-rights laws (*Romer v. Evans,* 1996)

The prominent animus-based ruling in *U.S v. Windsor* (2013) invalidated Section 3 of the federal Defense of Marriage Act (DOMA), enacted in 1996. Section 3 declared that the government would recognize, for purposes of over a thousand federal benefit and regulatory statutes, only marriages that had opposite-sex, not same-sex, partners.

According to the dissenting justices in *Windsor* (who felt that the Court should have used rational-basis scrutiny)

>> The DOMA-passing Congress had several legitimate (and as one dissenter put it "downright boring") fiscal and public-administration interests for not allowing state recognition of same-sex marriage; arguably, if the ranks of marriages covered by federal law should be swelled, Congress — not states — should make that decision.

>> Section 3 legitimately prevented the need to answer difficult questions about how federal laws, such as tax laws, would apply when same-sex couples moved to a state that didn't recognize their union.

The animus interpretation produces a win for various disfavored groups, but it has a downside. The Court can invalidate an objectionable law without deciding whether the distinctions against the groups in question should receive heightened scrutiny. This lack of examination leaves some difficult questions unanswered, which we talk about in the section "Leaving LGBTQ+ Distinctions Unresolved," later in this chapter.

Dealing with disparate impacts

Equal Protection doctrines deal with laws that are neutral on their face but have differential effects on various racial, gender, or national-origin groups. For example, a minimum-height requirement might apply equally to all applicants for a government law-enforcement job. But because Mother Nature distributes height differently among men and women, and among various racial and national-origin groups, this apparently neutral height requirement has significantly *disparate impacts* (disproportionate effects) along gender, racial, or national-origin lines that would otherwise trigger heightened scrutiny.

The governing doctrines say that *mere disparate impact* (a legal term referring to this effect alone, without intent) doesn't provide enough reason to trigger strict or intermediate scrutiny. Equal Protection guarantees forbid only intentional discrimination. Many types of government distinctions that aren't intentionally discriminatory could have discriminatory effects because of disparities not of the government's making; therefore, government would have too large a burden if mere disparate impact alone merited heightened scrutiny.

Court decisions hold that a law or policy's disparate impact is an important starting point. But the Court usually needs other factors that suggest a discriminatory motivation, such as

>> The specific sequence of events that led to adoption of a challenged law or policy

>> The legislative or administrative history reflecting the possible reasons for or against intentional discrimination

>> Departures from the procedures or substantive rules by which government usually deals with an issue

The 1979 decision in *Massachusetts v. Feeney* illustrates these principles. In *Feeney*, the Court confronted allegations that Massachusetts' policy of giving an edge in hiring to applicants for state jobs who were veterans should be treated as gender-based discrimination that warranted intermediate scrutiny. On its face, the policy drew a veteran/non-veteran line, not a male/female line. But as Massachusetts was well aware, especially in the 1970s, the vast majority of veterans were male.

The *Feeney* decision said that the policy didn't warrant a heightened review. The Court maintained that the circumstantial factors didn't justify concluding that the state adopted the preference policy because of a desire to discriminate against women; at most, the state was only aware of the disparate impacts and pursued its policy in spite of them.

Providing equal protection to all persons

The Equal Protection guarantees apply to *persons* (rather than *citizens*, as some other constitutional provisions do). When government makes distinctions that treat citizens and non-citizens differently, complicated and shifting rules apply. (The Court decisions in this area apply to non-citizens who are legally present in the United States.)

The level of scrutiny applied to government distinctions depends on the basis on which the law regulates non-citizenship:

>> **Strict scrutiny:** State laws and policies that disadvantage legally present non-citizens in receiving government benefits (such as state welfare laws and professional licensing)

>> **Rational-basis scrutiny:** When states make citizen/non-citizen distinctions that are "bound up with the operation of the state as a governmental entity." For example, Court decisions allow states to impose exclusions on legally present aliens who seek government jobs as police officers, and probation officers, and teachers; part of the rationale states that persons performing these jobs exercise important governmental functions and require a high sensitivity to American values.

And federal legislation and presidential executive orders that draw citizen/non-citizen distinctions receive lesser scrutiny because of the special authority Congress and the president have over foreign affairs and immigration.

Leaving LGBTQ+ Distinctions Unresolved

Government making distinctions based on an individual's sexual orientation arguably deserves heightened scrutiny, but at the time of writing, the Court hasn't yet established guidance on how to analyze equal protection when a law involves lesbian, gay, bisexual, transgender, queer, and other (LGBTQ+) individuals.

Sexual-orientation minorities

In the section "Heightening scrutiny based on animus," earlier in this chapter, we discuss two cases in which the Court used an animus rationale to invalidate government distinctions that disadvantaged members of sexual-orientation minorities (lesbian, gay, and bisexual [LGB] individuals). In those cases, the Court avoided accepting advocate arguments and lower-court rulings that the Court use heightened scrutiny.

In 2020, in *Bostock v. Clayton County*, the Court accepted similar reasoning in a non-constitutional context. The Court held that, for purposes of the employment-discrimination prohibition from the Civil Rights Act's Title VII, discrimination *because of sex* included discrimination against LGB and transgender employees.

Transgender individuals

In June 2025, the Court punted the question of whether discrimination based on individuals because they don't identify with the gender assigned them at birth deserves heightened scrutiny. *U.S. v. Skrmetti* probed the constitutionality of a Tennessee law banning certain medical therapies that help transgender youth transition to the gender that they want to express. (The law allowed the therapies for other young persons seeking them for reasons other than transitioning.)

Opponents of Tennessee's law argued for intermediate scrutiny for the following reasons:

>> **Under a gender-discrimination theory.** In part, determining whether a young person was seeking to transition required a comparison between their desired gender expression and their gender at birth.

>> **Because it drew a transgender/non-transgender distinction.** Challengers pressed into service some of the arguments we talk about for LGB discrimination in the preceding section.

Six *Skrmetti* justices declined the invitation to use either basis for heightened scrutiny. Over objections from dissenters that their characterization was disingenuous, the majority held that Tennessee's law discriminated based on age and type of treatment. Hence, it only needed to pass rational-basis review and easily did. The Court explicitly declined to decide whether transgender distinctions merit intermediate scrutiny.

Three majority justices went further and stated that transgender distinctions don't merit such scrutiny. And the three dissenters said the opposite; they opined that the law discriminated based on transgender status and deserved intermediate scrutiny. At the time of writing, a definitive answer awaits a future case.

Seeing an answer on the horizon?

In its 2025-2026 term (still ongoing at the time we write this book), the Supreme Court is hearing a pair of cases that challenge Idaho and West Virginia bans on transgender athletes participating in women's sports. Among other issues, the Court may decide whether intermediate scrutiny is applicable under Equal

Protection. However the Court decides, this pair of cases provides an illustration of the difference that heightened scrutiny could make. (You can see the Supreme Court's latest cases and decisions on its website at www.supremecourt.gov.)

The level of scrutiny that the Court thinks is appropriate can effect the hurdles that the cases must clear:

>> **Importance and actuality of the states' concerns:** They would face more rigorous analysis under intermediate scrutiny than under rational-basis review.

>> **The interest serving the objective:** Intermediate scrutiny requires that the divisions that government creates be substantially related to its objectives. A rational-basis scrutiny requires only that it serve the interest to some extent, a much broader target.

>> **Justification:** If intermediate scrutiny looked for an "exceedingly persuasive justification," the scope of the different bans could affect the practical outcome. By contrast, rational-basis review would tolerate bans that went significantly farther than necessary.

Chapter **13**

Preventing Arbitrary Loss of Liberty and Property

The 5th and 14th Amendments prohibit federal, state, and local governments from "depriving persons . . . of life, liberty, and property without due process of law." (You can read more about these amendments in Chapter 2.) Although the term might seem technical, *due process* relates ultimately to "the Nation's basic commitment . . . to foster the dignity and wellbeing of persons within its borders," as the Supreme Court put it in the 1970 decision in *Goldberg v. Kelly.*

Under modern interpretations, the Due Process Clauses in these amendments provide two distinct types of protections against arbitrary deprivation: procedural and substantive due process. In this chapter, we explain the difference between these two types and focus on procedural due process. (Chapter 14 dives into substantive due process.)

We look at the nature and sources of liberty and property rights to figure out which rights are entitled to due process protection. We also determine what processes the government must provide and when it must provide them, taking into consideration what notice is required and whether any substitutes or exceptions apply. This chapter also notes non-constitutional provisions that supplement constitutionally required procedures. And we identify some unique procedural due process issues that arise in cases that involve immigration and national security.

Distinguishing Procedural from Substantive Due Process

A simple but helpful way to distinguish procedural from substantive due process is to think about procedural due process as *how* the government is doing something and substantive due process as *what* the government is doing:

>> **Procedural due process:** Starts with the basic premise that the government has the authority to do what it's doing, but it must go about it properly. It focuses on the fairness of the government's processes, requiring the government to provide notice, a hearing, and a neutral decision maker before depriving a person of liberty or property.

>> **Substantive due process:** Protects liberty and property interests from unjustified government interference; courts strictly scrutinize infringements on fundamental liberty interests (including property rights) to ensure that government's limitations are proportionate and necessary. (We talk about the levels of scrutiny in Chapter 12 and detail this form of due process in Chapter 14.)

The Due Process Clauses protect against arbitrary deprivation of "life." But the only way governments seek to deprive persons of life is through the death penalty, when it seeks to execute criminal offenders. In Chapter 21, we summarize the constitutional limits that seek to make imposition of the death penalty non-arbitrary; these rules primarily implement the 8th Amendment prohibition on cruel and unusual punishment.

As we discuss in Chapter 12, issues involving the Equal Protection guarantees arise whenever government makes distinctions in its laws and policies. By contrast, the Due Process Clause issues that we consider in this chapter and Chapter 14 pop up whenever government jeopardizes a liberty or property interest; the argument doesn't focus on the fairness of any distinctions that the government makes in restricting liberty or property.

A procedural due process example

As an example of procedural due process, in *Trump v. J.G.G.*, a Court decision from 2025, the plaintiffs argued that they didn't receive notice and a hearing before they were deported. The challengers didn't question the ultimate right of the government to deprive them of their liberty interest through fair procedures, they just claimed the procedures they received weren't sufficient to prevent the deprivation from being arbitrary. (We discuss the *Trump v. J.G.G.* case in greater detail in the section "Weighing Due Process, Immigration, and National Security," later in this chapter.)

A substantive due process example

A highly controversial case (which we talk a lot about in Chapter 14) — *Dobbs v. Jackson Women's Health Organization* — was a substantive due process challenge. A coalition of healthcare providers and women of child–bearing age challenged a Louisiana law that severely restricted access to abortion procedures after the 15th week of pregnancy. The challengers didn't claim that the state didn't provide proper procedures before it prohibited women from getting an abortion. Instead, the challengers argued that the 14th Amendment Due Process Clause imposed an ultimate (*substantive*) legal barrier that prevented Louisiana from restricting abortion so comprehensively.

A HYPOTHETICAL DUE PROCESS CLAIM

Suppose a high-school student reports that a fellow student has drugs in their backpack. The principal calls the fellow student down to the office, demands that they turn over their backpack, searches their backpack, finds drugs, and expels the student. That student might cry either procedural or substantive due process:

- **Substantive:** "You can't do that!" The student might argue that by expelling them, the school has wrongfully deprived them of their protected right to receive a public education. (You can see in Chapter 14 why courts would likely reject this claim.)

- **Procedural:** "You went about that in an unfair way!" The student could argue that the school didn't follow fair procedures such as giving them notice that the school intended the disciplinary action to lead to their expulsion and allowing them an opportunity to tell their side of the story before authorities expelled them. (This notice would give the student an opportunity to show, for example, that the drugs weren't theirs, that the student who reported it planted the drugs, and so on.)

Determining Whether Any Process Is Due

The government doesn't always have to provide notice and an opportunity for a person to respond before it deprives that person of a liberty or property right. Procedural due process protections kick in only when liberty or property interests protected by the Due Process Clauses are at stake. And, as interpreted by modern courts, some interests that you might think of as liberty or property remain unprotected by these clauses.

You can compare the Due Process Clauses to the Free Speech doctrines that we cover in Chapter 10. In the same way that the 1st Amendment leaves some categories of speech unprotected, the Due Process Clauses leave some liberty and property interests unprotected.

Finding the sources of a liberty or property right

Procedural due process requires the government to provide adequate notice and a fair hearing before depriving individuals of liberty or property, but the Due Process Clauses themselves don't specify what rights they protect. Here's a rundown of where these liberty and property rights come from:

>> **Liberty rights:** The Supreme Court has found that the Due Process Clause and various other constitutional provisions protect certain liberty interests such as marriage, travel, and students' rights to be free from corporal punishment.

>> **Property rights:** Property rights don't come from the Constitution but from other sources, such as state constitutions; federal and state laws, regulations, and policies; and case law. For example, the Supreme Court has held that where state law grants welfare benefits, those benefits are a property right that the state can't stop without notice and a hearing.

Lawmakers (or others acting in a rule-making capacity) don't have to provide procedural due process when they enact legislation that impacts liberty or property interests. Except in rare cases where a regulation affects an identifiable group of people, individuals can't challenge laws on the basis that those individuals didn't receive notice or a hearing before a legislative body voted on the laws or rules, or before they went into effect.

In the section "Supplementing Due Process Outside the Constitution," later in this chapter, we point out how non-constitutional sources, such as federal and state administrative-procedure acts, may require notice and hearing before government can adopt regulatory rules, even though the Constitution doesn't include such a requirement.

Determining what liberty rights are protected

Liberty traditionally means the right to be free from physical restraint or incarceration, but constitutionally protected liberty rights aren't limited to that context. The Supreme Court hasn't established a definition or test to determine whether an interest amounts to a protected liberty right, but its decisions upholding or rejecting due process claims give meaning to the term. The Court has said that liberty interests include the right to enjoy privileges recognized at *common law* (meaning the accumulated rights recognized in judicial decisions) as essential to the orderly pursuit of happiness; the freedom to use and enjoy your mental and physical abilities in all lawful ways, to live and work where you choose, to pursue any livelihood or career, and to enter contracts to achieve any of those means.

Criminal law and prisoner rights

Due process claims come up a lot in criminal and prisoner-rights cases because physical freedom is a protected liberty interest:

>> **Prison transfer:** Transferring a prisoner to a facility that has less favorable conditions doesn't deprive them of liberty.

>> However, if state statutes require prison officials to make certain findings before they can transfer prisoners, the government must use fair procedures to determine whether to make those findings.

>> **Parole:** A grant of parole or commutation of sentence doesn't require due process, unless denying it involves atypical or significant hardship; but revocation of probation or parole and loss of credits for good behavior qualify as deprivations of liberty that require due process.

>> **Disseminated information:** Posting accurate information on the internet regarding sex offenders doesn't infringe upon a liberty right.

>> **Forced medical treatment:** People have the right to due process before prisons or state hospitals can involuntarily medicate them.

Reputation

Although not all government action that affects someone's reputation infringes on a protected liberty interest, individuals do have a liberty interest in freedom from government impugning their reputation if doing so results in denial of an entitlement (such as the right to purchase alcohol) or imposes an additional harm (such as jeopardizing employment prospects).

Other liberty interests

The Court has found constitutionally protected liberty interests in a variety of other contexts:

- **»** **Corporal punishment:** School children have a liberty interest in being free from corporal punishment.

- **»** **Upbringing:** The rights of parents to make decisions about the upbringing of their children are liberty rights that require due process before those rights can be terminated.

- **»** **Travel:** People have a protected liberty interest in traveling between states.

Determining what property rights are protected

When it comes to property rights, the Supreme Court has established a test to determine whether constitutional process is due. A property right is protected

- **»** Where the government has created a *legitimate entitlement* (meaning a legitimate claim to a government-provided benefit).

- **»** Not where it has created a *mere unilateral expectation,* which means an abstract need or desire for a government-provided benefit.

Not every deprivation of a constitutionally recognized liberty or property right requires a formal process akin to a court hearing. The nature, degree, and formality of the process required depends on several factors, as you can read about in the following section.

Two Supreme Court cases illustrate the line between a constitutionally protected property right and an unprotected benefit:

- **Unilateral expectation:** In *Board of Regents v. Roth*, a public university refused to renew a teacher's one-year contract. The teacher claimed this refusal amounted to a deprivation of a property right (specifically, the right to continued employment), but the Court disagreed in its 1972 decision. Nothing in the contract, state law, university policy, or any government regulation gave the teacher a legitimate claim to have their contract renewed.

- **Legitimate entitlement:** In another case, *Perry v. Sindermann*, also in 1972, the Court reached a different conclusion. There, the school's written policies affirmatively promoted a tenure-like environment (even though they didn't provide actual tenure). Unlike in *Roth*, the teacher in *Sindermann* had a legitimate entitlement to continued employment. This was a property right that the school couldn't deny without fair procedures.

Figuring Out How Much Process Is Due, and When

If the government is trying to take away someone's constitutionally protected liberty or property interest, it must provide processes (as discussed in the section "Determining Whether Any Process Is Due," earlier in this chapter). What processes it needs depends on the specifics of the situation. Due process generally requires

>> Notice

>> An opportunity *to be heard* (meaning specifically an opportunity to present their positions in relation to the liberty or property interest the government wants to deny)

>> A neutral decision maker

But the required formality and degree of those processes differs depending on the government action and the type of right at issue. In other words, procedural due process isn't a one-size-fits-all remedy.

A range of processes are constitutionally adequate in various contexts. The Supreme Court uses a basic three-factor test for determining how formal the process must be and when it must be provided. We talk about this test in the section "Determining the formality and timing of process," later in this chapter. Given the vast array of liberty and property rights arising in countless different contexts, a variety of procedures (at varying levels of formality) may satisfy due process.

Seeing the range of acceptable process

Modern due process principles provide a wide range of constitutionally acceptable ways to provide fair notice, an adequate hearing, and an impartial decision maker.

Assuring adequate notice

Due process requires the government to give enough notice of the planned deprivation to the affected individual that the individual has sufficient time to contest it. If the attempt to give notice is unsuccessful, the government must take reasonable follow-up measures. The notice needs to include the following elements:

>> Information about what deprivation the government plans and what the individual can do to prevent it

>> The legal basis for the planned deprivation

>> The date, time, and location of any hearing

The Constitution doesn't specify a set period within which the government must provide notice. Courts usually regard notice as adequate when it provides the recipient with sufficient time to prepare a response.

Statutes, rules, and regulations may provide specific timeframes. For example, a government employment contract may provide that employees must be notified a certain number of days before a disciplinary hearing. Courts will uphold these timing requirements if they satisfy the constitutional standard of giving the recipient sufficient time to prepare a response. For example, a court would likely find that a civil-service rule that requires only one-day notice before a termination hearing is unconstitutional.

Providing an opportunity to be heard

The purpose of a *hearing* (an opportunity for interested parties to present their positions to an unbiased decision maker) is to protect a person from having their liberty or property arbitrarily taken or encroached upon. The right to be heard ensures that the person whose liberty or property is at stake gets a chance to tell their side of the story.

The type of hearing required, however, depends on the circumstances. The hearing doesn't always have to be a trial-type proceeding. In some cases, a summary or informal hearing suffices; even when the required hearing is more formal, it may allow for more relaxed evidentiary and procedural rules than a trial.

But any hearing must be fair and sufficient to serve the purpose of minimizing the unfair and mistaken deprivation of protected interests by enabling people to challenge the deprivation. Fairness generally requires that the individual have an opportunity to respond to the claims and present evidence.

Criminal prosecutions generally require the highest level of formality and the greatest number of procedural protections. As we discuss in Chapter 18, even a formal trial can't satisfy due process by itself in criminal cases; the government must also provide a speedy trial, a jury trial, turn over *exculpatory evidence* (evidence favorable to the defendant), allow confrontation, and provide a number of constitutionally mandated processes.

In other situations, abbreviated or summary proceedings satisfy due process, such as

>> Excluding an employee from a military site based on security concerns

>> *Fact-finding hearings* (to investigate and determine the facts), as opposed to *adjudicative hearings* (where a decision maker decides the outcome of a legal dispute)

>> Student disciplinary hearings

Guaranteeing an impartial decision maker

The due process requirement of an objective, unbiased decision maker, in both criminal and civil cases, preserves both actual and perceived integrity in the process.

For example, a juvenile-court judge who owns for-profit juvenile detention centers has a conflict of interest and can't act as an impartial decision maker if they receive a financial benefit from sending kids to juvenile detention facilities and may not fairly consider other options, such as probation, rehabilitation programs, or placement with family.

The *presumption of regularity* assumes that government agents are acting lawfully in the regular course of business. This assumption places the burden on the person claiming a conflict of interest to show that a decision maker is biased or unfair.

Procedural due process requires judges (and other adjudicators) to self-police. Although most conflicts don't rise to the level of due process violations, the Constitution requires that judges must *recuse* themselves (not participate in a decision) when they have a direct, personal, and substantial interest in a case.

Conflicts can arise in a variety of situations. Here are a few examples where the Supreme Court found the decision maker's conflict of interest violated an individual's right to due process:

>> *Caperton v. A.T. Massey Coal Co.* (2009): After a West Virginia trial judge entered a $50 million damage judgment against a company, the company's chairman spent $3 million to support the election of an appellate court judge who sat on the appellate panel and was the deciding vote in overturning the jury's verdict. The Supreme Court held that the judge's failure to recuse themselves violated the plaintiff's due process rights.

>> *Williams v. Pennsylvania* (2016): The Supreme Court found an unconstitutional conflict of interest based on a Pennsylvania Supreme Court judge's failure to recuse themselves from a post-conviction proceeding that affirmed a death-penalty judgment because the judge was previously a prosecutor who had given approval to seek the death penalty against the defendant.

>> *Ward v. Village of Monroeville* (1972) and *Tumey v. State of Ohio* (1927): A judge's failure to recuse themselves from cases where fines were imposed violated the offender's due process rights because the judge received a portion of the collected traffic fines.

TECHNICAL STUFF

The conflict inquiry is objective, focusing not on whether the individual judge harbors an actual bias but whether the circumstances create an unconstitutional potential for bias.

Determining the formality and timing of process

One important consideration in due process determinations involves the timing of process:

>> **Pre-termination process:** Receiving notice of a planned action allows individuals the opportunity to challenge a government's planned deprivation of liberty or property before it happens.

>> **Post-deprivation process:** May cause irreparable harm if the government takes away a person's liberty or property before the individual has an opportunity to challenge it.

Another important consideration is the type of hearing granted to the individual whose liberty or property right is threatened. The word *hearing* implies a degree of formality that's not necessarily required:

>> **Informal hearing:** In some circumstances, an informal hearing can achieve the purpose of the Due Process Clause (to prevent the arbitrary deprivation of property and liberty rights). The hearing in those cases may require only that the government provide the individual with an opportunity to explain or respond to allegations.

>> **More formal hearing:** Other circumstances may require a more formal, trial-like evidentiary hearing. Even these formal hearings may vary as to whether they require formal procedures, such as the right to counsel or the application of evidentiary rules.

To decide these timing and formality issues, courts evaluate cases on their individual facts by applying a balancing test that the Supreme Court developed in 1976 in *Mathews v. Eldridge*. The government terminated Eldridge's Social Security Disability benefits without a pre-termination hearing. He received notice and a post-termination hearing, but he argued that his due process rights entitled him to a pre-termination evidentiary hearing.

The Court noted that due process was flexible and that it demanded different protections in different cases. The Court developed a three-part balancing test, considering

>> The private interest affected by the official action

>> The risk of erroneous deprivation of such interest through the procedures used and the probable value (if any) of additional or substitute procedural safeguards

>> The purpose served by the government benefit at stake and the fiscal and administrative burdens that the additional or substitute procedural requirements would place on the government

Mathews v. Eldridge was about whether the notice and post-termination process in place was adequate, not whether any process was required. No one disputed that some process was required before the government could terminate Social Security Disability benefits because the court had previously held that eligible individuals have a protected property interest in retaining welfare-type benefits after government decides to grant them.

Also, as we cover in the section "Supplementing Due Process Outside the Constitution," later in this chapter, when it comes to Social Security and other government benefits, federal laws and regulations often provide additional procedural protections beyond what the Constitution requires.

Providing process before deprivation

The Constitution requires adequate notice and an appropriate hearing before the government can deprive an individual of a protected interest. One Supreme Court case shows why it's sometimes not enough to give a person the right to challenge a deprivation after the fact.

In *Armstrong v. Manzo* (1965), a divorced father sought to vacate a court order allowing his ex-wife's new husband to adopt the father's kids. Although the law required the biological father's consent before someone else could adopt the children, the consent requirement was excused if the father failed to pay child support for two years. The court ordered the adoption without notice to the father after wrongfully finding he had failed to pay child support (which, if true, meant no consent was needed).

The father had paid child support, but he didn't have any evidence to prove it. After the adoption order was entered, the father was granted a hearing, but without sufficient proof, his petition to undo the adoption was denied. The Supreme Court reversed the lower court's decision. It held that the father shouldn't have to lose his child first, and then prove that he paid child support to get the child back. A post-deprivation (adoption) hearing wasn't sufficient. These circumstances require a pre-deprivation hearing where the burden is on the government (not the parent) to prove the parent failed to pay before it terminates their parental rights.

Like all constitutional rights, the right to advance notice and a pre-deprivation hearing isn't absolute. Government officials must balance it against other rights and public interests, and it gives way during a true public emergency. Importantly, government officials don't need to delay protecting the public while they provide notice and a hearing. They may seize dangerous materials or stop dangerous operations; but after they deal with the emergency, they must provide post-deprivation hearings and risk paying damages if they initially assessed the situation incorrectly.

The Supreme Court established the emergency exception to pre-deprivation procedures in 1908 in the *North American Cold Storage Co. v. Chicago* case, where it upheld the government's seizure of tainted poultry from a poultry-processing company without a pre-deprivation hearing because of the threat to public safety. But that exception may no longer be necessary; analytically speaking, the public safety concern may now be included in the later-developed *Mathews v. Eldridge* test (which you can read about in the section "Determining the formality and timing of process," in this chapter).

Here's an example: In *Mackey v. Montrym*, in 1979, the plaintiff raised a due process challenge to a Massachusetts law that provided for an immediate 90-day driver's license suspension when someone who was arrested for driving under the influence refused to submit to a blood-alcohol test. The law provided no pre-deprivation process, but it did require authorities to provide an immediate post-termination hearing.

The Court found that a driver's license was a protected property interest but that no pre-termination hearing was required under the *Mathews v. Eldridge* factors. Balancing the government's interests with the burdens that additional or substitute procedures would entail, the Court found that the state had a compelling interest in highway safety, that the summary proceedings substantially furthered that interest, and that a pre-deprivation hearing wouldn't serve the public safety concerns.

Supplementing Due Process Outside the Constitution

The Constitution sets the *floor* (the minimum amount of process the government must provide), but it doesn't limit federal or state government bodies from adding additional procedural protections. Supplemental protections may come in the form of comprehensive legislation (such as the Administrative Procedure Act [APA]) or by individual statutes, rules, or policies that apply in specific situations.

The APA is a federal law that governs federal agencies. It sets forth the procedures by which agencies make formal and informal rules, as well as the legal standards for *adjudication* (deciding the legal outcome of a case) and review of final decisions. The APA requires federal agencies to provide more extensive processes than the Constitution in adopting legally binding rules. The APA generally requires the agency to provide the public with notice of a proposed rule and an opportunity to comment:

>> Notice must include the time and place of public-comment proceedings, the legal authority under which the rule is proposed, and the proposed rule (or at least the agency's perspective on the subjects and issues the rule seeks to address).

>> The public-comment requirement provides interested parties an opportunity to provide data, views, or arguments.

>> In finalizing its rule, the agency must explain how it responded to public comments.

Even in the absence of comprehensive legislation such as the APA, statutes, rules, and regulations may provide for more protective procedures than required by the Constitution's Due Process Clauses. These additional protections may supplement or substitute for the constitutional requirement of notice and a hearing. For example, in a case in which a government agency withheld payments during a dispute with a contractor, the Court found the state deprived the contractor of a property right. But the deprivation itself didn't require notice and a hearing because the contractor had an alternative remedy. They could sue to enforce the contract, and that alternative procedure would protect their interests.

REMEMBER

Just because a statute provides a process doesn't mean the process can withstand a due process challenge. Courts can test the process provided by statute to ensure it meets constitutional requirements.

Weighing Due Process, Immigration, and National Security

Immigration and national security present unique and complex due process problems. When it comes to noncitizens, the text of the Due Process Clause extends broadly to "all persons." And the Supreme Court has stated that "[a]liens, even aliens whose presence in this country is unlawful, have long been recognized as 'persons' guaranteed due process of law."

The question isn't whether due process protects noncitizens, but how much process the government must provide. Expedited removal proceedings near borders have long been authorized by federal law, but recent expansion of those proceedings to the entire country have been met by criticism (and lawsuits!)

alleging that the expansion involves a major departure from the norm of providing noncitizens with notice and a hearing when they face deportation.

In the 2025 decision in *Trump v. J.G.G.*, the Supreme Court reaffirmed that the 5th Amendment entitles noncitizens to due process in removal proceedings and that detainees are entitled to notice and an opportunity to be heard. (But the case was still a loss for the plaintiffs because they filed the wrong type of case in the wrong court.)

Deportation proceedings are civil, not criminal, so immigrants facing deportation do not have a right to appointed counsel (although they do have a right to be represented by counsel if they can provide their own attorney).

Special due-process principles also apply if United States citizens are detained as enemy combatants, as happened to two American citizens during the period following heightened security concerns after the September 11th attacks in 2001:

>> Due process required the government to provide notice of the factual basis of the enemy-combatant classification and a fair opportunity to refute the label.

>> But the important national-security issues at stake allowed the hearing to use less-exacting procedures, including relaxed evidentiary rules. (For example, the hearing could admit hearsay evidence that wouldn't be admissible in a criminal trial.)

Like the Due Process Clause, the 4th Amendment prohibition against unreasonable searches and seizures also protects all people, not just citizens. In the 4th Amendment context, the Supreme Court has signaled (but not decided at the time of writing) that the protection extends to all people on American soil, including undocumented immigrants. To see the latest Supreme Court decisions, go to www.supremecourt.gov.

Chapter **14**

Navigating Intimate Liberty and Privacy Issues

I n this chapter, we explore the U.S. Constitution's application to some of the most hotly debated issues today. Whether to recognize implied fundamental rights under constitutional liberty protections inevitably involves strongly held and competing views about major private choices — including avoiding or delaying the conception of children, engaging in sexual intimacy, marrying, and terminating a pregnancy through abortion. When courts make decisions about these and other intimate liberties, the rulings inevitably privilege some views about moral and even religious imperatives to the detriment of others. And these decisions go the heart of the current values of American society.

The modern Court has enhanced the constitutional protection of some, but not all, liberty interests linked to an implied right to privacy, including same-sex privacy rights. But, although past Court decisions strongly protected abortion rights, the 2022 overturning of those rights in *Dobbs v. Jackson Women's Health Organization* means significant changes for the future of abortion itself in the U.S. This chapter also examines what *Dobbs* may foretell about the fate of other implied privacy rights.

Analyzing Implied Privacy Rights as Substantive

Implied privacy rights (rights not explicitly stated but implicit in other rights), can be integral to substantive due process claims. The following sections examine the two-tiered scrutiny scheme to resolve these claims, clarify the importance of determining whether an asserted liberty interest is fundamental, and state the criteria for making that determination.

Defining substantive due process

The Court has for decades interpreted the Due Process Clauses by looking at whether someone is challenging the way government deprives people of liberty or property (procedural due process, as discussed in Chapter 13) or is challenging the government's basic ability to deprive those rights substantive due process, as discussed in this chapter.

To take a prominent example that we detail in the section "Changing Abortion Rights Protection," later in this chapter, the *Dobbs* challengers didn't argue that Mississippi's restrictive abortion law, which generally prohibited abortions after 15 weeks of pregnancy, was procedurally defective. They didn't see the problem as that Mississippi failed to give pregnant women a sufficient hearing by which to argue that they needed a later abortion. The challengers objected that Mississippi's law violated the substance of the special protections then in place for abortion choice.

Understanding the two-tiered scrutiny used for substantive due process

As detailed in Chapter 1 (which explains how different levels of scrutiny apply to government distinctions), substantive due process analysis uses the two levels of rational–basis and strict scrutiny to determine the constitutionality of a law or policy that restricts liberty or property rights:

>> **Rational-basis scrutiny:** Applies to any laws or policies that deprive a person or entity of either

- Any property interest

- Any non-fundamental liberty interest

As detailed in Chapter 12 (which explains how rational-basis analysis applies to governmental distinctions), whether the challenged law or policy can in some way serve a legitimate interest (which might have motivated its adoption) must be "at least debatable."

>> **Strict scrutiny:** At the opposite end of the scrutiny spectrum, rigorous strict scrutiny applies to any fundamental liberty interest (foundational and important). Essentially, strict scrutiny requires that a law or policy have the narrowest focus necessary to fulfill an actual compelling interest.

TIP

We talk about strict scrutiny in Chapter 10 (for content-based regulation of protected speech), Chapter 11 (for discrimination against the free exercise of religion), and Chapter 12 (for race and national-origin discrimination). Strict scrutiny applies any time case precedent defines a liberty interest as fundamental.

Seeing the fundamental fundamentals

Given the two opposite scrutiny levels available, labeling a liberty interest as *fundamental* via a two-part test (explained in the following section) makes a real, practical difference in the likely verdict on constitutionality. Characterizing a liberty interest as fundamental means that the law or policy that threatens that interest will likely fail; even if a court is willing to agree (or assume) that government is actually pursuing a compelling interest, government can usually find a narrower focus for fulfilling that interest. Finding a liberty interest to be non-fundamental likely allows government to meet low-level rational-basis review.

A high-profile example of this practical difference is the 1997 decision in *Washington v. Glucksberg*. In *Glucksberg*, doctors and seriously ill patients who were soon likely to die challenged a Washington State law making it a crime for physicians to assist any patient to die. The challengers argued that they had a fundamental liberty interest in choosing the circumstances and timing of their death. How the Court identified the interest had huge effects on its decision:

>> **Found non-fundamental:** The Court interpreted the challengers' liberty interest narrowly, concluding that no person has a fundamental right to die by suicide. Because the Court deemed the liberty interest non-fundamental, Washington only needed to pass the rational-basis test. The Court readily identified several at-least-legitimate governmental interests, including a broad "interest in the preservation of human life" to which Washington's law "at least reasonably related."

>> **If found fundamental:** If the Court had instead found the patients' liberty interest to be fundamental, strict scrutiny would have been the order of the

day. The Court would have confronted the question of whether a flat ban on all physician assistance to all persons is the narrowest option necessary to accomplish governmental interests.

Washington State would have had to show, for example, that it couldn't accomplish its goals to protect vulnerable patients by allowing physician assistance for a subgroup of terminally ill patients, backed up by significant safeguards (such as requiring a panel of other doctors to investigate and approve the assistance request). Washington would have had a significantly harder time meeting this alternative inquiry.

Determining what's fundamental

Because labeling a liberty right as *fundamental* raises the scrutiny level significantly, the criteria that courts use to apply the label — and how free they feel to do so — are very important and controversial.

Substantive due-process doctrines, which trace back to the 1937 decision in *Palko v. Connecticut,* now define fundamental liberty interests as those

>> Deeply rooted in the nation's history and tradition

>> Implicit in the concept of ordered liberty, such that "neither liberty nor justice would exist if [the interest] were sacrificed" (as stated in the *Palko* decision)

REMEMBER

The criteria in the preceding list are admittedly vague and subjective. To critics, these criteria run too great a risk that judges can confuse their preferences about what liberty ought to be with an objective reading of history and tradition. The *Washington v. Glucksberg* opinion warned that courts lack "objective guideposts" in the "uncharted area" of implied privacy rights; courts should "exercise the utmost care" before finding a liberty to be fundamental through a substantive due process theory.

To determine whether a liberty interest qualifies as fundamental, the Court must take into account how narrowly or broadly to frame the challenger asserted interest. (For example, in the preceding section, how the *Glucksberg* Court characterized the liberty interest asserted by terminally ill patients determined the outcome.)

>> The Court called the interest a right to be aided by doctors in committing "suicide." This characterization made the interest an unlikely candidate for fundamental status. Given long-standing legal prohibitions and moral and religious disapproval of suicide, you can't easily argue that American history and tradition deeply embody a fundamental right to end your life. And we you can imagine a free and orderly society that prohibits suicide.

Entering the New Era of Implied Privacy Rights

As a general matter, the 1960s ushered in robust issues of feminism and also the advent of many oral contraceptives. A Connecticut law that banned contraceptives became the focus of a court challenge.

The landmark 1965 decision in *Griswold v. Connecticut* struck down a Connecticut law making it a misdemeanor (punishable by a $50 fine or some jail time) for any person to use contraceptives or for doctors to assist them in obtaining contraceptives. The following sections explore how and why *Griswold* used heightened scrutiny to protect the rights of married adults, in particular, to use contraception.

TECHNICAL STUFF

The Connecticut law applied to all persons. But the *Griswold* challengers focused on how the law prevented married persons from accessing and using contraception in their marital sexual relations. This savvy move allowed the Court to credit the long-standing importance of the marital relationship.

Implied privacy rights and liberty of contract

Griswold v. Connecticut wasn't the first decision in which the Court used a substantive due-process approach to give heightened protection to a liberty interest. In 1905, the Court struck down a law that seems quite normal and justified to most modern eyes: New York forbade bakery workers from working more than 10 hours a day or 60 hours per week. But in *Lochner v. New York*, the Court held that this law unconstitutionally restricted the liberty of contract between a business entity and its workers.

This and other cases striking down economic regulations between 1897 and 1937 as unconstitutional didn't call the liberty of contract fundamental; nor did the Court apply strict scrutiny. But they certainly applied something more than modern rational-basis review. The Court rejected New York's interest in regulating labor conditions to protect workers and second-guessed New York's argument, which it backed up with occupational-health data, that bakery workers faced special health and well-being risks.

Today the Court would use rational-basis review and defer to New York's judgment about appropriate economic policies and uphold the law.

In 1937, as part of a broader shift in the Supreme Court's willingness to uphold economic regulation, the Court discredited *Lochner* and the liberty-of-contract line of cases.

Using heightened review for implied privacy rights

For almost 30 years after getting out of the business of strongly protecting liberty of contract (discussed in the preceding section), the Court declined to give any special protection to other liberty interests. Then came the *Griswold v. Connecticut* decision in 1965.

Connecticut authorities defended the State's law as protecting the marital relationship — making contraception unavailable would discourage married people from cheating on their spouses by increasing the risk of unwanted pregnancies. From the viewpoint of the rational-basis standard (you can find discussion of the different Court scrutiny levels in Chapter 12), the legislature could have found it at least debatable that lack of access to contraception would discourage some would-be marital cheaters from straying, especially in an era in which extramarital pregnancy came with a very serious social stigma for the child.

The *Griswold* Court nevertheless held that the Connecticut law violated substantive due-process protections. The Court didn't explicitly label the asserted liberty right of married people to access contraception as fundamental; nor did it formally invoke the strict scrutiny currently used for fundamental implied privacy interests. But the Court condemned Connecticut's legal prohibition as "sweep[ing] unnecessarily broadly and thereby invad[ing] . . . protected freedoms." (This assessment implicitly employs the second requirement of strict scrutiny, that government draw a law as narrowly as possible to meet its interests.)

Griswold generated four different opinions by the seven justices who agreed to invalidate the Connecticut law. The different points that these justices made illustrate why they found the state's prohibition not narrowly drawn. Key among these reasons was that the law appeared

>> **Not necessary:** The state already had laws forbidding adultery and sex between unmarried people.

>> **Over-inclusive:** It denied access to contraception for the large group of married persons who sought it for controlling pregnancy within their marriage.

>> **Under-inclusive:** The Connecticut law exempted from its prohibition condoms (in 1965 language, devices "sold for the prevention of disease"). Exempting the most readily available form of contraception from the law's reach obviously undermined its supposed ability to deter extramarital affairs.

Applying the fundamental zones-of-privacy rationale

The *Griswold* Court used a two-step process to explain why the right of married people to use contraceptives was entitled to special protection, which we explore in the following sections.

Implying a right to privacy

The Court held that the liberty protected by the Substantive Due Process Clauses includes certain implied rights to privacy. The Court started by observing that several constitutional amendments "create zones of privacy." (For example, the 4th Amendment protects against unreasonable searches and seizures) Along with the 9th Amendment's recognition that the Constitution protects certain rights beyond those enumerated, the Court concluded that these and other privacy-protecting amendments threw *"penumbras"* (shadows) broader than their literal reach.

Identifying interests that have a right to privacy

The Court explained why the interests of married persons seeking contraception fell within the special zone of privacy it identified. The Court emphasized that the marital relationship was deeply rooted and "intimate to the degree of being sacred." The Court also noted that, "in forbidding the use of contraceptives, [the law] seeks to achieve its goals by means having a maximum destructive impact upon that relationship."

Evoking the importance of home privacy, the Court asked rhetorically, "Would we allow the police to search the sacred precincts of marital bedrooms for telltale signs of the use of contraceptives?" Answering its own question, the Court concluded, "The very idea is repulsive to the notions of privacy surrounding the marriage relationship."

Strengthening Protection for Some Privacy Interests

The Supreme Court *Griswold v. Connecticut* decision (which we talk about in the section "Entering the New Era of Implied Privacy Rights," earlier in this chapter) began a decades-long process of expanded protection for certain implied privacy rights.

Constitutional provisions may protect privacy in a variety of contexts. For example, governmental officials seizing your cellphone would raise issues under 4th Amendment search-and-seizure rules, which stem from a concern about "reasonable expectations of privacy." (See Chapter 19 for more about the 4th Amendment.) Court rulings have given expanded protection to a number of forms of implied privacy rights.

For contraception access, specifically, the Court expanded the right beyond married people to include

>> Unmarried adults (*Eisenstadt v. Baird,* 1972)

>> Minors under the age of 16 (*Carey v. Population Services International,* 1977)

>> Persons seeking contraception other than through a pharmacist (*Carey v. Population Services International,* 1977)

The Court also recognized certain aspects of family rights as worthy of special protection through heightened scrutiny. Key decisions include

>> Protecting an unmarried father, who had been bringing up his children in a stable, long-standing relationship, from having his parental rights automatically terminated upon the death of the children's mother (*Stanley v. Illinois,* 1972)

>> Broadening the deeply rooted constitutional protection afforded to the family to include the right of *extended family members* (meaning family members other than parents and siblings) to live together, notwithstanding a city's restrictive zoning laws (*Moore v. City of East Cleveland,* 1977)

And in a major 1990 right-to-die decision, *Cruzan v. Director, Missouri Department of Health,* the Court recognized the right of a *competent adult* (an adult who can make sound healthcare decisions) to terminate their own medical care, even if their life ends earlier than would happen if they received continued care.

The Court hasn't expanded the zone of privacy to robustly protect rights against government disclosure of personal, medical, or economic privacy. (Of course, many important federal, state, and local laws and regulations fill in the gaps.)

Expanding Same-Sex Privacy Rights

Two important and controversial areas of substantive due process decision-making deal with decisions protecting the sexual intimacy of same-sex couples and expanding their fundamental right to marry.

Establishing a right to same-sex intimacy

In 2007, the Court used a substantive due process/implied privacy rights rationale to protect consenting adults from state laws that criminalized same-sex intimacy. In *Lawrence v. Texas*, the Court overruled the 1986 precedent in *Bowers v. Hardwick* (which upheld a law that criminalized certain acts between consenting adults) in part because the *Bowers* Court denigrated the rights in question as a non-fundamental "right [of] homosexuals to engage in sodomy."

Lawrence didn't call the interest in sexual intimacy of consenting same-sex adults fundamental. But the Court spoke of the importance of the right in elevated terms, calling same-sex sexual activity "but one element in a personal bond that is more enduring." Echoing *Griswold*'s reliance on intimacy and home privacy (which you can read about in the section "Entering the New Era of Implied Privacy Rights," earlier in this chapter), the *Lawrence* Court noted that laws that criminalize same-sex intimacy have "far-reaching consequences, touching upon the most private human conduct, sexual behavior, and in the most private of places, the home."

Although *Lawrence* didn't specifically state the level of scrutiny it applied, the Court seemed to many observers to be using more than low-level rational-basis review. (Flip to Chapter 12 for discussion of the different levels of scrutiny the Court can apply to cases before it.) Texas presumably could have justified its law under rational-basis review as a measure providing partial protection to some residents against the dangers of sexually transmitted disease (which would certainly have been a legitimate governmental interest). And, although the Court might have argued the law reflected animus against sexual-orientation minorities, the Court's statement that the Texas law "furthers no legitimate state interest that can justify its intrusion into the personal and private life of the individual" appears to require a stronger justification for laws that interfere with same-sex intimacy.

Identifying a right to same-sex marriage

Even before its 2015 ruling expanding the right to marry to same-sex couples (in *Obergefell v. Hodges*), the Court had already afforded the marital right special protection in several cases.

Beyond the *Griswold* case (see the section "Entering the New Era of Implied Privacy Rights," earlier in this chapter), especially noteworthy cases include

» *Loving v. Virginia* **(1967):** Employing both Equal Protection and substantive due process theories, the Court established that the fundamental right to marry extends to interracial couples.

» *Zablocki v. Redhail* **(1978):** Re-emphasizing the fundamental quality of the right to marry, the Court invalidated a state law that prohibited a non-custodial parent subject to a court child-support order from getting a marriage license without court approval. The Court found that the state law wasn't narrowly drawn to accomplish its purpose to enforce child-support obligations.

Still, the persons whose rights were vindicated in the cases in the preceding list and others were heterosexual. So it was big news when in 2015 the Supreme Court decided *Obergefell v. Hodges*, extending the fundamental right to marry to same-sex couples. The Court justified the expansion based on "four principles and traditions . . . demonstrat[ing] that the reasons marriage is fundamental under the Constitution apply with equal force to same-sex couples." Specifically, the *Obergefell* Court noted that

» "Choices about marriage shape an individual's destiny," which makes "the right of personal choice regarding marriage . . . inherent in the concept of individual autonomy."

» Marriage "supports a two-person union unlike any other in its importance to the committed individuals."

» Marriage "safeguards children and families and thus draws meaning from related rights of childrearing."

» "[M]arriage is a keystone to our social order," which is why, said the Court, governments offer both "symbolic recognition and tangible benefits to protect and nourish the union."

Obergefell was highly controversial at the time the decision was reached and continues to be so in some quarters at the time of writing. As we note in the following section, one big question in the aftermath of the 2022 *Dobbs* decision overruling abortion-rights precedents is whether the logic of *Dobbs* imperils

Obergefell and other decisions arguably not reflective of a long-standing tradition of legal protection. (These potentially vulnerable decisions include the *Lawrence* decision, discussed in the preceding section, which protects same-sex intimacy from criminal prohibition.)

Changing Abortion Rights Protection

Abortion rights have been and remain controversial. In the following sections, we chart how for almost 50 years the Court provided special protection for the rights of adult women to choose abortion in the first six months of pregnancy. In 2022, the Court reversed those precedents in its *Dobbs v. Jackson Women's Health Organization* decision, which has implications for abortion rights specifically and more generally for other implied privacy rights.

Establishing strong protection for abortion rights

Less than a decade after *Griswold* opened up an avenue of heightened protection for implied fundamental privacy rights (see the section "Entering the New Era of Implied Privacy Rights," earlier in this chapter), the Court applied the approach to the controversial area of abortion rights. The 1973 decision in *Roe v. Wade* had the effect of invalidating all state abortion laws in existence at the time. Although the 2022 *Dobbs* decision overruled *Roe* and a later key precedent, understanding *Dobbs* requires understanding *Roe* and its aftermath.

The *Roe v. Wade* protections

The first 17 years of strong protection for abortion rights ushered in by *Roe* had these main facets:

>> **Right to choose:** A pregnant adult woman had a fundamental right to choose abortion, in consultation with her doctor, up to the point of fetal *viability* (the point at which the fetus "has the capability of meaningful life outside the mother's womb," according to the decision).

>> **Strict scrutiny for exceptions:** Governments could restrict abortion choice only through laws that were narrowly drawn to achieve a compelling interest. The Court struck down many — but not all — restrictive laws passed after *Roe*.

For example, in 1983, the Court struck down one state-law provision requiring all abortions after the third month of pregnancy to be done in hospitals; many abortions during this timeframe could be effectively performed at less expensive and more readily available outpatient clinics, so the law wasn't narrowly drawn.

>> **Viability:** At the point of viability (generally the seventh month of pregnancy), governments could ban abortion except where necessary to preserve the life or health of the mother.

REMEMBER

The *Roe* Court denied taking a side in the centuries-old question of when life begins (whether at conception, birth, or somewhere in between). *Roe* character-ized the fetus at viability as having a *potential* life sufficient to give government a compelling interest in generally banning abortion:

>> States could more strictly regulate abortion access for pregnant girls under the age of 18.

>> States didn't have to affirmatively assist women in getting abortions. For example, a state could decline to fund abortions for poor women, even when medical-assistance programs funded the expenses of women who carried their pregnancies to term. And governments could decline to provide abortions in publicly funded facilities.

The *Planned Parenthood v. Casey* adjustments

In 1989, the Court significantly adjusted the matrix of abortion rights in *Planned Parenthood v. Casey*. Here are the main features of the post–*Casey* era:

>> **Kept the right to choose:** *Casey* reaffirmed *Roe's* central holding about the fundamental nature of an adult woman's choice pre-viability. This surprised many observers who predicted that the Court would reverse *Roe*.

>> **Undue burden standard:** However, *Casey* replaced strict scrutiny for pre-viability regulations with a less protective undue burden standard. Instead of examining the importance of government interests and the narrowness of the means of achieving them, the amorphous *undue burden* standard weighed how substantial an obstacle a law placed "in the path of a woman seeking an abortion."

The Supreme Court and lower courts wrestled with how to define when a law's burden was undue. Some restrictive laws still fell, but others were greenlighted, even though they wouldn't have met *Roe's* strict scrutiny.

The state law upheld in *Casey* itself required informed consent disclosures unrelated to the risks and benefits of the abortion procedure (such as information about adoption and enforcement of child support), followed by a waiting period. In a pre-*Casey* era, the Court struck down similar laws as not narrowly drawn.

Considering the rationale behind the *Dobbs* reversal

In 2022, the Court overruled the cases discussed in the section "Establishing strong protection for abortion rights," earlier in this chapter, in *Dobbs v. Jackson Women's Health Organization*. *Dobbs* upheld a Mississippi law that generally banned abortion after the 15th week of pregnancy (several weeks before the viability point at which *Roe* previously held that government could ban abortion).

TECHNICAL STUFF

Although six *Dobbs* justices upheld Mississippi's law, only five did so by overruling 49 years of abortion-rights precedents. A sixth justice (Chief Justice Roberts) held that Mississippi's ban was constitutional under the currently applicable undue burden test; in Roberts' view, overruling *Roe* and *Casey* was unnecessary and inappropriately activist.

Applying factors the Court uses to determine whether to overrule precedents, the *Dobbs* majority held that *Roe* and *Casey* were "grievously wrong" in their reasoning; that the standards they produced are unworkable and distort legal rules in other areas; and that insufficient evidence exists that women and men structure their personal lives in reliance on the availability of abortion in the event of contraceptive failure. (The dissenting *Dobbs* justices strongly rebutted these arguments.)

Three critiques lie at the heart of the *Dobbs* view that the view of fundamental rights in the *Roe* and *Casey* decisions is grievously wrong:

>> **No historical basis:** A right to choose abortion wasn't deeply rooted in the late 1860s, when the government enacted the 14th Amendment protection against the deprivation of liberty.

>> **Insufficient analogy to other liberty rights:** Other individual autonomy and privacy rights don't pose a "critical moral question" about "the destruction" of a potential life.

>> **Inappropriate interference with elected-official discretion:** The *Roe* Court inappropriately displaced the right that public officials generally have to regulate medical procedures in the name of patient safety and morality.

Justice Breyer's dissent, for himself and two colleagues, countered these points:

>> **Inappropriate historical basis:** Echoing the ongoing dispute between the original intent and evolving Constitution approaches to constitutional interpretation (covered in Chapter 4), the dissent asserted that "we in the 21st century" shouldn't be limited to the concepts of liberty that the ratifiers of the 14th Amendment held in the 1860s.

>> **Clearly an implied liberty right:** The dissent also found a privacy-based abortion right fully "embedded in core constitutional concepts of individual freedom and of the equal rights of citizens to decide on the shape of their lives."

>> **Outside of elected-official discretion:** As for interference with legislative discretion, the dissent rejoined that "the Constitution puts some issues off limits to majority rule."

Understanding *Dobbs*'s practical significance

The *Dobbs* decision has implications both for the future of abortion rights and other implied-privacy rights.

Abortion rights

The *Dobbs* decision has big consequences. As the majority writes, *Dobbs* "return[s] the issue of abortion to the people's elected representatives." The result, notes the dissent, is that "[a]cross a vast array of circumstances, a state will be able to impose its moral choice on a woman and coerce her to give birth to a child."

REMEMBER

Because laws restricting abortion rights are no longer subject to heightened scrutiny, state (and federal) laws that regulate abortion must merely meet the low-level rational-basis test, in the same way as laws that regulate other medical procedures. Restrictive laws are valid if regulators might have a legitimate interest that's served in some way by their limits. Even very strict abortion restrictions would seem to advance general state interests in protecting fetal life.

Specifically, *Dobbs* seems to clear the way for many state laws (already adopted or proposed) that

>> Pursue disputed theories that fetuses feel pain early in pregnancy.

>> Assume that medical abortions raise special risks.

>> Require often-unnecessary ultrasound tests or waiting periods as prerequisites to abortion.

>> Limit private-insurance coverage for the procedure.

Of course, other states may and do adopt laws strongly protective of abortion rights, creating regional patterns in abortion access.

Here are some aspects of the legal and practical implications of *Dobbs* to abortion access in America:

>> Restrictive laws that require pregnant women to face unreasonable risks of death or serious health impairment could face several constitutional arguments, including that they deprive such women of their right to life.

>> Other constitutional protections might limit the available range of options for other restrictive laws.

For example, in an important concurring opinion, one member of the *Dobbs* majority (Justice Kavanaugh) noted that restrictions on pregnant women leaving the state in which they live to access abortions in states that allow abortion would violate an Equal Protection–based right of interstate travel. (You can read about the Equal Protection guarantees in more detail in Chapter 12.)

>> Those challenging restrictive state laws might use the limitations on vague criminal laws that have ambiguous definitions or exceptions (which we discuss in Chapter 18).

>> Congress can pass national legislation (either protecting or restricting abortion rights) that preempts contrary state laws.

Other implied privacy rights

Critics of *Dobbs* both on and off the Court raise different and broader questions about the decision's ultimate implications. To what extent does the reasoning of *Dobbs* suggest that the Court might overrule any other implied privacy right precedents? Would a similarly narrow approach to 14th Amendment history mean that rights to contraception, or to same-sex intimacy and marriage, aren't deeply rooted in history and therefore aren't protected by heightened substantive due process scrutiny?

In a separate *Dobbs* opinion, Justice Thomas called for his colleagues to "reconsider" substantive due process precedents generally; he specifically pointed to the precedents protecting interests in contraception, same-sex intimacy, and same-sex marriage.

At various points in its opinion, the *Dobbs* majority repeated its view that abortion is different from all other implied-privacy rights (because it uniquely involves the fate of another potential life). Based on this, the majority emphasized several times that overruling *Roe* and *Casey* does not undermine the other precedents. And Justice Kavanaugh underlined in his concurring opinion that overruling *Roe* "does *not* threaten or cast doubt" on precedents about contraception, or interracial or same-sex marriage.

Still, many observers worry that the *Dobbs* dissent is correct that "all rights that have no history stretching back to the 19th century are insecure" under the *Dobbs* majority view. As often happens with constitutional rights, only time will tell.

4

Protecting Property, Gun Ownership, and Voting Rights

Delve into the ways the Constitution protects specific interests to promote stability.

Follow the evolution of the 2nd Amendment right to bear arms from its longstanding interpretation as a state right to support a militia to its recent reincarnation as a broad individual right to own guns.

See how the Constitution fortifies the democratic process by building in protections for voters, candidates and supporters.

Chapter 15

Promoting Stability by Safeguarding Specific Interests

We highlight some unique aspects of the Contract Clause in Article I, Section 10 of the Constitution, including its original purpose and its changing relevance over time. We also examine the primary features of the 5th Amendment Takings Clause, which prohibits government from taking private property except for public use and requires payment of just compensation. And we discuss the reach of the 14th Amendment Citizenship Clause, which prevents government from depriving individuals born on American soil of the benefits of U.S. citizenship.

The Contract Clause, Takings Clause, and Citizenship Clause have one thing in common: They promote stability and economic prosperity by ensuring that government can't unfairly interfere with specific interests.

Protecting Contract Obligations

The Contract Clause within Article I, Section 10, of the Constitution prevents states from "pass[ing] any law impairing the obligation of contracts." This clause doesn't apply to the federal government (although other provisions, such as the 5th Amendment Due Process Clause, which we discuss in Chapter 13, prevent the federal government from interfering with certain contracts). The Framers included the Contract Clause in the original Constitution as one of several limitations on state rights and powers.

The records of the Constitutional Convention don't say much about the Contract Clause, but the Supreme Court interpreted the Contract Clause's purpose as to prohibit states from passing debtor-relief legislation. According to the Supreme Court, the Framers worried that these laws threatened the economy by eroding confidence in interstate commerce and devaluing private-property rights. The Contract Clause sought to provide stability, reassuring individuals and businesses that the states wouldn't undermine their agreements.

The Contract Clause prevents interference with existing contracts. It doesn't prevent states from passing laws that govern future contracts.

As interpreted by the Supreme Court, the Contract Clause limits the states' powers to enact legislation that breaches or modifies that state's own contracts or regulates contracts between private parties.

Although it uses broad language, the Contract Clause doesn't prohibit all state interference with existing contracts for at least two reasons:

>> State involvement in existing contracts may be appropriate and necessary to carry out a state's duty to protect its citizens.

>> In the same way that the Contract Clause was written to address specific issues at a certain time in the nation's economic history, its interpretation has evolved with changing economic times.

Protecting business with Article I's Contract Clause

During the 1800s, the Supreme Court struck down most state laws challenged under the Contract Clause. For example, in the 1810 case of *Fletcher v. Peck*, the state of Georgia sold land grants to investors at a very low price. In response to public outrage that the land grants were tainted by corruption, the state passed legislation invalidating the land grants. But the Supreme Court held the new legislation violated the Contract Clause. *Fletcher* is one example of how the Court's early decisions broadly interpreted the Contract Clause to protect business interests from state interference.

In 1934, during the New Deal era, the Court substantially changed its approach to the Contract Clause in *Home Building & Loan Association v. Blaisdell* and gave states far greater power to influence private contracts through the states' police powers to protect the lives, health, comfort, morals, and general welfare of their people. For example, during the Great Depression, the Court upheld a Minnesota law extending the amount of time given to a homeowner to reclaim their property after a foreclosure.

Establishing a contract test

States don't have unlimited police powers. In the 1970s, the pendulum began swinging back from courts upholding legislation under a state's police powers (as discussed in the preceding section) to striking down laws under the Contract Clause. In 1983, the Supreme Court established a three-part test to determine whether state laws that interfere with contracts between private parties satisfy the Contract Clause:

>> The state regulation can't substantially impair a contractual relationship.

>> The state must have a significant and legitimate interest behind the regulation (such as fixing a broad social or economic problem).

>> The law must be reasonable and appropriate for its intended purpose (in other words, it must survive rational-basis review, which we talk about in Chapter 12).

State's efforts to modify their own contractual obligations are subject to higher than rational-basis scrutiny. In 1977's *United States Trust Co. v. New Jersey*, the states of New Jersey and New York issued bonds, promising investors that the states would use the money only to finance building the World Trade Center and to support certain specified rail operations. When New Jersey later attempted to pass a law to repeal the restrictive covenant and allow the states to use the money for purposes not authorized by the original agreement, the bondholders successfully sued and prevented New Jersey from passing the law.

REMEMBER

The Court held that the state's modification of its own contractual obligations must be both reasonable and necessary to achieve a legitimate public purpose. The Court found the modification wasn't essential and that the state had alternative means to accomplish its goal.

Explaining substantial impairment

In *Sveen v. Melin* (2018), the Supreme Court clarified the first part of the Contract Clause test (substantial impairment; see the preceding section), holding that whether a state regulation substantially impaired a contractual relationship involved balancing three factors — the extent to which the law

>> Undermined the contractual bargain

>> Interfered with a party's reasonable expectations

>> Prevented the party from safeguarding or reinstating their rights

Applying that test, the Court held that the Contract Clause didn't render invalid a state law declaring that life-insurance policies terminate upon divorce. The law was intended to carry out the decedent's probable wishes (to remove their ex-spouse as their life-insurance beneficiary) and didn't substantially impair a contractual relationship.

COVID-19 AND THE CONTRACT CLAUSE

During the COVID-19 pandemic (2020–2023), states enacted legislation to protect their residents. For example, California and Washington placed a moratorium on evictions, and New Jersey issued an executive order allowing security deposits to be applied to past-due rent. Many Contract Clause challenges to these measures failed because of the importance of curtailing the transmission of the virus and minimizing its economic consequences. In the face of devastation and uncertainty, most courts deferred to the states' police powers to protect their citizens' health and welfare.

But critics argued that relying solely on the importance of the public interest at stake to invalidate existing contracts effectively nullified the Contract Clause. And some state courts did strike down protective legislation as violative of the Contract Clause. The New York judiciary struck down a law that made commercial lease guarantees permanently unenforceable for rents that were due during a specific period. And a Minnesota court invalidated a pandemic-related eviction moratorium under the Contract Clause. Although most state courts have found that the public emergency posed by COVID-19 justified protective legislation, the split of authority could lead the Supreme Court to reexamine the three-part test in the context of this significant historical period.

Prohibiting the Government from Taking Private Property Unjustly

In Chapter 13, we look at how the Due Process Clauses of the 5th and 14th Amendments prohibit the government from arbitrarily depriving individuals of property. But when it comes to one specific property-taking scenario, another 5th Amendment clause kicks in: The Takings Clause prohibits the federal government from taking private property for public use without just compensation. The Takings Clause also applies to state governments because the Due Process Clause of the 14th Amendment incorporates it.

The Framers designed the Takings Clause to prevent the government from forcing an individual to bear a burden alone that in fairness should be borne by the public. In the following sections, we explore the three main questions that arise under the Takings Clause:

>> Did the government action constitute a taking of private property? (The Constitution requires compensation for both physical and regulatory takings.)

>> Was the taking for a public purpose?

>> Did the government pay a fair price ("just compensation")?

The Takings Clause applies not only to land, but to personal property, lesser interests in land (such as mortgages and leases), and intellectual property. Courts must decide whether government actions that affect these interests amount to *compensable* takings (meaning they qualify for payment).

Identifying government action as taking

The government *takes* private property when it confiscates it or interferes with a person's right to use and enjoy it. Either the government or the property owner can take legal action to address government takings:

>> **Condemnation:** Involves a formal, government-initiated action to take private property through the power of eminent domain (see the following section).

>> **Inverse condemnation:** Involves a property-owner-initiated claim that government action has resulted in a taking, which may be physical or regulatory (discussed in the section "Putting inverse condemnation in the picture," later in this chapter).

Understanding eminent domain

In 1875, the Supreme Court approved a state government's seizure of a parcel of private property to use for a post office. The Court affirmed that both federal and state governments have the power of *eminent domain* (to take private property for public use without the owner's consent).

In classic condemnation scenarios, the government initiates formal proceedings to oust property owners, completely depriving them of any use or possession of their property. For example, using its power of eminent domain, a city may notify homeowners of its intent to raze their homes to build a freeway. In such cases, you can easily see that the government is taking private property.

The government doesn't have to take over an entire parcel for a compensable taking to occur. For example, if the government seizes a portion of someone's front or back yard to put in fire-resistant landscaping in order to prevent the spread of wildfires, it has to compensate the landowner for the portion of land seized. Of course, the size and value of the portion of property taken affects what compensation the government (or the court, if the property owner challenges the government's valuation) determines is just.

Putting inverse condemnation in the picture

Inverse condemnation occurs when a private property owner claims the government took their property without initiating formal condemnation proceedings. The types of takings that can lead to inverse condemnation actions may include

>> **Physical takings:** For example, if the government installs a sewer line across someone's property without purchasing an easement. These takings that may give rise to inverse condemnation actions include temporary takings.

>> **Regulatory takings:** In rare cases, land-use restrictions (including zoning laws) rise to the level of takings. Zoning laws limit the way that property owners can use or develop their property. These laws may prohibit certain uses or limit the height, size, and location of structures in a particular area. Landowners have argued that these laws constitute takings because they diminish the economic value of the property.

Courts have mostly disagreed that these zoning laws rise to the level of constitutional takings because any civilized society requires rules governing certain aspects of property ownership. Most challenges to zoning laws under the Takings Clause fail because the courts find it unreasonable to require the government to pay money every time a homeowner's property is subject to a reasonable zoning regulation.

Common zoning and land-use regulations include

» Limiting use or development of property in certain areas designated as agricultural, historic, residential, single-family, commercial, or industrial

» Setting aside certain properties as environmental

» Requiring that properties provide a minimum number of parking spaces or not exceed a certain height

TIP

Individuals can challenge zoning regulations that amount to arbitrary deprivations or are based on unfair line-drawing under the Due Process and Equal Protection Clauses, in addition to the Takings Clause. (You can read more about these clauses in Part 3.)

REMEMBER

Police sometimes destroy property while performing their duties, such as breaking into a house to rescue someone. The Supreme Court hasn't decided whether the lawful use of police powers results in a 5th Amendment taking under these circumstances, and lower courts have reached conflicting decisions.

TAKING WITH REGULATIONS

In *Penn Central Transportation Company v. City of New York* (1978), the Supreme Court held that a law designating New York's train station as an historic landmark (preventing the owners from selling it for use as an office building) did *not* constitute a taking. But the Court clarified that the government does take private property when it passes land-use regulations that unreasonably interfere with the owner's use of the property. A law or regulation goes too far (and constitutes a taking) if it denies all economically beneficial or productive use of the land or it partially denies economically beneficial use, and an analysis of the following factors weighs in favor of finding a taking:

• The regulation's economic effect on the landowner

• The extent to which the regulation interferes with reasonable investment-backed expectations

• The character of the government action

Imposing conditions on development

Local-government agencies often require landowners to obtain permits as a pre-requisite to further development (such as erecting fences around a property or adding rooms in a house). When the government makes granting these permits conditional on the property owner's agreement to give up other property rights, the government's action may amount to a taking. The test is whether

>> The conditions on development further a legitimate state interest

>> An *essential nexus* (meaning connection) exists between the legitimate state interest and the permit condition

>> The state interest achieved is roughly proportionate to the extent of interference with the individual's property rights

Considering the public uses for land

The government can't take private property for just any reason. Even if it pays a fair price, the 5th Amendment prohibits takings except for public use. But this requirement no longer really limits the government's ability to take property because the Supreme Court has defined *public use* so expansively.

Before the early 20th century, courts interpreted the phrase *public use* literally. The courts considered takings legitimate only if the new purpose granted the public a right to actually use the property. But in *Fallbrook Irrigation District v. Bradley*, in 1896, the Court rejected this interpretation in a case that upheld a power company's taking of private land to generate and sell water power. Later decisions broadly expanded the definition of public use to include any legitimate exercise of the government's police powers.

REMEMBER

The phrase *police powers* refers to the government's authority to enact laws for the public good. Because this term is so broad, legitimate takings for public use can be based on safety, health, morality, peace and quiet, and law and order.

Public use may be more aptly described as *public interest.* It includes such things as

>> Facilitating transportation

>> Providing water

>> Preserving historical sites

>> Establishing public parks

>> Building low-cost housing

TAKING FROM ONE PRIVATE PROPERTY OWNER TO SELL TO ANOTHER

Governments implement redevelopment plans to create jobs, increase tax revenues, and spur economic growth; these plans have involved taking private property for public uses. But in the 2005 case *Kelo v. City of New London*, a homeowner claimed that a city, as part of its redevelopment plan, abused its eminent domain powers by transferring their home to private developers of a business complex. The homeowner claimed the government's forced transfer of ownership from one private party to another didn't constitute a public use within the meaning of the Takings Clause.

The Supreme Court disagreed. The Court held that the term *public use* didn't limit takings to situations where the public would actually use the property; rather more broadly, government satisfies public use whenever the takings serve a public purpose. Many judges, legal experts, and legislators have criticized the *Kelo* decision for effectively nullifying the Takings Clause's public use requirement. Dissenting justice Sandra Day O'Connor called the *Kelo* decision a "reverse Robin Hood" scenario.

>> Beautifying urban areas

>> Transferring land from lessors to lessees to address land-ownership inequities

Determining whether compensation is just

After the government (or a court, if a property owner challenges a government decision) establishes that the government's actions constitute a taking of private property, the property owner is entitled to "just compensation." Not surprisingly, property owners and government agencies often disagree on what amount of compensation qualifies as *just*.

The 5th Amendment, as interpreted by the Supreme Court, requires that landowners who have property taken by the government without their consent are entitled to the fair market value of the property based on its highest and best use:

>> **Fair market value:** You can calculate this value by using a variety of different methods. The parties often hire experts who provide competing opinions on the property's value.

>> **Highest and best use:** Entitles the landowner to compensation for the most profitable use of the property, not necessarily what the property is currently being used for.

Granting Citizenship to People Born on U.S. Soil

A particular section of the Constitution extends the benefits and privileges of American citizenship to all persons born on American soil. Section 1 of the 14th Amendment starts with a Citizenship Clause, which states that "All persons born or naturalized in the United States, and subject to the jurisdiction thereof, are citizens of the United States and of the State wherein they reside."

Although the 14th Amendment was written in the post–Civil War period with former slaves in mind (we talk about this amendment in more detail in Chapter 2), its broad language ("all persons") isn't limited to former slaves. This language has caused controversy in modern America over whether the Clause confers citizenship on babies born on U.S. soil to undocumented immigrants.

In 1898, the Supreme Court's decision in *United States v. Wong Kim Ark* established that individuals born in the United States to parents who aren't United States citizens are automatically citizens unless the parents are alien enemies or diplomats of a foreign state.

REMEMBER

A constitutional amendment could eliminate or modify the Citizenship Clause, but the Framers designed amendment to be intentionally difficult to accomplish, requiring a two-thirds vote in the House and Senate and three-fourths of the states to ratify it. (Flip to Chapter 1 for information on the Framers and decisions they made.) The Supreme Court can also change the understanding of the Clause.

Reworking the Citizenship Clause through executive order

On January 20, 2025, President Trump issued an executive order declaring that individuals born in the United States were ineligible for birthright citizenship if their mothers were in the country either without legal documentation or temporarily, and if their fathers weren't citizens or lawful permanent residents. This order represented a dramatic change from existing policies under the Citizenship Clause which (with a few exceptions) had previously been understood to confer citizenship on people born in the United States, regardless of their parents' immigration status.

Throughout the country, individuals and organizations challenged the executive order as unconstitutional, and federal district courts in several states (Washington, Maryland, and Massachusetts) issued universal *preliminary injunctions* (temporary court orders that prevent a government action from going into effect until the courts resolve the legal challenges) that applied nationwide. Anyone born in the country pending a final decision on the legality of the executive order wouldn't have their citizenship denied.

The federal government challenged the preliminary injunctions in the Supreme Court, in *Trump v. CASA, Inc.*, but the Court didn't interpret the Citizenship Clause or rule on the constitutionality of the executive order. Instead, the Court focused on whether court-jurisdiction statutes passed by Congress give federal district courts authority to issue nationwide injunctions. The Supreme Court held that they did not. This ruling could significantly impact the ability of lower courts to protect — at least temporarily — the victims of illegal government action.

Because the Supreme Court struck down the universal injunctions in *Trump v. CASA, Inc.*, federal district courts can independently decide whether the executive order is unconstitutional in relation to the specific plaintiffs in the case before it. This case-by-case decision-making could lead to a situation where one baby born in the United States is automatically a citizen, while another baby born on the same day under the same circumstances but in a different part of the country isn't. But several groups, including the plaintiffs in *Trump v. Casa*, took steps to prevent that from happening. They filed a class action lawsuit on behalf of all babies affected by the executive order, so when the district court issued a preliminary injunction in that case, it applied to them all.

Ruling on the Citizenship Clause

The original purpose of the Citizenship Clause was to grant citizenship to slaves newly freed under the 13th Amendment. (We talk about the post–Civil War amendments in Chapter 2.) As you can read about in the section "Granting Citizenship to People Born on U.S. Soil," earlier in this chapter, the *Wong Kim Ark* Court interpreted the Clause's reach to include anyone born in the country. Congress also enacted a federal law codifying the Clause's language.

Against this background, the Supreme Court, in its 2025–2026 session, is deciding the constitutionality of the executive order limiting birthright citizenship (see the preceding section). The Court hasn't issued a decision at the time we write this book (but you can go to the Supreme Court's website, www.supremecourt.gov, to see whether the Court has since issued a decision). Key issues in the litigation include

>> The meaning of the Citizenship Clause and the federal law

>> The proper application of the clause's phrase "subject to the jurisdiction thereof"

Chapter 16

Assuring the Right to Keep and Bear Arms

The 2nd Amendment grants a broad individual right to possess guns. It's a fundamental right, so federal, state, and local authorities generally can't pass laws that limit gun ownership or possession. The Amendment also significantly limits how these governments can regulate gun sales and use. The boundaries of this right are hotly debated in the media and among politicians and government officials, often in response to tragic gun-related events such as school and workplace shootings.

In this chapter, we examine the constitutional right to keep and bear arms. We look back to 2008, when the Supreme Court first recognized that the 2nd Amendment guarantees an individual right to own guns. We also examine how the Supreme Court has clarified its approach to figuring out whether gun regulations impermissibly infringe on that right. This chapter also considers the future and identifies some open questions that the courts may (or may not) resolve.

Protecting an Individual Right to Gun Ownership

The 2nd Amendment states, "A well regulated Militia, being necessary to the security of a free State, the right of the people to keep and bear Arms, shall not be infringed." The freedom to own and possess guns is one of the most highly charged constitutional topics. The debate tends to divide into two camps:

>> **Little regulation:** Argue that government should broadly interpret the right in order to prevent regulating guns except in very rare circumstances

>> **Regulation for safety:** Believe that the Constitution allows the government greater power to regulate guns in the name of public safety

Neither side disputes that the 2nd Amendment protects an individual right to bear arms; most disagreements center around whether gun-control measures go too far or not far enough in protecting or violating that right. But the right as the courts understand it today is quite new in the constitutional big picture.

Courts' interpretation of the 2nd Amendment in the past focused on the state militia aspect, but the 2008 Supreme Court decision in *District of Columbia v. Heller* first recognized that the 2nd Amendment protects an individual's right to bear arms. *Heller* left some questions unanswered, which creates challenges for lower courts assessing the constitutionality of gun regulations (discussed in the section "Applying *Heller* to Gun Regulations in Lower Courts," later in this chapter).

Assuming no individual right to bear arms

From at least as early as 1939 to 2008, the Supreme Court assumed that the 2nd Amendment protected a collective right to bear arms to defend the state against a tyrannical federal government, not an individual right to own guns for self-defense.

The text starts by referencing a "well regulated Militia," so the interpretation made sense. Before 2008, courts seemed to view history as also supporting this interpretation. Decisions that upheld federal gun-regulatory laws (such as *United States v. Miller* in 1939) explained that, although the Constitution granted Congress the power to create and maintain an army, the Framers harbored a strong distrust for peacetime standing armies, fearing that the federal government could use the army against its own people.

The Court interpreted the 2nd Amendment as guaranteeing soldiers and citizens the right to own guns for use in the state militia as a safeguard against a hostile federal army. The right to bear arms went no further than that.

Changing the 2nd Amendment interpretation

The militia interpretation lasted for nearly 70 years, until the Court rejected it in 2008. In *District of Columbia v. Heller*, the Court decided that the militia language was just *prefatory* (meaning it introduced a general idea), therefore it didn't limit the right to bear arms to state militia use. The Court held that the 2nd Amendment protected an individual right to own and possess guns.

In *Heller*, the plaintiff claimed that Washington, D.C.'s near-total ban on operative firearms in the home violated their 2nd Amendment right to bear arms. In a 5–4 opinion authored by Justice Scalia, the Supreme Court agreed. In its decision, the Court

>> Rejected the interpretation of the 2nd Amendment that limited protection to the militia and held that the amendment protected an individual gun ownership right for self-defense.

>> Reasoned that the right to self-defense in the home was a central and well-established national tradition in 1791, when the 2nd Amendment was adopted.

>> Acknowledged that the gun-ownership right was not unlimited and that it didn't preclude all regulation of guns. For example, the 2nd Amendment didn't protect *dangerous or unusual weapons* (interpreted by lower courts to mean weapons that law-abiding persons don't normally possess for lawful reasons, such as fully automatic firearms), and some regulations were presumptively lawful, such as laws that

   • Prohibited dangerous people from possessing firearms

   • Prohibited possession of firearms in sensitive places such as schools and government buildings

   • Imposed conditions on the commercial sale of firearms

The dissenters relied on the amendment's text and history to support their position that the more limited militia interpretation was correct.

Heller only prohibited the federal government from imposing gun restrictions because, at the time it was decided, the Supreme Court hadn't yet found that the 2nd Amendment was incorporated through the Due Process Clause of the 14th Amendment (which we talk about in the section "Extending to state and local gun safety laws," later in this chapter). State and local governments became subject to the Amendment in 2010's *McDonald v. City of Chicago* decision.

Seeing what *Heller* decided and didn't decide

The *Heller* majority opinion and two dissenting opinions take up 154 pages, but the case left open many questions that courts have struggled to work out:

>> **What scrutiny standard applies:** In its decision, the Court generally side-stepped the question of what scrutiny standard applied to gun regulations because it held that the D.C. law at issue (which was a near-total ban on handguns in the home) didn't satisfy the 2nd Amendment under any standard of review. Without direction from the Supreme Court, lower courts decided inconsistently whether intermediate or strict scrutiny applied.

   Heller did rule that courts can't use the lowest rational-basis scrutiny standard in cases relating to gun regulations. (Flip to Chapter 12 for a description of the different levels of scrutiny that the Court applies.)

>> **What guns are protected:** The *Heller* majority opined that the 2nd Amendment protects weapons that were in common use at the time it was drafted but does not protect dangerous and unusual weapons. Lower courts reached different conclusions about what weapons were in common use during the 18th century, depending on how broadly they generalized various types of weapons. They also inconsistently interpreted what weapons qualified as dangerous and unusual.

>> **Types of gun regulations allowed:** *Heller* acknowledged that the right to bear arms wasn't unlimited and didn't preclude all gun regulation. The opinion listed various categories of regulations that were presumptively valid, including laws that impose conditions on the commercial sale of firearms, but did not specify the extent to which regulations that don't amount to total bans (such as background checks and registration requirements) fell into these categories.

>> **Whether gun ownership and possession outside the home are protected:** *Heller* held that the 2nd Amendment established an individual right to own and possess handguns in the home for the purpose of self-defense. It did not address whether the right applied outside the home.

Applying *Heller* to Gun Regulations in Lower Courts

In the absence of a directive from the Supreme Court about what level of scrutiny to apply to gun regulations after the decision in *District of Columbia v. Heller* (see the section "Changing the 2nd Amendment interpretation," earlier in this chapter), lower federal courts had to develop their own rules. They generally followed a two-step process:

>> They asked whether the law at issue burdened conduct protected by the 2nd Amendment.

>> They applied either strict or intermediate scrutiny, depending on whether the law burdened the core protection of the 2nd Amendment.

Handling post-*Heller* havoc

Lower federal courts upheld most, but not all, gun regulations in decisions not long after *Heller*. But without a standard of review, outcomes were inconsistent.

Some regulations upheld after *Heller* include

>> A ban on juveniles possessing firearms

>> A lifetime firearm prohibition for convicted domestic abusers

>> Pre-sale background checks

>> A *suitable person* (nonviolent, as determined by police) or *proper cause* (proof that a person has a special need for a firearm) standard for carrying a concealed weapon

>> A law requiring payment of fees for gun licenses

>> Bans on sawed-off shotguns

Federal courts struck down some regulations after *Heller*:

>> Zoning laws that prohibited shooting ranges

>> Firearm bans on persons convicted of non-violent misdemeanors

>> Limitations on the issuance of concealed-carry licenses to people who had a special need for self-defense (such as high-risk employment or receiving threats)

The courts' decisions discussed in this section in relation to what qualifies as constitutional shows only how the court was interpreting the constitution during a short window of time — a modern court likely wouldn't have the same interpretations.

Extending to state and local gun safety laws

Just two years after *Heller* (discussed in the section "Protecting an Individual Right to Gun Ownership," earlier in this chapter), in *McDonald v. City of Chicago* (2010), the Supreme Court once again dramatically expanded the 2nd Amendment's reach. *McDonald* involved a Chicago law banning handguns in the home, similar to the one struck down in *Heller*, but the city of Chicago argued that the 2nd Amendment didn't apply to the state.

McDonald examined historical evidence about the importance of guns during the 18th century and decided that gun ownership was deeply rooted in the nation's traditions, so it held that the 2nd Amendment was a fundamental right that applied to the states through the Due Process Clause of the 14th Amendment. (We talk about due process in Chapter 13.)

Balancing gun rights against public safety concerns

In the 15 years after *McDonald*, the Supreme Court decided three 2nd Amendment cases, first expanding the right to bear arms even further than *Heller* and *McDonald*, and then seemingly setting some limits. In the following sections, we take a closer look to see how the Court developed and later clarified the legal standards for evaluating gun regulations.

The right to bear arms as modern Americans know it is less than 20 years old. That's brand new in terms of the Constitution. Table 17-1 shows at a glance how the law around gun rights has developed so far.

Protecting modern, non-lethal guns

Caetano v. Massachusetts in 2016 was the Supreme Court's first post-*Heller* 2nd Amendment case. In *Caetano*, the defendant borrowed a stun gun from a friend to protect herself against an abusive former boyfriend. She was convicted under a law prohibiting the possession of stun guns. In a *per curiam opinion* (a brief opinion of the Court not attributed to a particular judge), the Court held that the law was unconstitutional because the 2nd Amendment protects stun guns. The

Court said that stun guns don't qualify as *unusual* (as presented in the *Heller* decision) simply because they're modern; *Heller* itself stated that protected weapons aren't limited to those in existence at the time the country was founded.

 2nd Amendment Supreme Court Cases Since 2008

Case	Year	2nd Amendment Application	Gun Protection
District of Columbia v. Heller	2008	Establishes an individual right to possess guns in the home for self-defense	Expanded
McDonald v. City of Chicago	2010	Applies to the states through the 14th Amendment Due Process Clause	Expanded
Caetano v. Massachusetts	2016	Protects modern and non-lethal guns	Expanded
New York State Rifle and Pistol Association v. Bruen	2022	Permits gun regulation only where the law has an historical equivalent	Expanded
United States v. Rahimi	2024	Historical comparison under *Bruen* requires a close analogy, not an historical twin	Narrowed

Extending gun rights to public spaces and limiting gun regulations

In 2022, the Supreme Court again expanded the reach of 2nd Amendment protection. In *New York State Rifle and Pistol Association v. Bruen*, the Court struck down a New York law that required people applying for gun permits that allow them to carry guns outside the home to prove that they had proper cause to carry a gun, meaning they had a special need for self-defense (such as protection against a specific threatening individual), compared to the general self-defense concerns of other members of the community.

Bruen clarified *Heller* and *McDonald* (discussed in the section "Extending to state and local gun safety laws," earlier in this chapter); and, in doing so, it developed 2nd Amendment law in two important ways. It held that

>> The constitutionality of a modern regulation depended on whether it was consistent with the 2nd Amendment's text and historical understanding (although the modern-day regulation didn't need to exactly match its historical precursor).

>> The 2nd Amendment protected the right to possess guns outside the home in public spaces.

Bruen maintained that the modern law didn't have to exactly match an historical law, but it provided no guidance about how broadly a court should generalize or analogize to historical laws. Nor did it provide guidance for courts dealing with new technology, such as guns created through 3D printers and assault weapons that didn't exist at the time the country was founded.

Removing the need for an exact match for a gun law

After *Bruen* (see the preceding section), gun-law opponents went into court to challenge well-established and previously unquestioned gun regulations. But lower courts found *Bruen's* history-and-tradition test difficult to apply. In 2024, the Court clarified the *Bruen* test and provided guidance to courts in drawing historical comparisons in *United States v. Rahimi.*

The Court upheld a law that prohibited individuals subject to domestic-violence restraining orders from possessing guns. In an 8–1 opinion, the Court clarified that the challenged law must be "relevantly similar" to historical laws and tradition. The Court observed that lower courts that interpreted *Bruen* (including the lower court in *Rahimi*) applied too rigid a standard for determining whether an historical precedent existed for a gun regulation. In the same way that the 2nd Amendment protected firearms that didn't exist in the 18th century, it permitted regulations that didn't exist in the 18th century.

The opinion focused the inquiry on the purpose of the regulation and the burden it imposed on the right to bear arms. If an historical law regulated firearms to address a certain problem, modern firearm restrictions addressing the same problems would likely be upheld if they didn't create excessive burdens compared to the burdens imposed by earlier laws.

Regarding the restraining-order ban at issue in *Rahimi*, the Court reviewed English and American history and found two sets of laws instructive:

>> Historical laws that required people who were believed to be dangerous to post a bond that would be forfeited if they engaged in violence

>> Historical laws that punished people who threatened others with guns

Although these regulations were different than the one *Rahimi* was subject to, they confirmed that, historically, when an individual posed a clear threat of violence to another, the government could prohibit them from possessing guns. The comparison standard required an historical analog, not an historical twin. Justice Thomas (who wrote the *Bruen* opinion) was the lone dissenter. He did not think that the historical laws relied upon by the majority were sufficiently analogous to the one at issue in the case.

Justice Sotomayor's concurring opinion in *Rahimi*, joined by Justice Kagan, pointed out the importance of a test accounting for societal changes over time. For example, at the time of the founding, the law protected abusive husbands and didn't hold them accountable, so no historical equivalent to the law at issue in the case exists, and requiring a too-narrow analogous regulation would subvert justice.

Rahimi was the first post-*Heller* Supreme Court case to uphold a challenged gun regulation. The near-majority opinion, and the agreement of most (but not all) of the concurring justices that *Bruen's* historical analog inquiry is a generalized, principle-focused comparison, suggests that *Bruen's* history and tradition test may permit more regulation than courts and gun-safety advocates initially believed.

GUN REGULATION CASES NOT REFERENCING THE 2ND AMENDMENT

The Court decided two other cases involving gun regulations in 2024 and 2025, but neither decision directly references the 2nd Amendment. In the 2024 decision, *Garland v. Cargill*, the Court held that *bump stocks* (accessories for semi-automatic firearms) don't convert such firearms into machine guns; this avoided opening up semi-automatic weapons to even more rigorous regulation. But in 2025's *Bondi v. VanDerStok*, the justices held that *ghost guns* (unregistered guns assembled from kits) qualify as firearms within the meaning of the main federal gun-control law. This interpretation subjected ghost guns to significant regulation.

Although justices' attitudes about 2nd Amendment rights may have influenced the decisions in both cases, the justices decided these cases based on complicated non-constitutional issues about the proper interpretation of federal statutes and how much deference administrative experts should receive. So *VanDerStok* and *Cargill* may not necessarily influence the development of 2nd Amendment legal standards. (Of course, courts and other observers still scour the decisions for subtle clues about the Court's inclinations!)

Identifying Future Areas for 2nd Amendment Challenges

The Supreme Court decisions in *Heller* (see the section "Changing the 2nd Amendment interpretation," earlier in this chapter), and *Bruen* and *Rahimi* (discussed in the section "Balancing gun rights against public safety concerns," earlier in this chapter), laid out the contours of the individual right to bear arms. But many issues remain undecided. Gun laws quickly change while legislatures respond to developing Supreme Court precedent. And guns themselves are changing while new technologies develop weapons that have capabilities the Framers could have never imagined.

While lower courts and state courts interpret Supreme Court standards and apply them to different scenarios, those decisions can provide more clarity and guidance on questions such as

>> What qualifies a weapon as *dangerous or unusual* and therefore unprotected under *Heller*?

>> Do areas other than schools and government buildings qualify as *sensitive places* where government can ban firearms?

>> Where does government draw the line between laws that impose conditions on the sale of firearms (which the Court has said are presumptively valid) and unconstitutional infringements on the 2nd Amendment right to bear arms?

We can predict to some degree what questions the Supreme Court will soon answer, as of the time we write this book. The following sections delve into our thoughts and predictions for the future of the 2nd Amendment interpretations by the Supreme Court.

Considering cases on the Supreme Court's 2025–2026 docket

By the time you read this book, the Supreme Court may have issued its decision in two 2nd Amendment cases that it agreed to review during the 2025–2026 term. (Check out the Supreme Court's website, www.supremecourt.gov, for the latest on the Court's decisions.) One pending case involves the constitutionality of bans in certain locations, and the other involves the constitutionality of bans in relation to a particular class of people. Broadly speaking, these two cases can help draw lines to define some of the categories that allow for gun regulation.

Potential impact on sensitive-place laws

In *Wolford v. Lopez*, the Court will decide the constitutionality of a 2023 Hawaii gun law that includes a provision that prohibits people from possessing handguns on private property open to the public unless the gun owner gets permission from the property owner. The law at issue in *Wolford* was enacted in response to language in *Heller* that regulations in sensitive places were presumptively permissible.

The sticking point in *Wolford* is not whether private property owners can ban people from carrying guns on their property — they can. But the Hawaii law is structured so it bans gun possession unless the person who has the gun gets permission in advance from the landowner. The question is whether the default of a ban, because it puts the burden on the gun owner, violates the 2nd Amendment.

REMEMBER

The only question before the Court in *Wolford* is the constitutionality of Hawaii's provision regulating firearms on private property open to the public. But that provision is part of a broader Hawaiian sensitive-places law that goes beyond *Heller's* examples of schools and government buildings; Hawaii's law includes parks, beaches, and playgrounds as sensitive places. Other states' sensitive-places laws cover zoos, stadiums, financial institutions, and places that serve alcohol.

The role of historical comparison

The decision in the *United States v. Hemani* case on the 2025–2026 docket will likely further develop the standards that courts should apply when comparing current laws to historical ones. Hemani was prosecuted under a federal law making it illegal for drug users or addicts to possess guns. He claims the law violates his 2nd Amendment rights because no historical precedent exists for prohibiting gun possession based on past drug use. Although historical laws did prohibit people who were impaired from possessing guns, no evidence shows that Hemani himself was impaired at the time he possessed the gun.

The Court could avoid the constitutional issue and decide *Hemani* based on federal law alone (finding, for example, that the law should be interpreted as applying only to people who are currently addicted to drugs). But if the Court reaches the 2nd Amendment question, its ruling can have a widespread impact because federal and state laws prohibit drug users — including marijuana users in states where such use is lawful — from possessing guns.

Flagging other 2nd Amendment issues that may soon be resolved

Petitions filed by parties requesting Supreme Court review of lower court and state court decisions provide clues about what cases the Supreme Court may hear in the near future. Recurring issues or ones that result in a split of authority may signal areas that are ripe for review:

>> Whether the 2nd Amendment allows states to prohibit or restrict sales to adults under 21 years old

>> Whether a statute barring felons from possessing firearms is unconstitutional as applied to felons convicted of non-violent felonies

>> Whether the 2nd Amendment permits a state to ban specific guns and ammunition, such as AR-15s, short-barreled rifles, semiautomatic rifles, ghost guns, or guns that have their serial numbers obliterated or that use large-capacity magazines

>> Whether prosecution for unregistered, homemade firearms violates the 2nd Amendment

>> Whether the 2nd Amendment prohibits background checks for ammunition

>> Whether limits on the number of firearms that an individual can purchase or the imposition of waiting/ cooling-off periods violate the 2nd Amendment

The Supreme Court hasn't directly addressed whether the 2nd Amendment allows background checks, but some experts think *Bruen* (discussed in the section "Extending gun rights to public spaces and limiting gun regulations," earlier in this chapter) makes it clear that it does. Justice Kavanaugh's concurring opinion in *Bruen*, joined by Justice Roberts, said so explicitly.

Chapter **17**

Guaranteeing Rights for Election Participants

resident Abraham Lincoln famously described American democracy as a government "of the people, by the people, for the people." Such a government requires participation, and participation inevitably involves power struggles between people trying to maintain the status quo and people trying to change it.

This chapter explores how the Constitution protects participation in the political process for voters, candidates, and political supporters. You can see what the Constitution says (and doesn't say) about the right to vote, including amendments that protect voters and empower Congress to safeguard voting rights. This chapter also goes into how the electoral college works and explores redistricting and *gerrymandering* (rigging electoral maps to favor a political party), delving into recent and pending redistricting controversies.

In this chapter, we also scrutinize how the 1st Amendment broadly protects campaign speech and spending.

Seeing What the Constitution Does (and Doesn't) Say about Voting Rights

The Constitution doesn't grant citizens a right to vote. Citizens have no federal constitutional right to vote. But several constitutional amendments (discussed in the following sections) imply a right to vote and ensure fairness in state-granted voting rights.

Leaving voting rights to the states

You may be surprised that the Framers didn't grant citizens a federal constitutional right to vote. After all, the Constitution makes it clear that the president and members of Congress are elected. In Article I, Section 2, the Framers gave states the power to decide who can vote. The effect of this delegation was to give states free rein to disenfranchise certain citizens and exclude them from the political process. Why would the Framers, who were so vigilant about protecting individual rights, leave it to the states to decide who could vote, instead of enshrining a right to vote in the Constitution itself?

History seems to suggest three reasons (with one underlying theme — the retention of power). The Framers

>> Were White men, most of whom were educated, wealthy landowners who would have lost power by granting all Americans a Constitutional right to vote

>> Believed that the elite class of White men was more vigilant in safeguarding individual rights than a poor, racially diverse, uneducated majority

>> Believed that land ownership was necessary to ensure that voters were sufficiently invested in the betterment of society

REMEMBER At the time the Constitution was ratified, voting was considered a privilege, not a right. Many of the Framers were slave owners who supported the Three-Fifths Compromise (counting slaves as three-fifths of a person for purposes of taxation and representation, while giving slaves no rights). Their strong beliefs in individual liberties didn't include racial or gender equality, which may shed light on their unwillingness to create a constitutional right to vote.

Article I, Section 2 of the original Constitution said that whatever qualifications states required for voters to vote in their state elections would also apply to elections for Congress. In other words, if states prohibited certain groups of people from voting for members of the state legislature (which states were perfectly free to do), then those same groups would be excluded from that state's federal elections. For decades following the Constitution's ratification, *suffrage* (the right to vote) was limited, and states had widely varying rules about who could vote. Many states granted the right to vote only to free male citizens, excluding women, slaves, Native Americans, and free Black men.

The Court upheld these discriminatory voting practices, even after the 14th Amendment was ratified. In 1872, Susan B. Anthony and hundreds of other women suffragists went to the polls and demanded to vote. They claimed that the 14th Amendment's Privileges and Immunities Clause prohibited states from interfering with women's right to vote. One woman sued the registrar after she was denied the right to register. The case made its way to the Supreme Court. In 1874, in *Minor v. Happersett*, the Court held that voting isn't a right of national citizenship and states don't violate the Constitution by limiting voting to free White men.

Protecting state-granted voting rights

Widespread discrimination in state-granted voting rights that followed the Constitution's ratification set the stage for several voting-related amendments. In the early 1800s, while some states expanded voting rights for White men by removing property-ownership requirements, they doubled down on their exclusion of women and Black men. Some states further limited suffrage by adding obstacles to voting, such as requiring people to pre-register or pay poll taxes.

After the Civil War, states enacted discriminatory laws to prevent newly freed slaves from voting. For example, vagrancy laws enabled the government to imprison Black people who then lost the right to vote because of their criminal conviction.

Over time, ratification of several constitutional amendments prohibited discriminatory voting restrictions and expanded voting rights:

>> **14th Amendment:** The Equal Protection Clause includes an implied right to vote in federal and state elections.

>> **15th Amendment:** Prohibits denying or restricting voting rights based on race, color, or previous condition of servitude.

» **19th Amendment:** Prohibits voting discrimination based on sex, effectively granting women the right to vote.

» **23rd Amendment:** Grants voting rights to Washington, D.C. residents.

» **24th Amendment:** Prohibits poll taxes in federal elections. (Poll taxes in state elections violate the 14th Amendment Equal Protection Clause.)

» **26th Amendment:** Prohibits voting discrimination based on age for citizens who are over 18 years old.

EVER-SHIFTING VOTING RIGHTS STANDARDS

What standard of scrutiny the Court applies to claims that voting restrictions are unconstitutional seems to change depending on what's at stake. (We talk about the standards of scrutiny and how they work in Chapter 12.) A few examples can help illustrate the confusion:

- In 1966, in *Harper v. Virginia Board of Elections*, the Court applied strict scrutiny to strike down poll taxes, finding that wealth-based line drawing wasn't legitimately related to voter qualifications.

- In 2000, in *Bush v. Gore*, the Court didn't announce or apply a clear standard but held that a Florida court's order to recount *undervotes* (ballots that included a vote for lower offices but not president) to see whether the ballots showed signs that the voter attempted to vote for a particular presidential candidate arbitrarily valued one person's vote over another in violation of the Equal Protection Clause because no regulations existed to govern how to count votes.

- In 2008, in *Crawford v. Marion County Election Board*, the Supreme Court applied a more deferential and flexible approach, considering the constitutionality of an Indiana law that required citizens to show photo identification before voting. The Court held that government must justify any burden, however slight, by relevant and legitimate state interests sufficiently weighty to justify the limitation. In the case of voter ID, the Court found that the state had a valid interest in deterring and detecting voter fraud, and that the burden did not "represent a significant increase over the usual burdens of voting."

The "usual burdens of voting" standard may have replaced strict scrutiny for equal protection challenges in voting rights cases. In 2021, in *Brnovich v. Democratic National Committee*, the Court cited the "usual burdens of voting" language to uphold several Arizona voting restrictions against Constitutional claims.

Summarizing federal voting rights laws

Each of the voting-expansion amendments listed in the preceding section includes a clause that authorizes Congress to enforce the amendment's provisions by appropriate legislation. Using these powers and others (such as its spending power and its authority to regulate the time, place, and manner of elections), Congress has enacted laws to safeguard the right to vote and make it easier for people to exercise that right.

Any voting rights discussion should include a brief overview of the laws that Congress enacted in exercising its constitutionally granted voting-rights enforcement authority:

>> **The Civil Rights Act of 1866:** A precursor to the 14th Amendment (see Chapter 2 for discussion of this amendment). This act established birthright citizenship and acknowledged that all U.S. citizens have certain inalienable rights, including the right to make contracts and own property.

>> **The Enforcement Acts of 1870 and 1871:** Designed to prevent the Ku Klux Klan from harassing and intimidating Black voters.

>> **The Voting Rights Act of 1965 (VRA):** A landmark civil rights law that prohibited discriminatory voting practices and imposed compliance requirements on states.

The Supreme Court struck down a portion of the VRA as unconstitutional in the case *Shelby v. Holder* in 2013, and the Court is deciding a case in its 2025–2026 session, *Louisiana v. Callais,* that involves a constitutional challenge to another part of the VRA. We discuss the status of the VRA in greater detail in the following section.

>> **The Voting Accessibility for the Elderly and Handicapped Act of 1984:** Requires that state and local election officials ensure that polling places are accessible to elderly and disabled voters and requires states to provide elderly and disabled voters with registration and voting aids for federal elections.

>> **The National Voter Registration Act of 1993:** Makes voter registration easier by requiring states to offer voter registration opportunities at their motor vehicle offices and through the mail. It also requires states to maintain accurate registration lists and promptly transmit completed registration applications to election authorities.

>> **The Help America Vote Act of 2002:** Establishes the Election Assistance Commission (EAC), which is an independent, bipartisan commission that supports voting officials and voters, and provides for funding, research, and improvements to voting equipment and practices.

Seeing the effects of the Voting Rights Act of 1965

Racial discrimination in voting continued after ratification of the 15th Amendment. The Supreme Court interpreted the amendment narrowly, finding that it didn't prohibit voting restrictions that on their face appeared neutral, such as literacy tests, grandfather clauses, and poll taxes. These practices, along with harassment and intimidation, severely restricted Black people's ability to register and vote.

The Voting Rights Act of 1965 (VRA) was the culmination of organized efforts by Civil Rights leaders who demanded legislation to enforce the 15th Amendment. This act prohibited discriminatory regulations and practices such as literacy tests that denied the right to vote based on a person's race, color, or language.

WARNING

Legislative district map drawing often leads to vote-dilution claims under the VRA. We cover redistricting in the section "Affecting Voters' Choices," later in this chapter, and *gerrymandering* (using redistricting to manipulate election outcomes or discriminate against certain voters) in the section "Fighting Against Gerrymandering," later in this chapter.

One of the most significant aspects of the VRA was its *preclearance* provision, which prevented states from making changes without federal approval:

» Section 4 of the VRA set forth a formula to determine whether a state had a history of voting discrimination.

» Section 5 required states that Section 4 showed to have such a history to obtain federal government approval before changing their voting laws.

For several years following the passage of the VRA, the Supreme Court upheld Section 5 and validated the preclearance requirement for all types of voting regulations. The VRA had an immediate impact, substantially increasing the number of registered Black voters.

Removing the VRA's preclearance requirements

In 2013, in *Shelby v. Holder*, the Supreme Court struck down the VRA's preclearance requirements. The Court held that the requirement violated the principle of equal state sovereignty by placing unfair burdens on some states because the formula for determining whether a state was covered was outdated. According to the Court, when Congress passed the VRA, blatant discrimination was prevalent, but current needs no longer justified the formula. Dissenting Justice Ginsburg observed that ending preclearance was like "throwing away your umbrella in a rainstorm because you are not getting wet."

The *Shelby* decision immediately released covered jurisdictions from the preclearance requirement. Some states responded by passing laws that likely wouldn't have passed preclearance. For example, Texas immediately enacted a statute imposing burdensome identification requirements. Since *Shelby*, states have adopted photo identification requirements, reduced mail-in and early voting, closed polling locations, and enacted other voting restrictions that disproportionately impact voters of color.

Whether those practices violate Section 2 of the VRA (prohibiting voting practices that have a discriminatory effect) requires a case-by-case analysis of the totality of circumstances. The results so far are mixed:

>> ***Brnovich v. Democratic National Committee* (2020):** The Court upheld Arizona's practice of discarding ballots of voters who voted at the wrong precinct and its criminalization of collecting ballots from a third party.

>> ***Allen v. Milligan* (2023):** The Court issued a preliminary injunction after it found that Alabama's redistricting plan had a discriminatory effect and likely violated Section 2 of the VRA.

Removing Section 2 of the VRA?

As discussed in the section "Racial gerrymandering," later in this chapter, the Court took the rare step in its deliberations in 2025 of requesting a second oral argument in *Louisiana v. Callais* to address whether a map drawn to comply with Section 2 of the VRA violates the 14th or 15th Amendments. (At the time of writing, the Court hasn't issued a decision in this case. You can go to the Supreme Court's website at www.supremecourt.gov to see the case's status.)

The states have the right to decide who gets to vote and what restrictions to impose, but they must do so in compliance with the Constitution and federal law. For example, states vary widely on the issue of voting rights for people who have felony convictions. Some states prohibit them from voting altogether. Some states don't restrict them at all. States can decide how to handle voting rights for people who have criminal convictions because no federal constitutional principle or law prohibits it.

Seeing the Electoral College's Role in Presidential Elections

The *electoral college* isn't a college at all, but a system that the Framers created to elect the president and vice president. As originally established in Article II, Section 1 of the Constitution, the system was a compromise between those who distrusted government (and thought that the president should be elected by a popular vote) and those who distrusted the masses (and thought that the president should be elected by Congress). The Framers designed the electoral system to address both groups' concerns by allowing states to choose presidential electors whom neither Congress nor the people elected.

CHANGES TO ELECTION PROCEDURES

The original procedure for electing the president and vice president involved awarding the first-place winner the position of president, and the second-place winner became vice president (which forced political opponents to work together). This procedure led to problems after the 1796 election when John Adams was elected president, and his political rival Thomas Jefferson became vice president. The 12th Amendment, ratified in 1804, changed the procedures for these elections. This amendment provided for electors to cast separate ballots for each, which generally led to a more harmonious outcome because electors cast their votes for presidential and vice-presidential candidates who were politically aligned. It also established a tie-breaker procedure that gives the House of Representatives the power to elect the president and the Senate the power to elect the vice-president.

Choosing and tallying electoral votes

Article II, Section 1 of the Constitution provides that each state gets a number of electors equal to its number of Senators and Representatives. Federal law sets the number of representatives at 435. Each of the 50 states has two senators, for a total of 100, bringing the number of electoral votes to 535. And the 23rd Amendment gives Washington, D.C. 3 electors for a grand total of 538 electors. A candidate needs 270 electoral votes to win the election. If there's a tie, the House of Representatives elects the president, with each state getting one vote.

TECHNICAL STUFF

State laws and political-party rules determine who can be an elector, subject to the constitutional limitations (from Article II and the 14th Amendment) that no Senator, Representative, or person holding federal office can be an elector, and no state official who has engaged in insurrection or rebellion against the United States or provided aid and comfort to its enemies can be an elector.

Seeing how the electoral college elects presidents

The electoral college works by following these general steps:

1. **Each state receives electors equal to its total number of federal legislators; and Washington, D.C., gets three.**

   Before the general election, every party that has a presidential candidate on the ballot chooses a slate of potential electors. These individuals, usually party loyalists, may include state officials and party leaders.

2. **During the general election, voters cast votes for president and vice president.**

   These popular votes actually apply to the slate of potential electors that their candidate's political party nominated.

3. **In 48 states and Washington, D.C., the winning candidate's full slate of potential electors become that state's presidential electors.**

   Nebraska and Maine allocate electors proportionately and may end up with split electors.

4. **After the election, state officials prepare a certificate of ascertainment that is sent to election officials.**

   The *certificate of ascertainment* identifies the individuals appointed as the state's electors.

5. **The electors meet in their respective states on the first Tuesday after the second Wednesday in December.**

   This meeting occurs after the general election, which happens the Tuesday following the first Monday in November.

6. **The electors vote separately for president and vice president.**

7. **The electors record their votes on a certificate of vote.**

8. **Each state sends its sealed certificate of vote to the seat of government.**

   In this circumstance, the *seat of government* is Washington, D.C. The president of the Senate (who is also the current vice president) safeguards these reports.

9. **On January 6 of the year following the general election, members of the Senate and the House of Representatives meet to conduct the official count.**

   This count occurs in the House chamber during a joint session of Congress. As Senate president, the current vice president presides over the count.

10. **The vice president opens the sealed ballots and delivers them to tellers, who read them out loud.**

    Tellers are people previously appointed by Congress who read the vote certificates in the presence of both houses.

11. **The vice president then announces the winners of the presidential and vice-presidential elections.**

    The vice president's role in presiding over the vote count is purely ceremonial. Congress considers and decides any objections to electoral votes, and Congress hasn't sustained any objections since federal law first established the rules in 1887.

12. **The Chief Justice of the Supreme Court swears the newly elected president into office on January 20.**

WHEN ELECTORS GO ROGUE

An elector votes for someone other than the candidate who put them on the slate exceedingly rarely. Nevertheless, in most states, parties require electors to sign a loyalty pledge as a condition of serving as an elector, and states can immediately disqualify and replace *faithless electors* (meaning electors who don't vote for the candidate the majority of their state voted for) with an alternate who votes for the winner of the state's popular vote. Nothing in the Constitution prohibits these loyalty pledges.

Affecting Voters' Choices

Who appears on your ballot depends on a variety of factors, including your *legislative district* (the designated geographical area where resident voters elect officials for that area) and whether any laws or regulations prevent a candidate from running. In the following sections, we examine what the Constitution has to say about district map drawing and candidates' access to the ballot.

Drawing state and federal legislative districts

Redistricting means redrawing maps to change the boundaries of districts. The Constitution mandates redistricting in Article I, Section 2, requiring that the House of Representatives be apportioned based on population as determined by the United States census every 10 years.

Although the Constitution requires redistricting according to a census taken every 10 years, it doesn't prohibit mid-decade redistricting. Under the Elections Clause in Article I, Section 2, the states draw the maps (although Congress can make or alter state regulations, including those involving redistricting).

The "one person, one vote" principle implicit in Article I, Section 2, and in the 14th Amendment Equal Protection Clause, requires that congressional districts have equal populations.

Determining who draws the maps

Whoever draws the maps of legislative districts must do so in accordance with the Constitution, the Voting Rights Act (which you can read more about in the section "Summarizing federal voting rights laws," earlier in this chapter), and their own state constitutions and statutes. Who does the drawing depends on the particular state:

>> **State legislatures:** In most states, the legislature draws congressional and state-legislative districts.

>> **Advisory commissions:** Some states use advisory commissions to draw congressional and state-legislative districts. These commissions may include legislators or non-legislators who draw maps for legislative approval.

>> **Independent commissions:** Some states use independent commissions made up of non-lawmakers. These commissions draw and approve the final maps.

>> **Political appointee commissions:** Some states use committees appointed by elected officials or political parties.

>> **Courts:** When redistricting processes fail or are successfully challenged, courts can play a role in drawing district maps.

Traditional criteria used by states in map-drawing include compactness, contiguity, preservation of counties and other political subdivisions, preservation of communities of interest, preservation of previous districts, and avoiding *pairing incumbents* (drawing lines that require current holders of elected offices to run against each other). When states draw lines based on other criteria (such as politics or race), other issues arise. You can read more about these issues in the section "Fighting Against Gerrymandering," later in this chapter.

Governing candidate ballot access and selection

The Constitution doesn't just protect voters; it seeks to ensure that the people they want to vote for aren't unfairly left off the ballot. Restrictions on ballot access may bump up against rights of free speech and association under the 1st and 14th Amendments, as well as the 14th Amendment Equal Protection Clause.

When it comes to ballot-access challenges under the 1st (and 14th) Amendments, the Court must weigh the character and magnitude of the asserted injury against the asserted state interests:

>> **Strict scrutiny:** If the regulation subjects the individuals' rights to severe restrictions, it must be narrowly drawn to advance a compelling state interest.

>> **Reasonable-basis scrutiny:** If it imposes only reasonable, nondiscriminatory restrictions, it needs to reflect only important regulatory interests.

Applying these two standards, the Court has issued inconsistent rulings on ballot access issues, such as state laws requiring certain candidates to file petitions with a certain number of signatures, prohibiting them from running as independents or appearing on multiple party's ballots, prohibiting them from running for office before completing their term, and imposing strict filing deadlines.

Fighting Against Gerrymandering

The primary objective of redistricting (discussed in the section "Affecting Voters' Choices," earlier in this chapter) is fairness in elections, but sometimes districts are redrawn in ways that are very unfair. *Gerrymandering* uses redistricting as a tool to manipulate election outcomes or discriminate against certain voters. It can be racial or *partisan* (political), and unscrupulous district mappers can accomplish it in different ways, such as

>> **Cracking:** Splitting members of a group among multiple districts so that they have insufficient power to elect their preferred candidate in any one district.

>> **Packing:** Putting members of the same group into one district (or as few districts as possible) so that they have strong political power in a few districts but diminished political power overall.

Voters, political parties, candidates, incumbents, and civil rights organizations can challenge district maps that they say violate the 14th Amendment Equal Protection Clause and the 15th Amendment prohibition against racial discrimination.

Racial gerrymandering

As we write this book, the Supreme Court is preparing to issue its opinion in *Louisiana v. Callais*, a case that may dramatically change the law on racial gerrymandering. (To see whether the Supreme Court has issued this opinion, check out www.supremecourt.gov.) In the following sections, we look at the legal backdrop leading up to the dispute in *Callais*, summarize what's at issue, and consider the potential outcomes and their implications.

The legal landscape leading up to *Callais*

These legal principles apply to racial gerrymandering claims, a potential conflict between which constitutes the primary issue in *Callais*:

>> **The 14th Amendment Equal Protection Clause:** Prohibits race-based classifications unless they're narrowly tailored to further a compelling state interest (the strict scrutiny test).

>> **The 15th Amendment:** Prohibits the federal government or any state from denying or abridging the right to vote based on race, color, or previous condition of servitude.

>> **Section 2 of the Voting Rights Act of 1965:** As amended in 1982, prohibits states from denying or abridging the right to vote based on race. Importantly, Section 2 prohibits states from acting in ways that result in discrimination, regardless of the lawmakers' intent.

>> **Supreme Court decisions:** Based on the holdings in three Supreme Court cases between 1993 and 1995 (*Shaw v. Reno*, *Miller v. Johnson*, and *Bush v. Vera*), when race is the predominant factor motivating the legislature's map-drawing, the 14th Amendment Equal Protection Clause requires the map to survive strict-scrutiny review.

Reconciling the Voting Rights Act, and the 14th and 15th Amendments

After Louisiana drew new congressional maps with the 2020 census information, it faced racial–gerrymandering challenges:

>> *Robinson v. Landry:* Approximately one-third of Louisiana's population is Black. When state legislators drew up maps with only one Black-majority Congressional district out of the state's six, a group of citizens filed a lawsuit that claimed the plan violated Section 2 of the VRA because it had a discriminatory effect on Black voters. The lower federal court ruled that the plaintiffs were likely to succeed at trial.

>> *Louisiana v. Callais:* Instead of fighting this ruling, the Louisiana legislature redrew the maps to create a second Black-majority district. Another lawsuit ensued, *Callais,* this time involving non-Black plaintiffs challenging the new maps as an unlawful racial gerrymander motivated predominantly by race in violation of the 14th Amendment Equal Protection Clause.

The case initially focused on reviewing the lower court's decision that the redrawn map violated Equal Protection principles. But the Court took the unique step of ordering additional briefing and a second oral argument to answer a broader question: Whether the state's intentional creation of a second majority-minority congressional district violates the 14th or 15th Amendments. The Court heard oral argument on that question in October 2025 and is expected to issue its ruling in the spring of 2026. The Supreme Court website (`www.supremecourt.gov`) has the latest information on its decisions.

Seeing possible outcomes of *Callais*

The maps at issue in *Callais* were redrawn because a court ruled that the original maps likely had a discriminatory effect on Black voters, in violation of Section 2 of the VRA. The Court could base a decision on its interpretation of the VRA's Section 2:

>> **Provides compelling state purpose:** Because it appears beyond dispute that race was a predominant consideration in drawing the new map, the Equal Protection Clause applies, so the Supreme Court may decide that the Louisiana legislature's compliance with Section 2 constitutes a compelling state purpose.

>> **Violates Equal Protection:** The Court could rule that Section 2 violates the Equal Protection Clause of the 14th Amendment to the extent it requires map drawing that's predominantly race-based.

However the Court finds, the *Callais* decision will be far-reaching, affecting state and local map drawing, in addition to congressional redistricting:

>> **Upholding the redrawn maps:** If the Court finds that the state has a compelling interest in bringing its map into compliance with the VRA, the decision will provide strong new protection against race-based voting discrimination.

>> **Finding the redrawn maps unconstitutional:** If the Court finds that Section 2 is unconstitutional, the decision may immunize states from consequences for racial gerrymandering and invalidate legislation that has been called the crown jewel of the Civil Rights Movement.

Two past Supreme Court decisions can likely influence the outcome of *Callais*:

>> ***Shaw v. Reno* (1993):** After the North Carolina Attorney General rejected a congressional map that created only one Black-majority district, the state submitted a second plan with a bizarrely drawn second Black-majority district. Residents challenged the map saying its purpose was to elect Black representatives. The Supreme Court held that even if the map was created with good intentions, it went further than necessary separating voters on the basis

of race. This decision suggests that even when a map is drawn to correct racial inequities, the new map itself may violate the Equal Protection Clause.

>> ***Allen v. Milligan* (2023):** Struck down Alabama's map under Section 2 weighs in favor of the statute's constitutionality.

Partisan gerrymandering

A 2019 Supreme Court case, *Rucho v. Common Cause*, seems to have opened the door to unchecked political gamesmanship, including *partisan gerrymandering* (drawing maps to give one party an unfair political advantage). But the Legislature may step in to clear things up.

In *Rucho*, the Court held that partisan gerrymandering claims present *nonjusticiable questions*, meaning they're outside the reach of the federal courts. The Court noted that districting had always involved politics and concluded courts had no way to draw a line between permissible and impermissible partisan line drawing.

The substantial impact of *Rucho* became clear in late 2025 when the Court issued an unsigned emergency ruling (called a *shadow docket*) in *Abbott v. League of United Latin American Citizens (LULAC)*. In anticipation of the 2026 midterm elections, Texas redrew its congressional districts to favor its predominant political party. Other states, including California and North Carolina, followed suit. Texas citizens challenged the new districts that the Texas government drew, claiming the legislature's motive was predominantly racially based. A district court agreed, but the Supreme Court reversed the district court's decision based on *Rucho's* holding that the case qualified as partisan gerrymandering, which is nonjusticiable.

Partisan gerrymandering cases may make it harder for racial gerrymandering claims to have their day in court. The plaintiffs in *Abbott* raised a racial gerrymandering claim, but the Court refused to consider it, citing its 2024 holding in *Alexander v. South Carolina State Conference of the NAACP* that where race and politics are closely correlated, the Court must presume that the legislature acted in good faith, and the plaintiffs must show that race was a predominant motivating factor.

The Legislature has so far voted down proposed legislation prohibiting mid-decade redistricting and partisan gerrymandering. Some think that Congress will reconsider in light of the post-*Rucho* redistricting frenzy. At the time of writing, this question remains unresolved.

Fitting Free Speech into Elections

The 1st and 14th Amendments protect freedom of speech for all political participants. (Chapter 10 dives deep into the Constitution's role in freedom of speech for all.) Candidates and their supporters don't give up their rights to free expression just because they put their name on the ballot or contribute money to a candidate or cause. To the contrary, political speech is a highly valued and zealously safeguarded form of constitutionally protected speech.

Citizens have a constitutional right to vote, but they don't have a corresponding right to receive full and accurate information. Voters or opposing political parties generally can't do much to stop candidates and supporters from exercising their own constitutional rights in a way that misleads or even deceives the public. The burden falls on voters to educate themselves about the candidates and issues on the ballot by consulting various sources and considering various viewpoints.

Protecting political free speech

Misinformation, disinformation, and lies during political campaigns can cause real harm to voters. But for the most part, the Supreme Court has concluded that the 1st Amendment protects false information in politics. The Court is concerned that prohibiting speech can have a potential *chilling effect* (meaning that regulating speech can deter people from speaking lawfully to avoid inadvertently crossing the line into prohibited territory) if false statements are against the law.

Cases that deal with 1st Amendment rights often involve concern about regulations having a chilling effect on speech.

Although the Constitution protects the right to lie, that right isn't absolute. Government can regulate certain types of false speech by candidates:

>> **Defamation:** Requires proof that a person knowingly made false statements that harmed someone's reputation

>> **Fraud:** Such as misrepresentations that a person has authority to act on behalf of a political candidate

>> **Voter suppression:** Including false statements about how, when, and where to vote

Constitutionalizing campaign spending

When it comes to politics, spending is a protected form of free expression, according to the Court's decision in 1976, in *Buckley v. Valeo*, a landmark campaign-finance case.

Buckley was a complicated case that involved challenges to multiple provisions of the Federal Election Campaign Act (1971) and the Presidential Election Campaign Fund Act (1966). The Court upheld the constitutionality of laws that limit contributions to candidates and require disclosure, but it found other provisions unconstitutional, including limits on expenditures by candidates from their personal funds. The Court concluded that

>> The contribution and disclosure rules safeguarded the integrity of the electoral process without directly impinging on the rights of citizens and candidates.

>> The expenditure limitations violated the 1st Amendment right to free speech. The limitation on a candidate's use of personal funds unconstitutionally interfered with the protected right of an individual "to engage in the discussion of public issues and vigorously and tirelessly to advocate his own election."

The Court reaffirmed *Buckley* in 2000, when it held in *Nixon v. Shrink Missouri Government PAC* that the government can limit contributions by individuals, political action committees (PACs), and corporations directly to political campaigns if the restrictions aren't so extreme that they make the contribution pointless.

Opening the door for campaign contributions

In addition to candidates themselves, supporters (including PACs, corporations, and labor unions) enjoy 1st Amendment rights to advocate for or against candidates and causes. Although these supporters must be independent of any candidate they support (meaning they can't coordinate with the candidate about how to spend their money), they have a constitutional right to spend as much money as they want, and they can (and often do) join forces to create Super PACs and other groups that wield tremendous political power.

A highly controversial 2010 case, *Citizens United v. Federal Election Commission*, opened the door for corporations to move tremendous amounts of money into politics. Citizens United, a politically conservative nonprofit organization, planned to release a documentary shortly before the 2008 election that was critical of Democratic presidential candidate Hillary Clinton. Citizens United sought injunctions to prevent the federal government from applying a federal law that prohibited corporations and unions from using their general funds to make independent expenditures for "electioneering communications" or speech advocating for the election or defeat of a candidate.

In its *Citizens United* decision, the Court held that corporations and unions had the same free-speech rights — and therefore the same independent-expenditure rights — as other advocates. The law at issue amounted to a ban on political speech, and the law failed the strict scrutiny test. (Flip to Chapter 12 for a rundown of the levels of scrutiny courts can apply to cases.)

In the wake of *Citizens United*, corporations, PACs, and wealthy individuals now spend billions of dollars on elections, concentrating political power in the hands of a small number of wealthy people and making it hard for government to monitor or enforce regulations that require transparency and prohibit corruption.

Predicting the future of campaign spending

A case pending before the Supreme Court at the time of writing could open the door to even more money in politics by eliminating *Buckley's* distinction between expenditures and contributions and holding that the 1st Amendment prohibits restrictions on *coordinated contributions* (contributions made in consultation with the candidate).

In *National Republic Senatorial Committee v. FEC*, the plaintiffs argue that the Federal Election Campaign Act's prohibition on coordinated spending violates the 1st Amendment. In 2001, the Court rejected that claim, but it agreed to revisit the issue based on the plaintiff's arguments that the circumstances have changed. The Court has since recognized that campaign-finance regulations are subject to 1st Amendment protections and that extensive political spending, including unlimited spending by PACs, has become the norm. At the time of writing, the case is pending. You can see the latest on Supreme Court decisions by going to its website (www.supremecourt.gov).

5
Creating a Fair Criminal Justice System

Explore why the Constitution tips the scales of justice in favor of individuals suspected and accused of crimes.

See how the Constitution limits government power to investigate, prosecute, and adjudicate crimes.

Discover how the Constitution keeps both state and federal criminal prosecutions fair.

Dive deep into the constitutional rights of the convicted.

Chapter **18**

Protecting Criminal Suspects and Defendants

The stakes are high in criminal cases, and the power differential between government and individual is stark. Criminal laws give government officials the power to arrest, fine, imprison, and in some cases execute violators. Given the Framers' intent to break free from the oppressive tactics of the British government, the Constitution has something to say about almost every aspect of the criminal process. And much of what it says is that individual rights come first.

In this chapter, we take a panoramic view of the Constitution's substantial role in the American criminal justice system. The Constitution is primarily concerned with ensuring that criminal processes are fair. Although the Constitution establishes a few important ground rules for criminal laws, it mostly leaves it to Congress and state lawmakers to decide what conduct is illegal and how to punish that conduct. Of course, those laws must comply with due process, just as every other aspect of criminal law and procedure must.

We examine the civil aspects of due process (involving non-criminal matters) in Chapter 12. In this chapter, we see how due process lays like a blanket over criminal cases, making sure federal and state prosecutions are fundamentally fair.

Curtailing Government Abuse in Criminal Matters

The Constitution governs criminal procedure in all federal and state prosecutions. (In the following section, you can see why the federal Constitution applies to state criminal cases, even though states have their own constitutions.) We use the terms *criminal procedure* and *criminal law* with the following meanings:

>> **Criminal procedure:** About process. Rules of criminal procedure are generally aimed at government conduct and specify what government officials can and can't do in enforcing criminal laws. The Constitution sets limits on the government's procedures in investigating, prosecuting, and punishing crimes. For example, the 4th Amendment prohibits police from searching without a warrant.

>> **Criminal law:** About substance. Criminal laws are generally aimed at individual conduct and spell out what people can and can't do while they go about their daily lives. Criminal laws define what conduct is prohibited and set forth the penal consequences. For example, one federal criminal law provides that a person who willfully attempts to avoid paying taxes is guilty of tax evasion and may be fined up to $100,000 and/or imprisoned for five years.

Think of criminal procedures as the guardrails keeping government officials on track while they enforce the criminal laws.

Criminal procedures promote integrity in the process and instill confidence in the system, while criminal laws generally protect public safety and an orderly society. The Constitution is primarily concerned with procedure.

The Framers largely designed the provisions of the Constitution related to criminal procedure to ensure that the new government couldn't engage in some of the oppressive tactics that the colonists had endured under British rule, including:

>> Searching homes and businesses without warrants or probable cause

>> Coercing confessions through torture

>> Suspending jury trials

>> Imposing unjust punishments

Suppose police arrest for murder a person whom they suspect killed another person, and they take this person to the police station. There, officers read the suspect their Miranda rights (you can read more about these rights in Chapter 19) before asking questions about the crime. This scenario involves both criminal law and procedure:

>> **Criminal law:** Defines murder as "the unlawful killing of another human being without justification." Criminal laws are mostly *statutory* (enacted by statute of the legislative branch of state or federal government).

>> **Criminal procedure:** Officers must read an in-custody suspect their *Miranda* rights before asking questions, otherwise a constitutional prohibition makes anything the suspect says inadmissible in court.

Rules of criminal procedure can come from federal law (the U.S. Constitution or federal statutes) or state law (state constitutions or statutes), but no federal or state law can authorize conduct that's prohibited by the Constitution or deny any right protected by the Constitution. The Constitution is the supreme law of the land.

Setting Up Ground Rules for Criminal Laws in Article I

For the most part, the Framers left it to federal and state lawmakers to decide what conduct qualifies as criminal and what punishment government should impose.

Exceptions include the Constitution's Article III, Section 3, which defines treason (which we talk about in Chapter 2), and the 8th Amendment, which prohibits excessive fines and cruel and unusual punishment (discussed in Chapter 21).

But lawmakers can't make any law they want. All criminal laws must comply with certain constitutional requirements. Article I, Sections 9 and 10 prohibit Congress and the states from passing any:

>> **Bills of attainder:** A law that singles out a person or group of people for punishment. For example, the Supreme Court invalidated a law barring

three named federal employees from receiving compensation based on their association with subversive organizations. Bills of attainder infringe on the separation of powers because they involve legislative exercises of the judicial powers to adjudicate guilt and impose punishment. They also call for arbitrary government action which violates due process, as you saw in Chapter 13.

>> **Ex post facto laws:** Criminalize conduct that wasn't criminal when it occurred or increase punishment for a crime after the fact. They involve arbitrary and unfair government conduct by subjecting people to a change in the law that they couldn't have anticipated and that was outside of their control; ex post facto laws fail to give fair warning of the prohibited conduct or the potential penalties.

For example, if a person is convicted of a crime punishable by one year in jail, but the legislature changes the maximum punishment to two years before the person is sentenced, they can only be sentenced under the old law to one year or less because the two-year provision would be an ex post facto law as applied to them.

KEEPING PRESIDENTIAL RECORDS

After President Nixon resigned in the aftermath of the Watergate scandal, he entered into an agreement with the General Services Administration (GSA) to store presidential materials, including 42 million pages of documents and 880 recordings. The agreement included provisions for restricting access to the materials and eventually destroying them. Shortly after Congress learned about the agreement from the White House announcement, Congress enacted the Presidential Recordings and Materials Preservation Act (PRMPA), a law directing GSA to take custody of the documents and have them screened by archivists to preserve those items that had historical value and make them available for use in judicial proceedings.

The law specifically targeted Nixon's records, so he argued it was a bill of attainder. The Supreme Court disagreed. Although the law was directed at Nixon, he was "a legitimate class of one" because the documents of other presidents were already housed in presidential libraries. The law also wasn't intended to punish Nixon, but to preserve documents.

Applying Due Process Principles in Prosecutions

Chapters 13 and 14 discuss how the 5th and 14th Amendments prevent the government from depriving individuals "of life, liberty, or property without due process of law." Criminal cases deprive people of liberty and property through imprisonment, parole, probation, and fines, so criminal investigations and prosecutions must comply with due process.

If the death penalty is involved, the case also involves the deprivation of life. When it comes to the constitutionality of the death penalty itself, the 8th Amendment prohibition against cruel and unusual punishment tends to become the focus, rather than the due process discussion. We take a look at these issues in Chapter 21.

Due process can seem like an amorphous concept, but in criminal cases, it really boils down to two overriding principles:

>> **Selective incorporation:** The 14th Amendment Due Process Clause incorporates most of the protections in the first ten amendments (the Bill of Rights), making them applicable to the states. (You can read more about selective incorporation in Chapter 2.)

Selective incorporation has significant implications in the criminal context. For example, it means state and local police, prosecutors, and courts have to act in accordance with the 4th Amendment prohibition against unreasonable searches and seizures. They must honor the 5th Amendment privilege against self-incrimination and appoint counsel for defendants who can't afford to hire their own attorney, among other things.

>> **Fairness:** Due process prohibits government actions that qualify as fundamentally unfair, according to the Supreme Court. The government

- May not pass laws that infringe on constitutional rights

- Must give defendants notice of the charges and an opportunity to be heard before a fair decision maker

- May not obtain convictions through means that offend a sense of justice, shock the conscience, or offend the community's sense of fair play and decency

Prohibiting laws that infringe on constitutional rights

A criminal law that infringes on a person's constitutional rights is unconstitutional (which may seem obvious). For example, if Minnesota passed a law that said prosecutors can compel defendants to testify at their trials, it would be struck down as unconstitutional because it violates the 5th Amendment privilege against self-incrimination as applied to the states through the 14th Amendment Due Process Clause.

Lawmakers must avoid trampling on more than just the Bill of Rights. Some rights are so essential to justice and fair treatment that courts recognize them as fundamental, even though the Constitution doesn't expressly state them. For example, the courts will invalidate a law if it waters down the presumption of innocence, the requirement of proof beyond a reasonable doubt, or the prohibition against shifting the burden of proof to the defendant.

REMEMBER

A fundamental principle of American criminal law is reflected in a doctrine known as the Blackstone ratio: It's better that ten guilty persons go free than one innocent person receive unjust punishment. Simply put, the U.S. government considers it a far greater injustice to convict an innocent person than to let a guilty person go free. This philosophy is consistent with the broader constitutional goal of ensuring that individuals don't get steamrolled by powerful government forces.

The Due Process Clause:

>> Requires government to provide a strong justification for criminalizing conduct that falls within the fundamental constitutional right to privacy. (We talk more about this issue in Chapter 14.)

>> Prohibits vague or substantially overbroad laws:

- Vague laws may deter people from exercising their constitutional rights because they can't clearly tell whether their planned conduct is prohibited.

- Overbroad statutes include both criminal and constitutionally protected activity.

For example, a statute that prohibits loitering could be both vague in the way it defines the term and overbroad in that it could apply to a lot of constitutionally protected behavior (such as the 1st Amendment right to assembly).

Requiring notice and an opportunity to be heard

Procedural due process requires notice, an opportunity to be heard, and a neutral arbiter in criminal cases, as well as civil cases. (Flip to Chapter 13 for more information on procedural due process.) Government must give timely notice and make the charges specific enough to allow the defendant to prepare a defense.

Questions about due process can arise in all kinds of situations. Some examples include when a judge has a financial interest in a case, police seize property without disclosing what they took, a defendant is held in custody without a probable cause hearing, or the prosecutor calls a witness that was not on the witness list.

Disallowing government actions that "shock the conscience"

In 1952, the Supreme Court decided *Rochin v. California*, a landmark case that asserted due process prohibits outrageous government conduct. The legal standard for government conduct so extreme that it violates due process is stated in several different ways, including conduct that "shocks the conscience," "outrageous government conduct," "conduct that offends a sense of justice," and "conduct that offends a community sense of fair play and decency."

In the case of *Rochin*, police had information that Rochin was selling drugs. They entered his house through an unlocked door, then forced their way into his bedroom, where they saw two pills on a nightstand. Rochin put the pills in his mouth, and officers couldn't get them out of his mouth before he swallowed them. They arrested him and took him to the hospital, where they directed a doctor to pump Rochin's stomach against his will to recover the pills. The pills contained morphine and were entered into evidence against Rochin.

The Court reversed Rochin's conviction, stating, "This is conduct that shocks the conscience . . . this course of proceeding by agents of government to obtain evidence is bound to offend even hardened sensibilities. They are methods too close to the rack and the screw to permit of constitutional differentiation."

Other extreme and outrageous government conduct that may violate due process include:

>> A prosecutor's knowing use of false testimony

>> A prosecutor's failure to provide the defense with evidence that undermines the prosecution's case or a witness's credibility (called *exculpatory evidence*)

>> The use of visible shackles or restraints during trial unless the court makes a finding that restraint is necessary for safety

>> Forcing a defendant to go to trial in jail clothing

>> Introducing irrelevant evidence that renders a trial fundamentally unfair (for example, evidence of marital infidelity unrelated to the charges)

>> Trapping a defendant in a scheme where government agents involve themselves directly and continuously in the creation and maintenance of criminal operations

Appreciating the Differences in Criminal Cases

REMEMBER

What happens after law enforcement becomes aware of a potential violation of the law can vary widely. Despite these differences, most cases follow the same general path through the justice system (as discussed in the following section), in large part because the Constitution requires certain processes. Although Congress and state legislatures can enact laws granting more expansive protections than the Constitution requires, they can't pass any laws that limit those protections.

Criminal laws vary around the country for a number of reasons:

>> **State law differences:** Conduct that's criminal in one state may not be criminal in another. State criminal laws and procedures may reflect regional priorities, preferences, politics, and resources. Much the same way as California is known for its fish tacos, New York for its pizza, and Texas for its barbecue, history, geography, and culture create differences in criminal laws when it comes to subjects such as drug offenses, juvenile delinquency, and punishment for repeated offenders.

>> **Regional procedure differences:** You can also see differences in criminal procedures, even within the same state. For example, some elected county district attorneys may offer diversion programs for certain minor crimes, allowing defendants to maintain a clean criminal record; others may refuse to engage in plea bargaining at all, forcing every criminal case to go to trial.

REMEMBER

As an example of how state procedures may vary, many states don't use grand juries to file criminal charges, and the Constitution doesn't require them to do so because the 5th Amendment grand jury requirement (for federal cases) isn't incorporated into the 14th Amendment Due Process Clause (which states must obey). In the section "Adjudicative stage," later in this chapter, you can see the other ways prosecutors can charge criminal cases.

Looking at the Stages of a Criminal Case

Broadly speaking, a criminal case has three stages (which we talk about in the following sections):

>> **Investigative stage:** The fact-finding process, which often includes interviews, search warrants, and evidence review

>> **Adjudicative stage:** The formal process where a neutral decision maker determines the legal issues in the case (for example, a trial where a judge or jury finds a defendant guilty or not guilty)

>> **Post-conviction stage:** Proceedings that take place after a person's conviction and sentence when the defendant claims their sentence is unlawful (habeas corpus proceedings, for example)

REMEMBER

Many criminal matters never make it through all three stages. A case can be shut down during the investigative stage if police don't develop sufficient evidence to charge anyone with a crime. Cases also end during the adjudicative stage when defendants plead guilty, get their cases dismissed during pretrial motions, or are acquitted at trial. Defendants may also obtain relief at sentencing or during post-conviction litigation, including *habeas corpus* (a petition filed by a prisoner who claims their detention is unlawful), which we cover in Chapter 21.

Investigative stage

Investigations are fact-gathering missions where law enforcement agents figure out whether they have sufficient evidence to charge an individual (or corporation, or group of people) with a crime. Investigators first must figure out what potential crimes to investigate:

>> A dog finds a human bone in the woods. Was someone murdered? Or does the bone relate to an accidental death or something else entirely?

>> An elderly couple discovers their retirement account has been drained. It could be embezzlement or a simple accounting error.

>> A child shows up at school with a bruise in the shape of a handprint, and their teacher (a *mandated reporter,* meaning the law requires them to notify the police of suspected child abuse) contacts authorities. It could be child abuse, or maybe the kid has an aggressive older brother who tried to steal the ball during a basketball game.

>> Police observe suspicious activity when they pull someone over for a traffic violation and smell alcohol on the driver's breath.

Every crime is defined by a federal, state or local criminal law, and investigators must investigate to figure out whether they can find evidence that supports every aspect (or element) of a potential crime.

Identifying all the components of a crime

If you're an investigator trying to determine whether a person committed domestic-violence battery, you have to find evidence of all the elements of that crime:

>> A harmful or offensive touching

>> On a person who is a cohabitant, coparent, or is (or was) in a dating relationship with the defendant

If the investigation develops evidence that Person A punched Person B in the face, that evidence satisfies the harmful or offensive touching element. But if Person A and Person B work together and have no other relationship, you don't have sufficient evidence of the second element. So you don't have a crime of domestic violence battery. Of course, the first element alone can apply to a number of other charges. (In Chapter 20, we explain that the constitutional right to a fair trial requires proof of every element beyond a reasonable doubt.)

Investigation outcomes

The investigation can lead to one of a few potential outcomes:

>> **Case closed:** If the investigation establishes that a crime didn't occur or that further investigation won't be productive, the case is closed.

>> **Case open but inactive:** If the investigation hits a dead end but investigators hope that new evidence will come to light, they can keep the investigation open but inactive.

You probably know the term *cold case,* which applies to an investigation that has exhausted all known leads, but the crime remains unsolved. The investigations are dormant, but investigators occasionally reopen them to determine whether they can find any new leads or overlooked evidence.

>> **Case submitted to a prosecuting attorney:** If an investigation develops sufficient evidence that supports every element of a crime (as well as the identity of the perpetrator), investigators submit the case to a prosecuting agency (usually a city attorney, county district attorney, state attorney general, or federal agency such as the United States Department of Justice or the United States Attorneys Office). Investigators may also get an arrest warrant and take the suspect into custody.

Adjudicative stage

After investigators submit an investigation to a prosecuting agency (see the preceding section), prosecutors review the police reports and evidence to determine whether they have sufficient evidence to file criminal charges. If they don't, they may request that investigators pursue additional areas of investigation, or they may reject the case altogether. After sufficient evidence exists, they can file criminal charges. Or they may exercise their discretion not to file charges in the interests of justice, such as in cases that have extenuating circumstances (for example, if the defendant is terminally ill or the victim received restitution and doesn't want to prosecute).

The adjudicative stage starts when formal charges are filed, which may happen in different ways, depending on the jurisdiction:

>> **Grand jury:** In federal felony cases, the Constitution requires the prosecution to convene a grand jury and file an indictment to initiate formal proceedings. Some states require grand jury indictments for felonies, as well.

>> **Complaint and charging document:** Other states use a complaint and information process where the prosecutor or a law enforcement agent files a complaint, the case proceeds to a preliminary hearing, and after the court finds probable cause, the prosecutor files an official charging document (called an *information*) in the case.

The case is then set for trial. As the trial date approaches, parties may need to make a number of court appearances for various reasons, including pretrial motions and settlement discussions. If the case doesn't resolve, it proceeds to a jury trial (unless both sides waive the right to a jury and agree to a court trial; they might do this because the issues in dispute are more legal than factual or because of a belief that judges can better compartmentalize prejudicial evidence).

At trial, the prosecutor must prove the defendant's guilt beyond a reasonable doubt. Then the jury (or judge) determines the verdict:

>> **Not guilty:** If the jury finds the defendant not guilty, the case is over.

>> **Hung jury:** If the jury *hangs,* meaning jurors can't reach a unanimous decision, the court declares a mistrial and either sets a new trial or dismisses the case.

>> **Guilty:** If the jury finds the defendant guilty, the court sets a date for sentencing, and a defendant who was previously out of custody may be remanded into custody.

Post-conviction stage

After a defendant is convicted (by guilty plea, court trial, or jury trial; discussed in the preceding section), the case is set for a sentencing hearing.

Often, the probation department or other court services branch prepares a report for the judge, or the parties lay out all the information the judge wants to know before sentencing the defendant, including family history, substance-abuse issues, criminal history, victim information, and the circumstances of the crime.

The report usually sets forth the maximum penalties authorized by law for each conviction and includes a sentencing recommendation.

Hearing

At the sentencing hearing, the judge considers the probation report, any sentencing briefs submitted by the parties, and any letters of support or other materials sent on behalf of the defendant. The court may permit victims to give impact statements, and the defendant (and possibly the defendant's supporters) may speak on the defendant's behalf. The court then imposes a sentence within the sentencing parameters authorized by law.

Post-sentencing

Even after sentencing, the defendant has remedies available to address potential errors and injustices. For the most part, these post-judgment remedies aren't constitutionally mandated. Some jurisdictions may allow defendants to bring motions to dismiss, for a new trial, or to withdraw their plea.

Federal and state laws provide appeals processes that allow defendants to challenge their convictions and sentences. These processes vary greatly between jurisdictions and aren't constitutionally guaranteed.

Habeas corpus, on the other hand, is a constitutionally mandated remedy for individuals who can convince a judge that they are unlawfully imprisoned. (We talk about habeas corpus in detail in Chapter 21.)

Using Constitutional Principles to Govern Criminal Proceedings

The Constitution operates to protect individual rights at every stage of the criminal process:

>> **Enacting criminal laws:** Article I, Sections 9 and 10 prohibit bills of attainder and ex post facto laws (flip back to the section "Setting Up Ground Rules for Criminal Laws with Article I," earlier in this chapter, for discussion of these prohibitions).

>> **Conducting investigations:** The 4th Amendment prohibits unreasonable searches and seizures, and requires a warrant and probable cause. The 5th Amendment protects the privilege against self-incrimination, grants a right to counsel during custodial interrogation, and requires the government to advise a defendant of their Miranda rights (discussed in the section "Curtailing Government Abuse in Criminal Matters," earlier in this chapter) before using their statements in court.

>> **Charging defendants:** The 5th Amendment requires grand jury indictments to charge all federal felonies. (States can use alternatives that meet constitutional fairness requirements, such as filing criminal complaints and conducting preliminary hearings.) The 8th Amendment prohibits excessive bail.

>> **Prosecuting defendants:** The 5th Amendment prohibits double jeopardy, and the 6th Amendment grants a right to counsel at critical stages.

The 6th Amendment grants trial rights, including the right to a speedy and public trial, the right to a fair trial, the right to a jury trial, the right to present a defense, and the rights to compulsory process and confrontation.

>> **Sentencing and post-conviction:** The 8th Amendment prohibits cruel and unusual punishment and excessive fines. Article I, Section 9, guarantees the remedy of habeas corpus (which we talk about in Chapter 21).

In addition to the specific provisions in the preceding list, the Due Process Clauses in the 5th and 14th Amendments overlay every aspect of a criminal case. Flip back to the section "Curtailing Government Abuse in Criminal Matters," earlier in this chapter, for discussion of the ways the Constitution's due process rights protect the accused.

Interpreting Constitutional Principles in Criminal Proceedings

The constitutional text applicable to criminal cases is surprisingly brief; most of the concepts are expressed in just a few words, phrases, or sentences. Yet countless pages of court opinions interpret these provisions, from the lowest courts in every state to the Supreme Court itself. Still, disputes arise daily about the constitutionality of government conduct in criminal cases.

Changing Supreme Court interpretations

As we talk about in Chapter 4, what the Constitution says and what the Supreme Court says it means are two different things, and the Supreme Court's interpretation can change with the times and the interpretive theories of the sitting justices.

If you look at trends throughout Supreme Court history, you can see that, over time, the criminal-rights decisions swing like a pendulum, depending on what's going on in the world and the current philosophy of the Court. During some periods in history, the decisions seem to scrupulously protect the rights of people suspected or accused of crimes. At other times, the pendulum swings toward law and order.

Applying legal standards

When it comes to criminal procedure, the Constitution often requires a heavily fact-based analysis. Courts balance the competing interests of the government and the individual to determine whether the facts meet the legal standard that government agents acted reasonably under the totality of circumstances.

These standards leave room for varying opinions on what factors should carry the most weight in the analysis. For example, when faced with deciding whether officers unlawfully entered a person's home, one judge may find the entry was reasonable because police received a 911 call saying that someone was injured at that location, while another judge might find it unreasonable because police barged inside without knocking.

Changes in available technology

Technological advancements alter the balance between personal interests and law enforcement needs. For example, computers and cellphones can store vast amounts of personal information, potentially easy to access. The government's right to access this information raises questions under the 4th Amendment that the Framers couldn't have anticipated.

Chapter **19**

Checking Government Power to Investigate, Arrest, and Indict

Law enforcement agents wield tremendous power during the early stages of the criminal process. They can enter homes, seize property, and arrest and interrogate suspects with the full weight of the government behind them. These measures may be necessary to keep the public safe, but if abused, they can lead to privacy violations, false confessions, and unfounded criminal charges.

The Constitution lays out ground rules to reduce the power disparity between the government and the individual in the early stages of criminal cases. The rules principally protect individuals from heavy-handed law enforcement tactics, but they also preserve the government's authority to protect public safety using reasonable investigative methods.

Prohibiting Unreasonable Searches and Seizures

According to the language of the 4th Amendment, "The right of the people to be secure in their persons, houses, papers, and effects, against unreasonable searches and seizures, shall not be violated, and no warrants shall issue, but upon probable cause, supported by oath or affirmation, and particularly describing the place to be searched, and the person or things to be seized."

The term *people* in the 4th Amendment refers to both American citizens and documented immigrants, according to the Supreme Court. The prevailing view among lower courts is that it applies to undocumented immigrants, as well, and the Supreme Court has implied as much. But at the time of this writing, the Court hasn't directly addressed the question. (You can see the latest Supreme Court decisions and opinions at www.supremecourt.gov.)

Through the 4th Amendment, the Framers sought to put an end to the British government's practice of intruding into private homes without justification to search for smuggled goods. The Founding Fathers drafted the 4th Amendment to protect individual privacy by requiring agents to have probable cause and obtain warrants. As a fundamental right, the 4th Amendment applies to the federal government, and it applies to the states through the 14th Amendment Due Process Clause.

Identifying what qualifies as a search

The 4th Amendment prohibits unreasonable searches and seizures, so you first need to establish whether the government conducted a search or seizure.

Prior to 1967, a *search* occurred when a government agent trespassed onto private property to look for and seize tangible items. Trespasses remain searches in legal terms to this day. But in *Katz v. United States*, in 1967, the Supreme Court expanded the scope of protected searches by holding that the 4th Amendment "protects people, not places." It held that police conducted an unlawful search and seizure by putting a listening device in a public phone booth, even though they never entered private property.

Katz developed a two-part test for what constitutes a search:

>> Did the person exhibit an actual (subjective) expectation of privacy?

>> Is that expectation one that society accepts as reasonable?

The 4th Amendment prohibits only unreasonable searches and seizures, so courts start the 4th Amendment analysis by asking whether a search or seizure is involved. For example, say a homeowner puts their trash out on the street for collection. A police officer who has no reason to suspect any crime kicks over the trash can. To the officer's surprise, a gun falls out of the trash. Police determine the gun was used in a murder, and the district attorney prosecutes the homeowner. If the homeowner argues that the police violated their 4th Amendment rights, they lose that argument. Based on the two-part test, the officer didn't conduct a search when they kicked over the trash can, so even though their conduct was unreasonable, they didn't violate the 4th Amendment.

The 4th Amendment prohibits only government agents — not private parties — from conducting unreasonable searches and seizures. For example, if a neighbor breaks into your house, finds evidence of a crime, and turns it into police, you can't assert the 4th Amendment as a defense (but your neighbor can be prosecuted for burglary!).

There's no place like home

Above all else, the 4th Amendment recognizes that homes are sacred places deserving the highest level of privacy. In fact, the sanctity of the home under the 4th Amendment extends beyond its walls to the areas surrounding the home, such as gardens and porches, commonly referred to as *curtilage.*

To determine whether an area is curtilage, courts look at four factors:

>> Proximity of the area to the home

>> Whether it's contained within an enclosure

>> What the area is used for

>> Whether the resident has taken steps to protect it from observation

Areas that impliedly invite the public to enter, such as driveways and sidewalks, are generally not within a home's curtilage.

Open fields

On the other end of the privacy spectrum from homes and curtilage (see the preceding section), you have open fields and public spaces. It's not reasonable to have an expectation of privacy in places that are readily accessible to the public. Even if fields and open spaces are privately owned, the public can generally see and access them in ways that they can't see and access homes and curtilage. Examinations of these areas by government officials don't raise the same privacy concerns and therefore don't count as searches under the 4th Amendment.

The Supreme Court has found no reasonable expectation of privacy (and thus, no search) in the following situations. The police can lawfully

>> Search a trash bin left on the curb.

>> Conduct aerial surveillance from public airspace.

>> Seize a list of phone numbers dialed by a suspect by accessing a pen register installed at the phone company.

>> Obtain a person's physical characteristics that are exposed to the public, such as their handwriting or the sound of their voice.

>> Search areas of a business that are open to the public.

Determining whether someone has a reasonable expectation of privacy is uniquely challenging in the digital age, when individuals routinely share massive amounts of highly sensitive data (such as financial, medical, and location information) with corporations. Normally, voluntarily sharing information waives the right to privacy, but the Supreme Court has made it clear that people have a reasonable expectation of privacy in material accessed through their cellphones, so even after police lawfully seize a cellphone, they have to get a search warrant to review its contents.

Finding probable cause for a search warrant

The 4th Amendment generally requires government agents to obtain a warrant supported by probable cause to authorize a search. Before searching, investigators must obtain permission from a judge by providing an "oath or affirmation" setting forth their reasons for wanting to search. The judge signs a search warrant only if the agent shows that they have probable cause to believe a crime has been or is being committed and that they will find evidence of the crime in the place they want to search.

In the following section, you can see that the Court has recognized several kinds of searches that don't need a warrant. The same probable cause standard usually applies, however.

A warrant issued by a neutral and detached judicial officer serves as a safeguard between law enforcement officers eagerly searching for evidence of a crime and individuals whose privacy rights are at stake.

The Supreme Court defines *probable cause* as "a fair probability that contraband or evidence of a crime will be found in a particular place." Determining whether probable cause exists involves a flexible and common-sense process, considering the likelihood of finding evidence based on the totality of the circumstances. Probable cause exists if a reasonable person would believe the search will produce evidence of a crime.

Probable cause can't be quantified, but you can get a sense of how much proof it requires by looking at it in the context of other familiar legal standards. Different types of cases require different amounts of proof. The legal standards form a hierarchy, with probable cause falling close to the bottom (requiring the least amount of proof):

>> **Beyond a reasonable doubt:** The highest standard of proof, required to convict a person of a crime

>> **Clear and convincing evidence:** A heightened standard of proof that often applies when depriving a person of an important right, such as parental rights

>> **Preponderance of the evidence:** Often phrased as *more likely than not;* the most common standard in civil cases

>> **Probable cause:** A fair probability

>> **Unsupported hunch:** A guess based more on intuition than evidence

Applying exceptions

Both the warrant and probable cause requirements have some exceptions, in cases where the balance between individual privacy and public safety (including the fact that officers often must make split-second decisions) makes it reasonable to relax the rules. In the following sections, we look at situations where police don't require a warrant and/or they can conduct searches without probable cause.

Consent searches

A person's voluntary consent to search eliminates the need for probable cause or a search warrant. Consent searches are widely used and well accepted, giving law enforcement a tool to simply ask a person for permission to search under circumstances that would otherwise require a warrant.

Consent is *voluntary* when it's given by free choice. A surprising number of people consent to searches knowing that the area authorities want to search contains contraband or evidence of a crime.

Evaluating whether a person's consent is voluntary involves looking at the totality of the circumstances. Officers don't have to inform suspects of their right to refuse to consent, but if a person exercises that right, the prosecution can't use their refusal against them in court.

A person whom police detain or arrest can give valid consent to search, but the fact that they're not free to leave carries substantial weight in a court's assessment of whether their consent was voluntary under the totality of circumstances.

Search incident to arrest

Officers don't need a warrant or probable cause to search the area immediately surrounding a person who's lawfully arrested. These searches protect officers from suspects who may be armed and dangerous and allow for the collection and preservation of evidence that might otherwise be concealed or destroyed.

A search incident to arrest is limited to the arrestee's person and the areas within the arrestee's immediate reach. This is a fact-specific determination, but when it comes to vehicles, the Supreme Court has created a *bright-line rule* (an objective rule that resolves legal questions in a straightforward, predictable manner) that officers can search the entire passenger compartment of a vehicle if any of its occupants are lawfully arrested. They can also search any containers within the passenger compartment, but not the trunk.

A search incident to arrest is lawful only if the arrest itself is lawful. We cover lawful arrests in the section "Seizing people," later in this chapter.

Exigent circumstances

The *exigent circumstances* exception to the warrant requirement applies where police have probable cause to believe they'll find evidence in a particular place but taking the time to get a warrant threatens someone's safety or creates a risk of losing valuable evidence. Courts consider the totality of circumstances to determine whether an emergency requires an urgent police response.

Exigent circumstances may excuse the warrant requirement where

>> Police are pursuing a fleeing felon

>> Evidence may be imminently destroyed

>> The circumstances present a threat to officer safety

>> Officers need to render aid to victims or perform a community caretaking function

>> Evidence may degrade or disappear, such as evidence that may be found on or in the human body, including alcohol or drugs in the bloodstream or DNA under a suspect's fingernails

The automobile exception

Cars are different from homes in several ways that matter for 4th Amendment purposes:

>> Vehicles are heavily regulated by government agencies.

>> Their contents are often in plain view, so people have a reduced expectation of privacy in cars as compared to homes.

>> Vehicles move around, unlike homes, so a suspect can more easily escape with evidence while officers are trying to obtain a warrant.

For the reasons in the preceding list, officers can conduct warrantless searches of a car if they have probable cause to believe the car contains evidence of a crime.

After probable cause exists, a warrantless search can extend to anyplace in the vehicle that could contain the object of the search, including closed containers such as purses and glove compartments, without requiring probable cause as to each separate container. However, probable cause doesn't authorize warrantless searches of passengers in the car because of the greater personal intrusion involved. To search a passenger, officers must have probable cause that the particular passenger is concealing evidence on their person.

Inventory searches

Police may impound vehicles for any number of reasons. When they do, they may conduct inventory searches without warrants or probable cause. These searches serve several purposes, including accounting for and safely storing the owner's belongings, as well as ensuring that nothing hazardous remains inside an impounded car. Warrantless inventory searches must follow standard procedures, and officers can't use them as a pretext to investigate without probable cause.

The 4th Amendment permits administrative searches with somewhat relaxed requirements in settings that pose unique security concerns. For example:

>> Government officials may conduct administrative searches of businesses for regulatory compliance.

>> School officials may search a student's locker or backpack for drugs or weapons.

>> Jail officials may search cells and prisoners for contraband.

>> Border officials may search cars, containers, and people for evidence of smuggling.

Like with all 4th Amendment issues, the overriding consideration is whether the intrusion is reasonable under the totality of circumstances.

Figuring out what constitutes a seizure

The 4th Amendment prohibits seizures, as well as searches (which we talk about in the section "Identifying what qualifies as a search," earlier in this chapter). Both property and people can be seized:

>> **Property seizures:** Occur in a variety of different contexts. Sometimes police will take physical possession of property. Other times, they *seize* property by preserving it in its current state while they obtain a warrant to conduct a search. Hold-in-place seizures are generally considered less intrusive than confiscating and searching property and typically don't require a warrant.

>> **Person seizures:** When it comes to seizures of the person, police interactions with individuals are categorized into consensual encounters, detentions, and arrests (which we discuss in the section "Seizing people," later in this chapter).

Seizing property

Seizing property usually requires a warrant and probable cause, but in many cases, the Supreme Court has relaxed those requirements because they're impractical in the real world of police work. The *Plain View doctrine* allows officers who are lawfully present in a place to seize items in plain view without a warrant if the items are apparently evidence of a crime. However, the Court doesn't consider an item in plain view if the officer must make even the smallest additional intrusion to confirm that it's evidence.

For example, officers who respond to a medical call at someone's house may seize drugs that they see in plain view on the kitchen table, but if they see a computer that they believe is stolen, they can't flip it over to check the serial number without getting a search warrant.

Seizing people

Police perform countless services that put them in constant contact with the public, such as investigating crime, directing traffic, and responding to calls for assistance. Most of these interactions don't implicate the 4th Amendment because the person is voluntarily interacting with police. But when police interfere with a person's freedom to go about their business, the interaction becomes a seizure that must comply with the 4th Amendment.

Arrests require probable cause and warrants, but these requirements don't make sense when routine police interactions unexpectedly escalate. In Table 19-1, you can see that the types of seizure work on a kind of sliding scale; the more police restrict a person's freedom of movement, the more justification they need to have for doing so.

 Types of 4th Amendment Seizures

Type of Encounter	Definition	Level of Cause Required	Warrant Required?
Consensual encounter	A reasonable person would feel free to ignore police and go about their business.	None	No
Detention	The totality of circumstances, including the officer's words and actions, would lead a reasonable person to believe they have to comply.	Reasonable suspicion that criminal activity is afoot	No
Arrest	A person submits to a show of authority or is taken into custody for longer than a brief investigative detention.	Probable cause that a crime is being or has been committed	Yes, unless an exception applies

Probable cause is an *objective* standard (what a reasonable officer would believe), not a *subjective* standard (what the officer actually believes).

The following examples illustrate how the definitions in Table 19-1 work in the real world:

>> **Consensual encounter:** An officer approaches your friend in a parking lot and says, "Hey, can I ask you a question?" Your friend says, "Yeah, sure." They stick around to talk to the officer. The officer had no cause to stop your friend, but they didn't need cause. Your friend was free to leave.

>> **Detention:** An officer pulls your friend over and sees that they're not wearing their seatbelt, so the officer writes your friend a ticket and sends them on their way. The officer had reasonable suspicion to conduct a traffic stop, detaining your friend, to briefly investigate whether they were violating the law.

>> **Arrest:** An officer stops your friend to see whether they're wearing their seatbelt, but the officer sees a baggie of what looks like cocaine in plain view sticking out of the center console. The officer places them under arrest. The officer's reasonable suspicion developed into probable cause after they saw apparent contraband in plain view.

Detentions must be brief and last only long enough for an officer to confirm or dispel their suspicions. If detentions last longer, they turn into arrests and must meet the higher probable cause standard.

Courts look at the totality of circumstances to categorize a seizure as a consensual encounter, detention, or arrest. Some important factors include

>> The number of officers on scene

>> Whether the officer's tone or words were threatening

>> Whether the officer used or displayed a weapon

>> Whether the officer touched the subject or used physical force

STARTING STOP-AND-FRISKS

How do officers protect themselves when they stop a person they suspect is armed but don't have probable cause to search that person for weapons? In a landmark case in 1968, *Terry v. Ohio*, the Supreme Court confronted that very common situation. The Court held that an officer may conduct a limited pat-down search for weapons if they have reasonable suspicion to believe that someone they detain for a brief investigation is armed and dangerous. Because of this decision, courts commonly call these encounters *Terry stops* or *stop-and-frisks*. And officers can use *Terry* stops in only a limited scope that protects public safety.

Honoring the Privilege Against Self-Incrimination

The 5th Amendment provides that no person "shall be compelled in any criminal case to be a witness against himself." As a fundamental right, the privilege against self-incrimination applies to the federal government thanks to the 5th Amendment and the states through the 14th Amendment Due Process Clause. The primary purpose of the privilege is to ensure that the government bears the full burden of proving a criminal case. The Supreme Court has described the privilege as demonstrating a "fierce unwillingness" to force people suspected of crimes into the "cruel trilemma of self-accusation, perjury or contempt."

REMEMBER

Outside the constitutional context, *privilege* often means a benefit that can be taken away, as opposed to a *right* that is absolute; but that distinction doesn't apply when discussing the privilege against self-incrimination (also commonly referred to as the right to remain silent).

The 5th Amendment privilege also allows a non-defendant witness to refuse to testify in any proceeding about any matter that could get them into trouble with the law.

TECHNICAL
STUFF

A prosecutor can grant immunity to a witness by promising not to use their testimony against them. Immunity eliminates any risk that the witness's testimony will put them in legal jeopardy, so the privilege no longer applies and the government can compel the witness to testify.

These in-court applications of the privilege against self-incrimination are pretty straightforward. But the privilege also applies during the investigative phase of a criminal case, in the so-called interrogation room, where application of this privilege can get confusing. In the following sections, we clarify how the 5th Amendment applies in a criminal investigation.

Figuring out whether the privilege applies

At the heart of it, the privilege against self-incrimination prevents the government from forcing a person to act as a witness against themselves. In this context, it makes sense that the privilege applies only to

>> Communications that are *testimonial* in nature, meaning they disclose a person's thoughts, ideas, beliefs, or knowledge. But it doesn't apply to non-testimonial communications, such as a person's refusal to submit to a blood alcohol test.

>> Compelled statements, where the government forces a person to testify. Government compulsion can occur in various ways, such as through physical force or psychological coercion, the use of a subpoena, or threats such as the loss of employment.

Reading a suspect their *Miranda* rights

"You have the right to remain silent." You probably know this phrase from TV or the movies; while placing a suspect under arrest, a police officer reads them their *Miranda* rights (so named because the rights stem from the landmark 1966 case *Miranda v. Arizona*). Police officers give *Miranda* warnings to notify people that they have a 5th Amendment privilege during criminal investigations. The warnings ensure that people who are under arrest know that they can refuse to provide incriminating information to police by asserting their right to remain silent.

Preventing unreliable confessions

Federal and state laws provide that the prosecution can admit voluntary confessions in court because the court considers them reliable. For the most part, if a person freely admits they're guilty of a crime, they're probably guilty. But the key here is whether they volunteer their confession. If a suspect incriminates themselves because they feel pressured by police and don't know about their right to remain silent

>> The confession is less reliable.

>> The suspect provides evidence that helps the prosecution convict them, reducing the prosecution's burden of proving guilt.

>> Police are more likely to engage in improper tactics to extract a confession.

In *Miranda*, the Supreme Court attempted to balance these concerns by holding that if an in-custody defendant makes incriminating statements to police in response to questioning, those statements aren't admissible in court unless the defendant was advised of their *Miranda* rights and agreed to answer questions.

A defendant's incriminating statements may be inadmissible for a number of reasons. In the section "Suppressing evidence," later in this chapter, we discuss the Due Process Clause that requires courts to exclude *involuntary confessions* (confessions obtained by physical or psychological coercion) under any circumstances.

Making sure a suspect understands their *Miranda* rights

Although officers must give *Miranda* warnings before conducting a custodial interrogation, *Miranda* violations occur only if the authorities use the suspect's statement against them. Making incriminating statements alone doesn't put a person at risk of criminal punishment. It's only when the prosecution introduces the statements against a defendant in court that the defendant becomes a witness against themselves in violation of the 5th Amendment privilege.

Most police officers carry cards in their pockets that have the *Miranda* warnings printed on them so that they can ensure they recite the warnings in full before questioning a suspect after an arrest. Suspects must be advised that

>> They have a right to remain silent.

>> Anything they say will be used against them in court.

>> They have the right to consult with a lawyer.

>> The lawyer can be with them during questioning.

>> The court will appoint a lawyer free of charge if the suspect can't afford one.

Using *Miranda* with custodial interrogation

It goes without saying that a person can find being arrested and questioned by police intimidating. In *Miranda*, the Court decided that those circumstances are so inherently coercive that defendants may feel they have no choice but to tell police what they want to hear. This coercion makes the statement *compelled* for 5th Amendment purposes. But the inherent pressure exists only if the person is both in custody and interrogated. If both factors are present, the defendant's statement is admissible only if the police advised them of their *Miranda* rights and they agreed to waive those rights and speak.

These terms have a specific definition in relation to *Miranda* rights:

>> **In custody:** A person is in custody for purposes of *Miranda* when authorities arrest them or restrain their movement to the degree associated with a formal arrest. The Supreme Court lays out the question as whether a reasonable person in the suspect's situation would believe they were free to terminate questioning and leave, considering the totality of circumstances. The Court has held that the officer's subjective belief that the suspect was or wasn't free to leave — or the suspect's subjective belief, for that matter — are irrelevant.

>> **Interrogation:** Questioning initiated by police officers that's reasonably likely to elicit an incriminating response. It includes not only direct questions, but also words or actions. When an undercover officer questions a person, they don't conduct an interrogation because the suspect has no pressure to respond created by knowing the questioner is a law enforcement figure.

In the section "Seizing people," earlier in this chapter, we analyze restrictions on a person's freedom of movement to determine what level of cause authorities need to have to detain or arrest them under the 4th Amendment. Similarly, you consider restrictions on a person's freedom of movement to determine whether the person was in custody — and if authorities want to interrogate them, the 5th Amendment requires *Miranda* warnings.

Determining whether a suspect waives or invokes their rights

Like most constitutional rights, criminal defendants can waive their right to remain silent and/or to have a lawyer present during questioning. Before the prosecution can use a defendant's in-custody statement against them in court, they have to convince the judge that the defendant waived their *Miranda* rights.

Determining whether a person waived or invoked their rights can be tricky. Waiving *Miranda* rights can happen in two forms:

>> **Express:** You get the clearest answer when police ask the suspect two questions before questioning them:

- Do you understand your rights?

- Do you agree to waive those rights and talk to me?

If the suspect answers yes to both questions, they've expressly waived their *Miranda* rights, and the prosecution can use any statement they make after that point against them in court.

>> **Implied:** If the officer reads a suspect their *Miranda* rights and then jumps right into an interrogation without getting an express waiver, the prosecution may still admit the defendant's statement against them because a defendant who understands their rights and participates in an interview impliedly waives their *Miranda* rights.

To resolve questions about implied waivers, courts look at the totality of circumstances to determine whether the waiver was knowing, voluntary, and intelligent. The totality of circumstances includes the facts of the case, as well as the suspect's conduct and background.

However, if a suspect clearly invokes their right to remain silent or requests counsel, police must stop questioning immediately. This requirement applies only if the suspect makes an invocation so that a reasonable police officer under the circumstances would understand it as a request for an attorney or an assertion of the right to remain silent.

WARNING

If the suspect makes an ambiguous or equivocal statement (such as, "I'm not sure if I should get an attorney"), the police don't have to clarify (although it's good practice to do so because the officers and the court don't have to guess whether the defendant was trying to invoke their constitutional rights). The police also don't have to end the interrogation in the face of an ambiguous request. But after a suspect unambiguously expresses their desire to have an attorney present, police can't resume communications with them unless the suspect initiates the talks.

Examining the exceptions to the *Miranda* rule

A few exceptions to the *Miranda* rules allow the prosecution to use a suspect's statement against them, even if it would otherwise be excluded under *Miranda*:

>> The main purpose of the officer's question is to protect public safety (such as asking, "Where is the gun?" after a shooting).

>> The officer asks routine booking questions (such as, "What's your name, date of birth, height, weight, and address?")

>> The suspect testified inconsistently with their earlier statement to police. In that case, the prosecution can admit their prior statement to impeach them, even if *Miranda* otherwise requires exclusion. (But they can't admit the statement if the suspect gave it involuntarily under the Due Process Clause, which we talk about in Chapter 13.)

REMEMBER

The *Miranda* rule is designed to protect the privilege against self-incrimination, not to allow a defendant to lie on the stand.

Using (or not using) unlawfully obtained statements

Say that the police arrest a suspect for burglary where surveillance video shows a red car speeding away. Without advising the suspect of their *Miranda* rights, police ask what color car they drive. The suspect (while in custody) answers, "Red."

How, when, and if the prosecution can use this statement depends on whether the defendant lies on the stand:

>> **Denied by *Miranda:*** The prosecutor can't use that statement at trial to prove the defendant's guilt because doing so would violate *Miranda*.

>> **Allowed as impeachment:** But if the defendant testifies at their trial that they drive a blue car, the prosecutor can bring in the red-car statement for impeachment.

>> **Denied by due process:** If, however, the police obtained the red-car statement through physical or psychological coercion, the Due Process Clause of the 5th and 14th Amendments defines that statement as involuntary, and the prosecution can't introduce it for any reason, including impeachment.

Excluding Evidence

The Constitution sets out ground rules for police conducting investigations. Police conduct during investigations can have serious implications much further down the road in a criminal case. Long after police find the proverbial (or literal!) smoking gun during a search of a suspect's house, that suspect may be a defendant in a criminal case where the prosecutor wants to offer the gun (or a confession, or other material) into evidence to prove that the defendant is guilty as charged.

If police obtained the evidence during an unlawful investigation, using it against the defendant in court only compounds the harm done. The *exclusionary rule* avoids this additional harm by preventing the use of evidence against a defendant that was discovered through unconstitutional means during an investigation.

THE EXCLUSIONARY RULE IN ACTION

Typically, a criminal case is well underway by the time a question arises about the legality of the investigation. While the parties prepare for trial, the defense may file a suppression motion that argues that officers violated the defendant's constitutional rights and that the court should exclude the evidence obtained as a result of the illegality. The court holds a hearing and determines the legality of the officers' conduct and the admissibility of any evidence they found. If the court invokes the exclusionary rule, the prosecution has to prove its case without the evidence (or any mention of the evidence) — or, if the prosecution doesn't have a strong enough case without the excluded evidence, the prosecution has to dismiss the case.

The exclusionary rule serves different purposes in different contexts. Excluding statements that violate *Miranda* prevents a 5th Amendment violation because it ensures that a person's compelled statements aren't used to incriminate them in court. But excluding evidence discovered during an unlawful search doesn't prevent a 4th Amendment violation because the violation is the unlawful search itself, which is over and done with.

Excluding critical evidence after an unlawful search doesn't fix the privacy violation. It just ties the prosecutor's hands and gives the defendant a benefit in order to punish a police officer for their misconduct or mistake.

In the 4th Amendment context, the exclusionary rule operates as a remedy, based on the theory that throwing out unlawfully obtained evidence deters officers from conducting illegal searches and seizures in the future. By excluding the evidence from criminal cases, courts negate the benefit of unlawful police conduct and promote confidence in the judicial system.

In the section "Applying exceptions to the exclusionary rule," later in this chapter, you can see that exceptions to the exclusionary rule apply in circumstances where exclusion probably won't deter future police misconduct.

Determining whether the defendant has standing

Your 4th Amendment rights are personal; you can't assert them through someone else. And when you think about the reason for the rules, that limitation makes perfect sense.

Say that the police conducted an unlawful search of Person A's house. Within the meaning of the 4th Amendment, homes are the most sacred spaces, where people have a clear expectation of privacy. During the search, police find a gun that they believe another person (Person B) used to commit a murder. When Person B is arrested and charged with murder, they move to suppress the gun as the product of an unconstitutional search. But Person B didn't have a reasonable expectation of privacy in Person A's home. The search violated Person A's constitutional rights, but not Person B's. So Person B can't move to exclude whatever evidence was found in Person A's house.

This concept is called *standing*, the right to bring a legal challenge that arises from having a personal interest. A person facing criminal charges has standing to seek the exclusion of evidence only if the search or seizure violated their personal 4th Amendment rights, not a third party's rights.

Suppressing evidence

The exclusionary rule serves the important public interest of deterring police officers from violating a suspect's constitutional rights during an investigation. But
it comes at a cost, forcing prosecutors, juries, and courts to ignore trustworthy,
sometimes critical, evidence. These competing concerns underlie Supreme Court
decisions that establish the breadth and boundaries of the exclusionary rule.

When the Supreme Court first established it in 1914, the exclusionary rule applied
only to defendants in federal criminal cases. In *Mapp v. Ohio* in 1961, the Supreme
Court held the exclusionary rule also applies to state prosecutions through the Due
Process Clause of the 14th Amendment. It also clarified that the exclusionary rule
prohibited the introduction of evidence that directly or indirectly flowed from an
illegality, unless the prosecution can show that only a weak connection exists
between the illegal search and the evidence discovered.

Courts refer to this interpretation of the exclusionary rule as the "fruit of the
poisonous tree." (The *poisonous tree* is the illegal search or seizure, and the *fruit* is
the evidence discovered as a result.) For example, say an officer illegally searches
a suspect's pockets and finds cocaine. When they pull the baggie out of the
suspect's pocket, the suspect exclaims, "That's my coke, all right. I guess I'm
busted." The cocaine must be excluded because it flowed directly from the unlawful search. And the defendant's statements must also be excluded as the fruit of
the poisonous tree.

Applying exceptions to the exclusionary rule

Like almost all rules, the exclusionary rule comes with several exceptions, mostly based on the idea that excluding evidence under certain circumstances would do little to promote the goal of deterrence:

>> **Inevitable discovery:** The police would have found the evidence even without violating the 4th Amendment.

>> **Attenuation:** The connection between the illegal activity and the evidence is too weak to serve the purpose of the exclusionary rule.

>> **Independent source:** Evidence that authorities obtained in an unlawful search which they also obtained separately from a lawful, independent source.

>> **Good faith:** The police reasonably relied on a search warrant that was later found to be invalid or case law that was later overturned.

Exclusion is a remedy, not a constitutional right. Under the law, trials must be fair but not perfect, and police officers can make innocent mistakes. Given the purpose of the exclusionary rule to deter police misconduct, the courts generally don't apply it where it's unlikely to deter police from acting unlawfully in the future.

Filing Criminal Charges

After law enforcement officers develop probable cause that a crime was committed and a particular person (or corporation, or group of people) committed it, they turn the case over to prosecutors to decide whether to pursue criminal charges. In Chapter 18, we look at how prosecutors go about making that decision. In this section, we look at some constitutional provisions that kick in to protect a defendant after an investigation becomes a prosecution.

Investigations don't end when the prosecution files charges. The 4th Amendment right to be free from unreasonable searches and seizures, and the 5th Amendment privilege against self-incrimination, continue to apply while officers work on cases that make their way through the criminal justice process.

Securing an indictment

The 5th Amendment provides that "[n]o person shall be held to answer for a capital, or otherwise infamous crime, unless on a presentment or indictment of a Grand Jury" — except in certain cases involving the military and wartime. To figure out what this provision means, first consider the terms used in it:

>> **Grand jury:** A group of citizens who reviews the evidence to determine whether the authorities have probable cause to charge a person with a crime

>> **Infamous crime:** Any federal felony

>> **Presentment:** A written accusation initiated by the grand jury itself; not enough to start a prosecution without an indictment

>> **Indictment:** Also called a *true bill;* a sworn document originating with a prosecutor, presented by a grand jury, formally charging a person with a crime

In Chapter 18, we explain the difference between grand juries and trial juries. In Chapter 20, you can read about jury trials in greater detail.

In practical terms, the 5th Amendment grand jury requirement means that authorities can't charge a person with a felony in federal court unless they follow this basic procedure:

1. **The prosecution prepares a draft indictment and presents the evidence to a grand jury.**

2. **The grand jury deliberates and returns an indictment when it finds probable cause to support the charges.**

   An indictment is also called a *true bill.*

3. **The prosecution files the indictment in court.**

   This process formally charges the defendant with the listed crimes.

4. **The indictment initiates a criminal case.**

The grand jury ensures that prosecutors have probable cause before they charge a person with a crime. It serves an important role in carrying out one of the primary purposes of the Constitution, to protect individuals from oppressive government tactics. However, prosecutors have a lot of control over grand juries because neither the accused nor their attorney has the right to be present when the prosecutor presents their case to the grand jury.

WARNING

A New York Supreme Court Justice once famously said, "A prosecutor could get a grand jury to indict a ham sandwich." The quote reflects a common criticism of the grand jury system that grand juries don't serve their protective function but operate as a rubber stamp for the government.

TECHNICAL STUFF

Grand juries have broad investigative powers, including the power to subpoena witnesses and documents. They can use these powers to obtain and consider evidence beyond that presented by the prosecutor.

Grand jury proceedings are conducted in secret to avoid stigmatizing someone who doesn't get indicted, to protect witnesses, and to preserve evidence.

REMEMBER

The U.S. Constitution doesn't require states to use grand juries. Some state constitutions require grand juries, and others give prosecutors the option of proceeding by grand jury or preliminary hearing. You can read more about these alternative charging methods in Chapter 18.

Conferring rights at arraignment

After the prosecution files a criminal case, the defendant must formally answer to the charges by entering a plea of guilty or not guilty at *arraignment* (usually the first court appearance, where the defendant is informed of the charges against them).

TECHNICAL STUFF

Occasionally, instead of entering a plea at arraignment, a defendant files a *demurrer*, a formal statement that claims the court should dismiss the case against them because the charging document doesn't meet the legal requirements.

Various constitutional provisions kick in at arraignment:

>> **The 14th Amendment:** The court must advise a defendant of the trial rights they give up by entering a guilty plea before they enter such a plea. (We examine these rights in Chapter 19.)

>> **The 8th Amendment:** Says that "excessive bail shall not be required." *Bail* is money a defendant must pay to get out of jail after they enter a not guilty plea and while they await trial.

   The purpose of bail is to ensure a defendant returns to court to face the charges. The court refunds bail after the case is complete, if the defendant made all the required appearances. An amount higher than necessary to accomplish this goal violates the 8th Amendment.

The Constitution doesn't entitle defendants to bail. A defendant can be held without bail if the court determines that they pose a substantial risk to public safety.

>> **The 6th Amendment:** A defendant has the right to be informed of the charges against them, and to have the assistance of counsel.

Guaranteeing the right to counsel

In criminal prosecutions, where the stakes for a defendant may include death or imprisonment, the 6th Amendment right to counsel is paramount to ensure fairness in the adversarial system. It levels the playing field and provides assurances that the courts obtained a conviction through a fair process.

The Supreme Court strongly discourages self-representation. Without lawyers, defendants untrained in the law usually can't effectively evaluate the validity of criminal charges, determine whether evidence is admissible, or figure out whether they have a viable defense. They may give up constitutional rights that they don't know they have or fail to pursue remedies that could reduce their punishment or result in lesser charges. (See the section "Having a fool for a client — the right to self-representation," later in this chapter, for the reasons courts inform defendants of the risks of self-representation.)

Retained attorneys are hired by defendants at their own expense. The government hires and pays for *appointed counsel* to represent defendants who can't afford an attorney. The Supreme Court established the right to appointed counsel in *Gideon v. Wainwright* (1963); and in *Scott v. Illinois* (1979), the Court clarified that the right extends to any case where a person is sentenced to imprisonment, including misdemeanors. A defendant who wants the court to appoint counsel to represent them fills out a financial statement to prove that they don't have the means to retain counsel on their own.

The 6th Amendment protects a defendant's right to

>> **Retain their attorney of choice.** Of course, the defendant must be able to afford the attorney, the attorney must be available and willing to represent the defendant, and the attorney must be free from any conflicts of interest (such as representing a codefendant who plans to point the finger at the defendant).

>> **Receive effective assistance of counsel.** They have the right to a lawyer who takes their adversarial role seriously to ensure the defendant receives a fair trial.

Aside from custodial interrogations (which we talk about in the section "Using *Miranda* with custodial interrogation," earlier in this chapter), suspects who are under investigation generally don't have a constitutional right to counsel. Courts look at two factors to determine when the 6th Amendment right to counsel applies (which we discuss in detail in the following sections): Has the right to counsel attached, and is the case at a critical stage of the proceedings?

Attaching the right to counsel

The 6th Amendment right to counsel *attaches* (begins) when the prosecution files formal charges. At this point, the government moves from an investigative role to a prosecutorial role, and adversarial judicial proceedings begin. As we discuss in Chapter 18, the prosecution can bring formal charges by complaint, information, indictment, or preliminary hearing. Prior to that time, the 6th Amendment right to counsel doesn't apply.

Identifying critical stages

Even after the right to counsel attaches (see the preceding section), it applies only at critical stages of the prosecution. Courts look at whether the proceeding is a trial-like confrontation, where the advice and presence of counsel can help to ensure the defendant's rights are protected. The Supreme Court has held the following points in a criminal proceeding qualify as critical stages, and therefore the 6th Amendment right to counsel applies:

>> **Post-charging lineups:** Where police present a suspect, in line with other similar-looking individuals to a witness for identification.

>> **Arraignments:** See the section "Conferring rights at arraignment," earlier in this chapter.

>> **Preliminary hearings:** See Chapter 18.

>> **Plea negotiations:** Where the prosecution and the defendant attempt to resolve the case without a trial.

>> **Trials:** Check out Chapter 20 for further trial information.

>> **Sentencing:** We discuss post-conviction procedures in Chapter 21.

>> **Appeals as of right:** Every defendant has the right to a first appeal, as opposed to subsequent appeals, which courts can decline to consider. (Chapter 21 discusses the appeals process.)

But the Supreme Court has ruled that the 6th Amendment right to counsel doesn't apply in certain circumstances, considered not critical stages:

>> **Grand jury proceedings:** See the section "Securing an indictment," earlier in this chapter.

>> **Photo lineups:** Where police present a suspect's photo, along with other photos of similar-looking individuals, to a witness for identification.

>> **Handwriting exemplars:** Where police take a sample of a person's handwriting.

>> **Discretionary appeals:** Unlike appeals as of right, courts can choose whether to consider a defendant's case after their first appeal. (Flip to Chapter 21 for more on the appeals process.)

Having a fool for a client — the right to self-representation

The Supreme Court has affirmed an old adage that says, "A man who represents himself has a fool for a client." The 6th Amendment right to counsel guarantees that defendants unskilled in the law don't have to defend themselves against a powerful government. But if defendants choose to go it alone, the court can't force an attorney upon them.

In 1975, in *Faretta v. California*, the Supreme Court held that the Constitution protects the right to self-representation for defendants who voluntarily and intelligently choose to go forward without counsel. (In this context, *intelligently* doesn't mean that the person is making a smart decision, only that they're aware of the dangers and disadvantages of self-representation and made their choice with their eyes wide open.) This right applies to both federal and state prosecutions under the 6th Amendment right to counsel and the 14th Amendment Due Process Clause.

The 6th Amendment right to counsel applies to a specific offense. If a defendant who's facing charges for one case is under investigation in a different case, they don't have a 6th Amendment right to an attorney when the police question them about the uncharged case. For example, the 6th Amendment doesn't prevent investigators from interviewing a defendant charged with murder in California about a bank robbery in Florida (but if the defendant is in custody, they may have a 5th Amendment right to counsel, which we talk about in the section "Honoring the Privilege against Self-Incrimination," earlier in this chapter).

Chapter **20**

Guaranteeing Fair Trials

The right to a jury trial appears twice in the Constitution. Article III, Section 2, Clause 3 provides that all crimes except impeachment shall be tried by jury trial in the state where the crime was committed. The 6th Amendment adds additional protections for the accused: the right to a speedy trial and a public trial, to be informed of the nature and cause of the accusation, to be confronted with the witnesses against them, and to have compulsory process and the assistance of counsel for their defense.

In this chapter, we delve into each of the trial rights packed densely into the 6th Amendment, illustrating why the Framers thought the right to a jury trial was important enough to mention twice.

Offering a Quick Rundown of Trial Elements

The mechanics of a trial and the roles of the participants are important elements to understand if you want to appreciate constitutional trial rights. The parties in a criminal case are:

» **The citizens:** Represented by a prosecutor, who may refer to their client as "the People" or "the State," and who files criminal charges against the defendant.

>> **The defendant:** The person charged with crimes. If they enter a not guilty plea, the case will be resolved by a jury (or judge, if the parties agree to a bench trial).

The process of a trial follows these basic steps, where the prosecution must meet its burden of proving the case beyond a reasonable doubt:

1. **The prosecution starts presenting its case-in-chief by calling witnesses to testify on direct examination.**

   Percipient witnesses testify to their personal observations. *Expert* witnesses offer opinions on their subjects of expertise. *Character* witnesses may provide insight into someone's behavior and reputation.

2. **The prosecution may also present physical evidence or demonstrative evidence.**

   For example, they can introduce items retrieved from the scene of the alleged crime or explanatory documents such as maps and diagrams.

3. **The defense cross-examines the witnesses.**

4. **The prosecution rests its case.**

   Resting refers to the prosecution officially concluding its presentation of evidence.

5. **The defense may move to dismiss if it believes the prosecution didn't meet its burden of proof.**

   The defense has no burden to present a defense, but it has the right to defend.

6. **If it chooses to do so, the defense then puts on its case-in-chief.**

   The defense follows the same procedures as the prosecution in Steps 1 through 4, with the defense being the active party. The defendant has a constitutional right to testify if they choose to do so and a constitutional right to remain silent if they don't want to testify.

7. **After the defense rests its case, the court instructs the jury on the law.**

8. **The jury deliberates and reaches its verdict.**

9. **If the jury finds a verdict of guilty, the judge sentences the defendant within the parameters set by law.**

The jury's role includes deciding what the facts are, figuring out who's telling the truth, and deciding whether the defendant is guilty.

The judge's role includes ruling on legal issues, such as whether evidence is admissible; instructing the jury on the law; and imposing sentence if the jury convicts the defendant.

Granting a Speedy and Public Trial

Applying to federal trials, the 6th Amendment begins: "In all criminal prosecutions, the accused shall enjoy the right to a speedy and public trial." Speedy trials and public trials are fundamental rights that apply to the states through the Due Process Clause of the 14th Amendment.

The right to a speedy trial

The 6th Amendment speedy-trial right applies only after authorities arrest a person or file formal criminal charges. Or, as the courts put it, the right protects against only "post-accusation delay."

REMEMBER

Different rights kick in at different times. In Chapter 19, we talk about the fact that the right to counsel attaches when authorities file formal charges. But the speedy-trial clock can start ticking earlier, at the time of arrest, before the right to counsel attaches. Even though both rights are in the 6th Amendment, they attach at different times because they serve different purposes:

>> **The right to counsel:** Protects a defendant's right to present a defense

>> **The right to a speedy trial:** Protects the accused from experiencing the emotional stress of living with pending criminal charges (which may come with pretrial confinement or the loss of employment or reputation), as well as the potential loss of favorable evidence

The 6th Amendment doesn't specify exactly how speedy a trial has to be; it doesn't require a trial to occur within a specific number of days (although state and federal statutes may impose such requirements). Instead, to determine whether a violation occurred, courts balance four factors:

>> The length of the delay

>> The reason for the delay

>> Whether the defendant asserted their right to a speedy trial

>> Whether the defendant suffered any prejudice

You may have heard the phrase, "The wheels of justice turn slowly." Ironically, the 6th Amendment right to a speedy trial does little to make them go faster. The Supreme Court has approved trials that were anything but speedy. In one case, after the defendant was arrested for murder, his trial was delayed for more than five years. The Court rejected the defendant's claim that the delay violated their speedy-trial right because the defendant didn't object to the delay for more than three and a half years, and they couldn't show any *prejudice* to their case (meaning unfair harm) from the delay.

The right to a public trial

Different players get constitutional protection when it comes to a public trial:

>> **The accused:** The 6th Amendment guarantees the accused a public trial; the Amendment generally protects the defendant's interest in fair treatment through transparency.

>> **The public (including the media):** A similar right protected by the 1st Amendment — the right to access court proceedings and documents. The right to access also promotes accountability through transparency, but for the broader purpose of curtailing government abuse of power and promoting public confidence in the proceedings.

Neither right is absolute; courts can close or limit access if necessary to serve a compelling government purpose.

The Supreme Court has a four-factor test to determine whether a court closure or restricted access violates a defendant's 6th Amendment right to a public trial (conveniently, a very similar analysis applies to determine whether it violates the public's 1st Amendment rights):

>> The party seeking to close the hearing must advance an *overriding interest* (something more important than a public trial, for example, witness safety) that's likely to be *prejudiced* (meaning harmed) by keeping the trial open.

>> The closure must be no broader than necessary to protect that interest.

>> The trial court must consider reasonable alternatives to closing the hearing.

>> After considering evidence on these factors, the trial court must make findings to support the other three factors in this list.

Prosecutors have asserted various overriding interests to justify court closures. Although the interests may be substantial (such as privacy for child sexual-assault victims or witness safety), most closures are overturned on appeal because the court made them broader than necessary.

TIP

Courts can close some types of proceedings because they're not prosecutions. For example, juvenile delinquency cases are considered rehabilitative, and grand-jury proceedings are investigative.

Providing for Trial by Jury

The Framers protected individuals against arbitrary government action by requiring jury trials for federal trials. Jury trials provide for citizen participation in the judicial process, inserting members of the community in between the judge and the defendant to promote fairness and accountability. The right to a jury trial is a fundamental right that applies to the states through the Due Process Clause of the 14th Amendment.

(Not really) all criminal prosecutions

The 6th Amendment says that the right to a jury trial applies "[i]n all criminal prosecutions." Yet the Supreme Court has made it clear that the right applies only to serious offenses, as opposed to petty offenses, and defined serious offenses as those that are punishable by more than six months in custody.

The Supreme Court acknowledged the six-month *bright-line rule* (meaning an objective rule that resolves legal questions in a straightforward, predictable manner) was somewhat arbitrary. But most states drew the line at that point, and the Court decided it properly balanced the competing interests of the individual (to have the participation of their peers in the process) and the government (to ensure the efficient administration of justice).

Impartial juries

The courts summon jurors from the community randomly from voter registration lists or driver's license records. From this *venire* (panel of potential jurors), the court selects a *petit jury* (or trial jury) to hear the case.

An *impartial jury* requires the jury to represent a fair cross-section of the community. To show a violation of the fair cross-section requirement, a defendant must present proof that

>> The jury selection excluded a distinctive community group.

>> The representation of the group in the venire isn't fair and reasonable in relation to the number of group members in the community.

>> Underrepresentation occurred because of systematic exclusion in the jury process.

A defendant doesn't have to show purposeful discrimination, nor do they have to be a member of the excluded group to raise a fair cross-section challenge. For example, a man could challenge a local court policy allowing women to opt out of serving on a jury if that policy resulted in women being underrepresented.

An impartial jury also means that individual jurors are unbiased. The process of *voir dire*, meaning the questioning of potential jurors by the court or the attorneys, helps uncover any areas of potential bias and furthers the goal of an impartial jury. The jurors' answers help the parties decide whether to exercise a challenge to excuse the juror from serving.

Each party can dismiss potential jurors either by establishing legal cause or as a peremptory challenge (which don't require explanation).

Not surprisingly, the parties can't exercise their peremptory challenges in a discriminatory manner. Although this rule applies to both the prosecution and the defense, the defense most often raises this prohibition, claiming the prosecution has exercised its peremptory challenges to exclude jurors based on a protected characteristic such as race, ethnicity, gender, or religion. The defendant doesn't need to be a member of the excluded group to raise the challenge.

Constitutional elements of jury trials

The constitutional right to a jury trial includes certain requirements.

- **»** The federal government and most states require 12-person juries, but the Constitution sets a 6-juror minimum.

- **»** Jury verdicts in criminal cases must be unanimous.

- **»** Only a small percentage of cases go to trial. In most cases, the defendant waives their right to a jury trial by entering a knowing, voluntary, and intelligent guilty plea.

Protecting the Right to Present a Defense

The 6th Amendment gives the accused the rights "to have compulsory process for obtaining witnesses in his favor" and "to be confronted with the witnesses against him." This fundamental right applies to the states through the Due Process Clause of the 14th Amendment. These rights are often referred to as the right to present a defense:

- **»** **Compulsory process:** Gives the defendant the right to subpoena witnesses, present evidence, and testify. The Court hasn't written a whole lot about the right itself because compulsory process questions are usually framed as due process issues and come down to whether the defendant's right to produce evidence is outweighed by the government's interest in fair and efficient trials.

- **»** **Confrontation Clause:** The Confrontation Clause is mainly intended to protect a defendant's right to cross-examination, which has been called "the greatest legal engine ever invented for the discovery of truth." The following sections delve into this clause and its uses.

Examining the Confrontation Clause

The Confrontation Clause protects a defendant's right to conduct face-to-face cross-examination of every witness against them. That requirement seems simple enough: A person testifies for the prosecution, then the defense gets a chance to cross-examine them. But the protection involves so much more than cross-examination.

The Confrontation Clause covers not only witnesses who testify at trial, but also people who make statements outside of trial that the prosecution uses against the defendant during the trial. If a witness testifies at trial that, "John told me that the defendant stole the car," John becomes a witness against the defendant without ever stepping foot in the courtroom. When someone accuses the court of violating their Confrontation Clause rights, they focus on these out-of-court statements; the problem in this example arises if the prosecution doesn't call John as a witness so that the defendant can't cross-examine him.

If you watch a lot of shows or movies about legal proceedings, introducing the statement John made to the witness may immediately prompt the thought, "Objection! Hearsay!" *Hearsay* is commonly defined as a statement made outside of the trial that's offered to prove the truth of the matter asserted in the statement. The witness offered John's statement to prove that what John said was true — that the defendant stole the car. Objection sustained! The statement is inadmissible hearsay. The hearsay rule (and exceptions) come from state and federal evidence laws, separate from the Constitution. Many statements that are admissible under the Confrontation Clause are still excluded under hearsay rules.

Under the Confrontation Clause, if John testifies at trial, another witness can testify about John's out-of-court statement that the defendant stole the car because the defense can ultimately cross-examine John about the statement.

Interpreting the Confrontation Clause

In 2004, the Supreme Court's decision in *Crawford v. Washington* explained that the Confrontation Clause is a procedural right that entitles defendants to face-to-face confrontation.

We take a closer look at the factors involved in the following sections, but simply stated, *Crawford* held that the admission of an out-of-court statement violates the Confrontation Clause if both the statement was testimonial and the witness doesn't testify at trial. The court makes an exception if both the witness is unavailable and the defendant had a prior chance to cross-examine the witness.

Defining a testimonial statement

The *Crawford* Court didn't define testimonial, but it looked at the historical purpose of confrontation and said that at the very least a statement qualifies as testimonial if the witness gave it at a preliminary hearing, grand jury, trial, or police interrogation. Later cases establish that the character of the statement depends on

>> Its primary purpose of establishing past facts potentially relevant to later criminal prosecution

>> The formality of the interview

>> The intents of both the interviewer and the interviewee

THE CONFRONTATION CLAUSE IN ACTION

Say that a domestic violence victim calls 911 and tells the operator that their partner punched them in the face. Police arrive, arrest the partner, and take them to jail. A responding officer interviews the victim, who again says that their partner punched them in the face.

The prosecutor doesn't call the victim as a witness at trial. Instead, they call witnesses to testify about what the victim said

- **The 911 operator:** Admissible under the Confrontation Clause because circumstances surrounding the call suggest the victim's primary purpose was to get help, so it's not testimonial.

- **The responding officer:** Inadmissible. By the time the victim spoke to the officer, the primary purpose was to establish past facts for potential prosecution, therefore this statement is testimonial.

After a court determines that an out-of-court statement doesn't violate the Confrontation Clause, the court must then decide whether it's admissible under hearsay rules. Although the Constitution protects a defendant's rights to confront witnesses, hearsay rules are designed to protect the integrity of the trial by keeping out potentially unreliable statements.

For example, if a witness makes a statement to police for the primary purpose of assisting in an emergency, the statement is nontestimonial.

Unavailability and prior cross-exam

Courts can still admit testimonial statements without violating the Confrontation Clause, even if the declarant is unavailable to testify as a witness — if the defense had a prior opportunity to cross-examine them. This situation happens occasionally when a witness who testifies at a preliminary hearing becomes unavailable for trial.

Unavailable doesn't mean the person can't make it to court, it means unavailable to testify as a witness. A person may be unavailable, for example, if they have a privilege not to testify or a medical condition that prevents them from speaking or remembering.

Getting Effective Assistance of Counsel

As we note in Chapter 19, the 6th Amendment right to counsel begins as soon as authorities file criminal charges and applies at all critical stages of the proceedings. Because trial obviously is a critical stage (some might argue it's the most critical), this section briefly discusses the right to counsel specifically at trial.

The Constitution guarantees not just a right to counsel but also the *effective assistance* of counsel. A defendant is deprived of the effective assistance of counsel when their attorney's conduct falls below reasonable standards of professional judgment. A defendant may claim ineffective assistance of counsel based on their attorney's failure to

>> Conduct an adequate investigation before trial.

>> Present *mitigating evidence* (evidence that may show the defendant is less culpable and more deserving of lenience).

>> Object to inadmissible, prejudicial evidence.

>> Bring a motion or make an argument that may have produced a better outcome.

>> Advise a defendant of the consequences of pleading guilty (such as deportation).

REMEMBER

Any decision or action that an attorney makes during their representation of a client can potentially become the subject of an ineffective-assistance claim, from failing to advise a defendant of their rights at arraignment to failing to raise a claim on appeal, and everything in between.

In any situation, defense attorneys may choose from a wide range of reasonable options, and the law gives them room to make tactical decisions based on all kinds of variables and unknowns.

Fortunately, the 6th Amendment doesn't require attorneys to make the right decision, only that they exercise reasonable professional judgment in the decision-making process based on the information that they have at the time they make the decision, not how things turned out. And if a defendant claims they were convicted (or a higher sentence was imposed) because their attorney was ineffective, the court won't reverse the conviction or sentence if the totality of the circumstances suggests that the defendant would get the same result even with an effective attorney.

The 6th Amendment right to counsel imposes an obligation on the court to appoint counsel for defendants who can't afford to pay for an attorney, but only in certain circumstances:

>> **Potential custody:** The right to counsel applies to misdemeanors where the defendant is *actually* sentenced to serve time in custody, but this backward-looking standard is problematic because the proceedings are over by the time the court decides on the sentence. As a practical matter, most courts appoint counsel at the outset for misdemeanors that carry a *potential* custody sentence.

>> **Appeals:** The Constitution doesn't grant a right to appeal, but due process requires the appointment of appellate counsel for indigent defendants for *appeals as of right* (first appeals, which a defendant is entitled to by law, as opposed to discretionary appeals where the court can decide whether to take the case).

Ensuring Due Process and a Fair Trial

The 6th Amendment doesn't mention the right to a fair trial explicitly, but all of its protections relate to a fair trial. The trial rights it does mention exist for the very purpose of ensuring that trials are fundamentally fair.

Any time a court or government official violates any of the explicitly mentioned trial rights, they also violate fundamental notions of fairness, meaning due process. Courts often use the terms *due process* and *fair trial* generically and interchangeably when talking about other substantive rights. Some of the more common due process challenges that arise during trial involve claims that

>> Police used an unduly suggestive identification tactic to influence a witness to identify the defendant.

>> The judge is biased.

>> The prosecutor committed misconduct.

>> Jury instructions wrongly shifted the burden of proof to the defense or watered down the burden of proof or the presumption of innocence.

Chapter **21**

Safeguarding Rights after Judgment

In the same way that the Framers prioritized individual rights over government power in the early stages of the criminal process (which we talk about in Chapters 18, 19, and 20), they sought to keep the government in check after courts resolved the question of guilt. In the post-judgment context, the Framers balanced several competing concerns: preventing arbitrary and unlawful imprisonment, ensuring just punishment, and expanding upon the guarantee against repeated prosecutions for the same offense. At the same time, the Framers respected the finality of judgments, and they needed to preserve the government's ability to protect public safety.

In this chapter, we delve into the 5th Amendment prohibition against double jeopardy, including the exceptions to the general rule that a person can't be tried twice for the same crime. We also look at some provisions that kick in at sentencing, such as the 8th Amendment prohibition against cruel and unusual punishment and the 6th Amendment right to a jury trial for certain sentencing factors.

Prohibiting Double Jeopardy

The prohibition against double jeopardy was widely accepted in English common law at the time of the American Revolution, but it only applied to felonies punishable by death or life in prison. When drafting the 5th Amendment Double Jeopardy Clause, the Framers chose language that seems to capture that limitation if taken literally; the provision states that no person shall "be subject for the same offense to be twice put in jeopardy of life or limb." But, even though the language suggests otherwise, the Supreme Court has interpreted the Double Jeopardy Clause as applying to all crimes because it prevents people from suffering the anxiety and expense of repeated prosecutions and promotes finality of judgments.

In the following sections, we look at the three main questions that you need to answer to determine whether a prosecution violates double jeopardy:

>> Is the proceeding another prosecution?

>> Has jeopardy attached?

>> Are the offenses the same?

The Bill of Rights applies only to the federal government, so the 5th Amendment applies only to federal prosecutions. But like most of the other Bill of Rights amendments, the 5th Amendment Double Jeopardy Clause applies to the states through the 14th Amendment Due Process Clause.

Avoiding another prosecution

Double jeopardy protects against multiple prosecutions for the same offense, but generally, it doesn't prevent further proceedings (including multiple trials) in the same case.

Later trials and other proceedings in the same case don't qualify as separate prosecutions, but continuations of the first prosecution.

Double jeopardy prevents:

>> Prosecution for the same offense after conviction or acquittal

>> Prosecution after a mistrial (unless the court granted the mistrial because of *manifest necessity*, meaning the mistrial is the only option and not the government's fault)

>> Multiple punishments for the same offense

Double jeopardy doesn't prevent retrial:

>> After a defendant successfully appeals their conviction.

   An important exception exists for cases that the court reverses because the evidence was insufficient to support a conviction. The prosecution has one chance to prove the case, so reversal on that basis prevents retrial.

>> After mistrial that was granted because of manifest necessity (such as the jury being unable to reach a unanimous verdict or several jurors falling ill without sufficient alternates to replace them).

Prosecutors can't appeal acquittals because even if they win the appeal, double jeopardy prevents them from prosecuting the defendant again.

Attaching jeopardy

Double jeopardy doesn't prevent a second prosecution unless jeopardy attaches the first time around. The Supreme Court says that jeopardy attaches when the court accepts the defendant's guilty plea, when the jury is sworn, or when the first witness is sworn in a bench trial. Double jeopardy doesn't prevent the prosecution from refiling a dismissed case if the dismissal occurred before the jury or any witnesses were sworn.

Comparing offenses

The Double Jeopardy Clause prevents a second prosecution for the same offense, but what constitutes the same offense isn't always clear. Criminal charges often arise from a course of conduct that doesn't neatly break down into discrete offenses. For double jeopardy purposes, according to the Court in *Blockburger v. United States* (1932), offenses aren't the same if "each provision requires proof of a fact which the other does not."

Suppose a person breaks into someone's home, rapes them, and takes off with their wallet. These crimes almost certainly satisfy the test for separate offenses because they each require at least one element that the others don't:

>> Burglary requires breaking into a home.

>> Robbery requires taking someone's property.

>> Rape requires sexual intercourse.

But in the common sexual-assault crime scenario where a defendant forces the victim to engage in various sex acts during a single encounter, double jeopardy may depend on the way the authorities charge the crimes:

>> Two counts of sexual battery that could be based on the same act would constitute a single offense.

>> One count of forcible rape and a second count of forcible oral copulation would avoid a double jeopardy bar.

Here are two common examples of how the same-offense test applies:

>> **Lesser included offenses:** The prosecution can't try a person for both a crime and a lesser included crime arising out of the same facts. For example, they can't try a single theft as both petty and grand theft.

>> **Dual sovereignty doctrine:** Double jeopardy doesn't prevent different governments (such as state and federal, or two different states) from prosecuting the same offense.

The Double Jeopardy Clause doesn't prevent a defendant from being sued in a civil-court action after they're prosecuted for the same incident. For example, a person who's acquitted of murder may be found liable for wrongful death in relation to the same events. Civil liability requires a lower burden of proof and results in money damages, not imprisonment. Former football star O.J. Simpson was famously acquitted at his criminal trial in 1995 but was later found liable in civil court and ordered to pay more than $30 million in damages for the wrongful death of victims Ron Goldman and Nicole Brown Simpson.

Ensuring Fair Sentences

Several constitutional provisions that kick in early in the criminal proceedings continue to protect defendants through sentencing, such as the rights to counsel and due process and the privilege against self-incrimination. Two specific provisions impact sentencing proceedings (and both amendments apply to states because of the 14th Amendment's Due Process Clause):

>> The 8th Amendment prohibition against excessive fines and cruel and unusual punishment

>> The 6th Amendment right to a jury trial for certain sentencing factors

Some constitutional rights don't apply at sentencing, such as the right to confrontation. (Flip to Chapter 20 to read more about this right.) This has significant practical implications because it allows courts to consider comprehensive reports (such as probation reports and psychological evaluations) that assist the court tremendously in deciding on an appropriate sentence but include information from individuals who aren't subject to cross-examination.

Participating in sentencing

Legislatures, courts, and sometimes juries have roles in sentencing:

>> **The legislature:** Passes laws setting forth the potential penalties for violating a particular penal statute. For example, the law may provide that auto theft is punishable by 18 months to 3 years in prison.

>> **The court:** Imposes a sentence within the range authorized by law. In selecting a sentence within the range, courts consider specific *mitigating factors* (facts that reduce a defendant's blameworthiness; for example, a defendant's young age) and *aggravating factors* (facts that increase a defendant's blameworthiness, such as a defendant's use of a weapon).

>> **Juries:** Make findings that permit the judge to increase the sentence. You'll see how this works when we talk about the right to a jury trial on sentencing factors in the section "Extending the 6th Amendment jury trial right to sentencing," later in this chapter.

Prohibiting excessive fines and cruel and unusual punishment

The 8th Amendment is surprisingly short, but it packs a big punch. It says, "Excessive bail shall not be required, nor excessive fines imposed, nor cruel and unusual punishments inflicted." You can see how the 8th Amendment applies to excessive bail in Chapter 19. This section looks at the other two prohibitions: excessive fines and cruel and unusual punishment. The Framers included them in the 8th Amendment as a check on the federal government's new power to create and punish federal crimes:

>> **Excessive Fines Clause:** Limits the government's ability to demand payment as punishment for an offense. The question of whether a fine is excessive comes down to proportionality; the amount of the fine must bear some relationship to the seriousness of the crime.

>> **Cruel and Unusual Punishment Clause:** To prevent Congress from passing laws that permitted the use of barbaric methods used in the past (such as public dissection, beheading, and burning alive) and to prohibit courts from imposing arbitrary and disproportionate punishment. But as you can see in the following section, it didn't prohibit the death penalty altogether.

REMEMBER

Cruel and unusual punishment is not limited to what the Framers had in mind when they drafted the 8th Amendment. It's a flexible standard based on "evolving standards of decency that mark the progress of a maturing society," according to the Supreme Court.

8th Amendment challenges to the length of a sentence rarely succeed. Courts defer to the legislature's role in setting the punishment for a crime, and the bar is high to prove a violation; in length-of-sentence cases, only extreme sentences that are grossly disproportionate to the crime violate the 8th Amendment.

Imposing the death penalty

When it comes to providing constitutional protections, the Supreme Court has often said, "Death is different." Proportionality is key. Most importantly, the government can impose the death penalty only for crimes resulting in the victim's death.

TECHNICAL
STUFF

If you believe that the death penalty is always cruel and unusual, you aren't alone. Several former Supreme Court justices have expressed that view. Capital punishment is among the most controversial constitutional topics, but it was considered a legitimate form of punishment at the time the Constitution was drafted.

The Supreme Court has held that the death penalty is not unconstitutional if sufficient procedural safeguards are in place to ensure that it's not arbitrarily imposed. For example, death penalty laws must

>> Provide for individualized sentencing processes (legislatures can never make the death penalty mandatory).

>> Include *narrowing criteria* (extra facts that make this murder worse than a regular murder) to ensure the court imposes the death penalty for only the worst of the worst crimes and defendants.

>> Include standards to govern the factfinder's exercise of discretion related to the circumstances of the offense and the character of the defendant (things the jury should consider, such as the defendant's prior convictions or mental illness).

The method of execution can be the subject of an 8th Amendment cruel and unusual punishment claim, but the prisoner bears a high burden to show that the state's chosen method is unconstitutional. The Constitution prohibits only methods that *superadd* (a term that the Supreme Court uses to mean compounding) terror, pain, or disgrace; even then, the defendant must show that known and available alternatives exist and that the state has no legitimate penological reason to refuse to use an available alternative method of execution.

Another constitutional protection for defendants facing the death penalty is the 6th Amendment right to a jury trial for certain sentencing factors. We cover that aspect in the section "Extending the 6th Amendment jury trial right to sentencing," later in this chapter.

Special rules for people deemed less personally responsible

Cruel and unusual isn't a one-size-fits-all standard. The Supreme Court has held that proportionality under the 8th Amendment requires special rules for young offenders and developmentally disabled people because their unique characteristics make them less personally responsible for their crimes. For example, according to the Supreme Court, authorities can't execute developmentally disabled people.

Juveniles (in most states, people under the age of 18) can't face the following punishments:

>> Execution.

>> Life in prison without the possibility of parole (LWOP) for non-homicide crimes.

>> Mandatory life without the possibility of parole in homicide cases. The Constitution doesn't forbid LWOP sentences for juvenile murderers (although the Supreme Court strongly discourages them). But it does prohibit legislatures from making LWOP mandatory for juveniles and requires courts to make case-by-case sentencing decisions.

Extending the 6th Amendment jury trial right to sentencing

In the section "Participating in sentencing," earlier in this chapter, we look at the roles of different players in the sentencing process. We take a deeper look at those roles in the following sections because they help illustrate how and why juries may become involved in sentencing, a function that's normally left to the legislature and the judge.

Sentencing by the legislature and the court

The legislature enacts laws that not only define crimes, but also set forth punishments. A statute that sets forth a punishment does two things:

>> Provides notice to the defendant about the potential punishment they're facing (due process, discussed in detail in Chapter 13, popping in to say hello!)

>> Authorizes the judge to impose the stated punishment

Importantly, the judge's power to punish comes from the criminal statute, and the statute sets the limits on what sentence the court can impose. Within those limits, however, a court can exercise its discretion to choose the right sentence by weighing and considering *aggravating* and *mitigating* factors (elements that make the defendant more or less culpable).

Involving a jury in sentencing

The legislature can potentially give the court conditional authority to impose a higher sentence, by saying something along the lines of, "This crime is punishable between [lower number of years] and [higher number of years]. But if [this additional fact] is true, the maximum punishment goes up to [higher number plus more years]."

This conditional authority gives the judge the power to impose a higher sentence if a certain fact is true. Because the length of the defendant's imprisonment depends on whether the fact is true, the Supreme Court ruled in *Apprendi v. New Jersey* in 2000 that the court needs to treat that fact as an element of the crime:

>> The 6th Amendment right to a jury trial applies to sentencing factors that increase the maximum punishment.

>> In the same way that a defendant is entitled to notice of the crimes charged, they're entitled to notice of the sentencing factors that may increase their sentence because of the Due Process Clauses of the 5th and 14th Amendments.

In an important exception, defendants have no right to a jury trial for sentencing enhancements based on prior convictions. Judges alone can decide whether a defendant has a prior conviction and if so, the judge can use that prior conviction to increase a defendant's sentence.

Seeing sentencing factors in practice

Before a judge can impose a sentence in a case that requires certain facts to be true, the following procedures must occur:

>> The prosecution must *allege* (state) the sentencing factors in the *charging document* (which may be an indictment, complaint, or information, as explained in Chapter 18).

>> The prosecution must present evidence that supports the sentencing factor.

>> The jury must find the fact is true beyond a reasonable doubt.

Examples of sentencing factors include:

>> The victim was particularly vulnerable.

>> The crime involved a high degree of cruelty or viciousness.

>> The defendant used a weapon.

>> The crime involved planning or sophistication.

>> The defendant had a prior conviction for the same offense.

>> The defendant's criminal conduct has increased in seriousness over time.

Following an example sentencing

Say a defendant is on trial for robbery. Under state law, the punishment for robbery is three years imprisonment. But state law also provides for two sentencing enhancements. The sentence can be increased by one year if the defendant has a prior conviction or used a weapon in the commission of the crime.

If the jury convicts the defendant on the robbery charge, the sentence the defendant receives depends on what additional facts, if any, the court and the jury find to be true beyond a reasonable doubt:

>> Without any additional findings from the jury, the judge can sentence the defendant to three years.

>> If the prosecutor alleged that the defendant has a prior conviction, the judge can find that the allegation is true and sentence the defendant to four years.

>> If the defendant also used a weapon, the judge can sentence the defendant to five years (rather than the four-year sentence relating to only the prior conviction) if both the charging document alleged they used a weapon and the jury returned a finding that the weapon allegation was true.

The 6th Amendment right to a fair trial allows a defendant to *bifurcate* (separate) the proceedings so that a jury doesn't hear about aggravating factors (such as a defendant's prior convictions) until they've already determined the defendant's guilt.

Letting Congress Provide Appellate Rights and Processes

An *appeal* is a legal process in which a party asks a higher court to review a lower court's ruling, find an error, and reverse the judgment (or grant some other remedy). The Constitution doesn't grant convicted defendants a right to appeal. The right to appeal is up to Congress and state legislatures to create and define through statutes. However, where federal or state laws provide for appellate processes, the procedures must satisfy the requirements of the 5th and 14th Amendment Due Process Clauses.

The federal government and every state provide for a first appeal *as of right*, meaning the defendant has an automatic right to appeal under state or federal law, and the appellate court must review the case. (Subsequent appeals are generally *discretionary*, meaning up to the court to decide whether to consider the appeal.) In *Griffin v. Illinois* (1955), the Supreme Court held that the fundamental fairness of statutorily granted appeal rights is a matter of federal constitutional concern.

The facts of the *Griffin* case demonstrate the importance of due process in statutorily granted appeals. Defendant Griffin was convicted of robbery. Illinois law granted convicted felons an automatic right to appeal; to obtain a full review, however, the defendant was required to provide a full record of the proceedings to the appellate court, including the trial transcript. To obtain the record, defendants (except in capital cases) had to pay for the transcripts. Griffin had no money and therefore couldn't pay.

The Supreme Court ruled that, even though the Constitution didn't provide Griffin with a right to appeal, the Due Process and Equal Protection Clauses prevented Illinois from discriminating against indigent people by limiting or preventing their access to a state-granted appellate right.

Since *Griffin*, the Court has also held that under the Due Process Clause (as opposed to the 6th Amendment right to counsel), defendants have a right to counsel on a first appeal as of right. But they don't have a right to counsel for subsequent discretionary appeals.

Understanding the appeals process

In criminal cases, most often, the defendant appeals their conviction or sentence and asks the appellate court to reverse it. (As noted in the section "Prohibiting Double Jeopardy," earlier in this chapter, double jeopardy prevents the prosecution from appealing an acquittal, although they may appeal other decisions, such as an improper sentence.) The appellate process varies among jurisdictions, but the appeal of a criminal conviction generally follows these steps:

1. **The defendant goes through arraignment, pretrial proceedings, and trial in court.**

2. **The jury finds the defendant guilty, and the court sentences them.**

3. **The defendant obtains and reviews the trial court record.**

   They want to identify what they believe to be errors that occurred during the trial court proceedings.

4. **The defendant files a brief in the court of appeal that argues their case and asks the court to reverse the conviction or sentence.**

   The party who files the appeal (the defendant, in this case) is called the *appellant.*

   Most states have two-tiered appellate systems, with an *intermediate appellate court* and a *court of last resort,* but some states' cases go directly from the trial court to the court of last resort.

5. **The prosecutor reviews the trial court record and files a brief.**

   This brief responds to the appellant's claims and asks the court to affirm the lower court's judgment.

   The responding party (the People, in this case) is called the *respondent.*

6. **The appellant may have an opportunity to file a reply brief responding to the arguments in the respondent's brief.**

7. **The appellate court reviews the trial court record and the parties' briefs.**

8. **The court then issues an opinion with its ruling.**

   It can either grant the requested relief, deny the requested relief, or order further proceedings.

9. **When a case raises new or important legal issues, the appellate court may publish the opinion.**

   Published opinions act as *precedent* (established law) that provide guidance to lower courts. Generally, lower courts in the same jurisdiction are bound by published opinions, meaning they must apply the published opinion when ruling on other cases.

10. **The party losing an appeal may file a petition in a higher court requesting review of the adverse appellate court decision.**

The higher court has discretion to grant or deny review. Both federal and state cases can ultimately end up in the United States Supreme Court, although the Court accepts only a small percentage of requests to take a case *(petitions for certiorari).*

Distinguishing appeals from other post-conviction remedies

Appeals are generally limited to claims of error that occurred during the trial-court proceedings. The parties usually can't bring in new evidence; the *appellant* (the person filing the appeal) must base their appeal on matters contained in the record of the lower court (motions, reporter's transcripts of oral proceedings, trial exhibits, clerk's notes, and so on). If a defendant's claim involves evidence outside the trial record, they must raise it through a different process, such as a petition for writ of habeas corpus, which we explain in the following section.

For example, suppose the defendant brings a motion in the trial court to exclude their confession, claiming it was obtained in violation of the *Miranda* decision's protection against self-incrimination (which we cover in Chapter 19). The trial court denies the motion and admits the confession into evidence, and the defendant is convicted:

>> **What you can appeal:** On appeal, the defendant can raise a claim that the trial court improperly denied their *Miranda* motion. The court of appeal will review the trial court record and decide whether the trial court's decision was correct. If it was incorrect, the court will then decide whether the error was *harmless* (meaning the defendant would have been convicted even without the error), and if not, it will reverse the conviction.

>> **What you can't appeal:** But suppose the defendant claims that the reason the trial court denied the *Miranda* motion is because the judge's son is trying to get a job with the prosecutor's office, and the judge was trying to curry favor. A court can't decide this claim of judicial bias on the record alone, so it's not appropriate for appeal. (But the defense can file a petition for writ of habeas corpus, discussed in the following section, that includes evidence of the judge's bias.)

Promising Relief from Unlawful Imprisonment

Even after a conviction is final, prisoners have a remedy to correct unlawful imprisonment by filing a petition in state or federal court to vacate their conviction or sentence. This petition requests a *writ of habeas corpus,* a court order to a law enforcement agency to produce a prisoner and justify the imprisonment against the prisoner's claims that their detention violates their federal constitutional rights.

The Framers wanted to preserve the writ of habeas corpus as it appeared in English law to provide a critical tool for protecting individual liberty but limit the opportunity for arbitrary denials and suspensions (which often happened in England). At the same time, they didn't want to tie the executive branch's hands in a way that would interfere with national security.

The result of this balancing act was Article I, Section 9, Clause 2, which states: "The Privilege of the Writ of Habeas Corpus shall not be suspended, unless when in Cases of Rebellion or Invasion the public Safety may require it."

Habeas corpus is a civil action to overturn a judgment presumed to be valid. Federal courts place a high value on the finality of judgments, so state prisoners must try various avenues without success (or establish that they have no available legal remedy) before a federal court will consider their petition.

The Part of Tens

Chapter **22**
Ten Key Dimensions of the Constitution

The Constitution sets out some ambitious objectives in its preamble: to form a more perfect union, ensure domestic tranquility, provide for the common defense, promote the general welfare, and secure the blessings of liberty. In this chapter, we look at ten facets of the Constitution that further those lofty goals.

Making the Constitution Supreme

Article VI declares that "This Constitution . . . shall be the supreme Law of the Land." (Flip to Chapter 2 for a full discussion of how the Constitution rules supreme.) *Constitutional supremacy* means that the Constitution is the foremost authority. The Constitution

» Applies to all federal government officials and actions, including treaties, presidential executive orders, court rulings, and federal regulations

» Is binding on state and local officials and their official government actions

Writing Brief (and Ambiguous) Provisions

The Constitution establishes all the details of a comprehensive government in words that take up fewer than 20 pages from a modern printer. Most provisions use terms so general that scholars and judges still debate, analyze, and interpret their meaning. Chapter 4 discusses the many aspects of constitutional interpretation.

Offering Negative Rights

The U.S. Constitution uniquely frames almost all of the rights it grants as negative, rather than positive. Here's what those terms mean in this context:

>> **Negative rights:** Require the government to refrain from interfering with an individual's exercise of their rights. For example, the 1st Amendment prevents the government from unjustifiably interfering with an individual's right to free speech.

>> **Positive rights:** Require government action. The Constitution does grant some positive rights, such as the right to a speedy trial and the right to counsel (which includes the right to have the court appoint counsel for indigent individuals), discussed in Chapter 20.

Leaving the Constitution Open to Interpretation

The Framers didn't specify how future generations should interpret the Constitution because they didn't agree on a method themselves. (We talk more about these two perspectives on constitutional interpretation in Chapter 4.) The two main approaches are

>> **Original intent:** Asks what the Framers had in mind when they drafted the provision. This approach focuses on historical records to determine the Framers' intent, then applies it to the current set of facts.

>> **Evolving Constitution:** Looks at the Constitution as adaptable to changing societal norms and values.

Establishing Checks and Balances

The separation of powers among three coequal branches of government is a defining feature of American democracy. The Framers took a risk in implementing a system of checks and balances that arose from the European Enlightenment and was largely untested. (Flip to Chapter 1 for a history of what inspired the Framers when they drafted the Constitution.) In addition to the Enlightenment's core concepts of inherent rights and freedom from authoritarianism, the Constitution implemented French philosopher Montesquieu's idea of checks and balances by separating powers among legislative, executive, and judicial branches. Chapter 8 examines the ways that the three branches interact under the Constitution.

Pairing National Authority with Independent States

In 1787, America was on the verge of economic and political disaster. The weak federal government created by the Articles of Confederation lacked the power to unify the states or execute federal policy. Political figures at that time divided into two groups (which we talk about in Chapter 1):

>> **Federalists:** Advocated for a strong federal government that had the power to tax, regulate trade, and create an army

>> **Anti-Federalists:** Feared that a strong federal government would lead to the very type of oppression the colonists had rebelled against

The Constitution involved compromises from both sides.

Making Government Accountable

Inspired by Magna Carta and the Enlightenment (see Chapter 1), the Framers envisioned a government that served the people and prioritized individual rights. These ideals were cemented with the *Bill of Rights* (the first ten amendments), which protected individual rights against government overreach.

The provisions about criminal procedure are perhaps the starkest in placing government accountability above individual accountability, cloaking criminal defendants in a presumption of innocence and requiring the government to prove guilt beyond a reasonable doubt. (Part 5 focuses on the Constitution's role in the criminal justice system.)

Leaving the Details of Crime and Punishment to Legislatures

The Constitution protects fundamental fairness in criminal prosecutions by requiring various procedures in criminal cases, such as notice of the charges against the defendant and requiring the police to get search warrants (discussed in Chapter 19). But the Constitution doesn't define crimes or designate their punishments; these details stem from laws enacted by Congress and state legislatures.

Avoiding Undeserved Windfalls for Criminal Defendants

Errors in criminal procedure typically come to light after a convicted defendant files an appeal. (Chapter 21 talks about the appeals process in detail.) The appellate court reviews the lower-court proceedings and, if it finds that the defendant's constitutional rights were violated, it must then decide what remedy is appropriate. But courts won't vacate convictions or sentences for harmless errors that didn't contribute to the outcome.

Promoting Majority Rule while Protecting Individual Liberties

People use *majority rule* (the larger number decides) to make all kinds of decisions, from what movie to watch to what crimes deserve capital punishment. It's a foundational constitutional principle, as well; generally speaking, the person who gets the most votes wins, and a bill passes or fails depending on whether a majority of legislators votes yay or nay. But some constitutional provisions protect the minority, such as the Bill of Rights, judicial review, and the supermajority requirement.

Chapter **23**

Highlighting Ten (or So) Landmark Cases

E very United States Supreme Court decision is important (after all, it's the highest court in the land!). But some decisions change the course of history. So-called *landmark* cases may announce a new rule, adopt a new test or legal framework, establish or abolish constitutional rights, or shift the balance of power. Here are ten (plus) examples.

Establishing Judicial Review

In 1801, a justice-of-the-peace appointed by an outgoing president filed a petition asking the Supreme Court to order the incoming administration to follow through on his appointment. The Judiciary Act allowed the plaintiff to file the case directly in the Supreme Court. Rather than decide the sticky political issue raised in the petition, in *Marbury v. Madison* (1803), the Court found the Judiciary Act unconstitutional because it went beyond the Court's Article III jurisdiction. In doing so, the Court established its power of judicial review, famously stating, "It is emphatically the province and duty of the judicial department to say what the law is." You can find further discussion on *Marbury v. Madison* in Chapter 7.

Granting Congress Implied Powers

In the 1819 case *McCulloch v. Maryland*, the state of Maryland argued that the federal government lacked the power to establish a national bank because the Constitution didn't grant any such power and that Article I, Section 8 limits congressional powers to those that are "necessary and proper." In its decision (which we talk about in Chapter 5), the Supreme Court found the Necessary and Proper Clause expands, rather than limits, congressional power, holding that Congress has broad implied power to use all "appropriate and plainly adapted" means to achieve its enumerated powers.

Expanding Commerce Clause Power

Two New Deal era cases (1933–1938) that we cover in Chapter 8 greatly expanded Congress's Commerce Clause power (which comes from Article I, Section 8):

» ***NLRB v. Jones & Laughlin Steel Corporation*** **(1937):** The Court held that the clause gives Congress the power to regulate intrastate matters (meaning commerce conducted completely within one state) if those matters have a close and substantial relation to interstate commerce.

» ***Wickard v. Filburn*** **(1942):** The Court held that Congress has the power to regulate purely intrastate activity, even activity that has a trivial effect on interstate commerce, if the activity viewed in the aggregate has a substantial effect on interstate commerce.

Limiting Executive Overreach

During the Korean War, President Truman issued an executive order that directed the Commerce Secretary to seize American steel mills to avert an imminent labor strike. In 1952, in *Youngstown Sheet & Tube Company v. Sawyer*, the Supreme Court found the order unconstitutional because it went beyond the president's powers and amounted to lawmaking, which was a power reserved to Congress exclusively. Chapter 6 goes into the details of this case.

Claiming Judicial Supremacy

Officials in some states refused to follow the Supreme Court's 1954 school-desegregation decision in *Brown v. Board of Education*. In *Cooper v. Aaron* (1958), the Court rejected state officials' claim that they could decide for themselves how to interpret the Constitution. *Cooper* established that federal-court interpretations of the Constitution are the supreme law of the land. Chapter 7 further discusses this case.

Appointing Counsel for Indigent Defendants

The 6th Amendment right to counsel is a fundamental right that applies to the states through the 14th Amendment Due Process Clause. In 1963, the Court held in *Gideon v. Wainwright* that state courts must appoint counsel for defendants who can't afford an attorney in felony cases. In *Scott v. Illinois* (1979), the Court applied the right to misdemeanors that could result in a jail sentence of any length. Flip to Chapter 19 for the details of these cases.

Interrogating Suspects in Custody

The 1966 decision in *Miranda v. Arizona* established rights to ensure that confessions are voluntary. (You can read more about these rights in Chapter 19.) Before interrogating in-custody suspects, police must advise them that they have a right to remain silent, anything they say can be used against them in court, and they have the right to the presence of an attorney during questioning. If police violate a suspect's *Miranda* rights, the suspect's statements are inadmissible at trial under the 5th Amendment privilege against self-incrimination.

Insulating Presidents from Lawsuits and Prosecution

As we talk about in Chapter 6, presidents have, in relation to their official actions, absolute immunity from civil liability (*Nixon v. Fitzgerald*, 1982) and criminal prosecution for their official acts (*Trump v. United States*, 2024). These protections are rooted in the Separation of Powers doctrine and arise out of concerns that the threat of lawsuits or prosecution may dissuade presidents from zealously performing their singularly important duties.

Protecting States from Federal Government Pressure

Three Supreme Court cases addressed when acts of Congress cross the line between lawful attempts to influence state governments and unconstitutional coercion (see Chapters 8 and 9):

>> *South Dakota v. Dole* (1987): The Court established a test for analyzing coercion claims.

>> *New York v. United States* (1992): The Court held that the 10th Amendment prohibited the federal government from forcing states to take title of radioactive waste if they refused to dispose of it in accordance with federal standards.

>> *NFIB v. Sebelius* (2012): The Court found that the Affordable Care Act (ACA) went too far by threatening to withhold all federal funding of Medicaid for states that refused to expand it.

Finding Punishment Cruel and Unusual

The 8th Amendment's prohibition against cruel and unusual punishment doesn't categorically prohibit the death penalty or life imprisonment, but those punishments are unconstitutional under certain circumstances. See our discussion in Chapter 21 about the Constitution's positions on punishments. Some examples of unconstitutional punishments include

>> Sentencing a person who has mental disabilities to death (*Atkins v. Virginia*, 2002)

>> Sentencing juveniles to death (*Roper v. Simmons*, 2005)

>> Sentencing a defendant to death for any crime other than homicide or treason (*Kennedy v. Louisiana*, 2008)

>> Sentencing juveniles to mandatory life in prison without the possibility of parole (*Miller v. Alabama*, 2012)

Index

fundamental liberty interests, 199–200

identifying action as deserving, 160–161

narrow tailoring requirement, 170

putting affirmative action under, 171

for race-based classifications, 252

reconsidering *Smith* with, 160–162

religious discrimination, 158

for speech regulation, 139

strictness, 170

use of, 169–171

using with parenting questions, 162

in voting rights cases, 242

student disciplinary hearings, 189

student speech rights, 145

stun guns as protected arms, 232–233

subject-matter regulation, 139

substantial-effects doctrine, 111

substantial impairment, of contractual relationships, 218

substantial overbreadth doctrine, 144

substantive due process

  doctrine, 198

  example, 183

  protection of liberty interests, 182

  reconsideration debate, 211

  and same-sex intimacy, 205

  two-tiered scrutiny used for, 198–199

subversive speech doctrine, 134

supplemental procedural protections, 193

supremacy and preemption, 42

Supremacy Clause (Article VI), 17, 26, 34, 51, 91, 123, 331

Supreme Court

  constitutional interpretation by, 2

  creation, 24

  interpretations, changing, 274

  nationwide constitutional interpretation authority of, 52

  original jurisdiction of, 93

Sveen v. Melin (2018), 218

symbolic speech doctrine, 144–145

"systematic unbroken practice," 82

T

Takings Clause, 215, 219

tariff delegation, 88

taxation without representation, 9

tax deductions, for private-school expenses, 156

taxing and spending

  constitutional restrictions to, 108–109

  enumerated power to tax (and spend), 107–108

  federal policies, 107–109

  identifying tax-related implied means, 108

Ten Commandments classroom displays, 152

Terminello v. City of Chicago (1949), 137

Terry stops, 286

Terry v. Ohio (1968), 286

testimonial vs nontestimonial statements, 39, 287, 310–311

Texas v. Johnson (1989), 144–145

"Thoughts on Government," 12

three-factor balancing test, for due process, 191

Three-Fifths Compromise, 64

three-scenario framework, 81–82

TikTok, 110

time, place, and manner restrictions, 139–140

timing and formality of procedural protections, 190–191

Tinker v. Des Moines (1969), 145

Title VII employment discrimination interpretation, 179

totality-of-the-circumstances test, 60

Town of Greece v. Galloway (2014), 153

traditional public forum doctrine, 141

transgender status discrimination debate, 179

treason, definition of, 24

Trinity Lutheran Church of Columbia v. Comer (2017), 161

true bill. *See* indictment

true threats doctrine, 136–137

Truman, Harry, 79, 80

Trump, Donald, 76, 86, 224

Trump v. Barbara (2026), 30

Trump v. Casa (2025), 34–35, 225

Trump v. Hawaii (2018), 115

Trump v. J.G.G. (2025), 183, 195

Trump v. United States (2024), 44, 79, 87, 99, 337

Tumey v. State of Ohio (1927), 190

two-tiered supermajority, 17

two-tier scrutiny framework, in substantive due process, 198–199

twelve-person jury practice, in criminal trials, 309

U

unconstitutional coercion, in federal funding, 121

unconstitutional searches and seizures, deterrence of, 293

undue burden standard, for abortion regulation, 208

unilateral expectation vs legitimate entitlement, 186–187

unitary system of government, 20

United Kingdom, 20

United States Trust Co. v. New Jersey (1977), 217

United States v. Hemani, 237

United States v. Lopez (1995), 112–114

United States v. Miller (1939), 228

About the Authors

Melissa Mandel is an award-winning prosecutor. As a Supervising Deputy Attorney General at the California Department of Justice, Melissa handled hundreds of cases at every court level — including the United States Supreme Court and the California Supreme Court — resulting in more than 70 published opinions. A recipient of both the California District Attorneys Association William James Award and the Attorney General's Award for Excellence in Prosecution, Melissa has extensive experience training prosecutors and law enforcement agents. Melissa devoted much of her career to fighting the abuse of government power by prosecuting public officials for misconduct, investigating excessive force claims, and drafting legislation signed into law by Governor Jerry Brown that closed critical gaps in California's bribery laws. As an International Fellow with the National Attorneys General Training and Research Institute, Melissa collaborated with officials from eight countries on public integrity initiatives. Melissa served as a Commissioner on the State Bar of California Judicial Nominees Evaluation (JNE) Commission. Her commitment to preserving our constitutional democracy inspired her to write this book.

Glenn C. Smith, J.D., LL.M., is an emeritus professor of constitutional law at California Western School of Law in San Diego, California. He also taught for decades as a visiting professor in the Political Science Department of the University of California, San Diego. In these roles, Professor Smith taught a nationally recognized course in which students reenacted Supreme Court cases, taking on the roles of attorneys arguing and justices deciding constitutional issues. He regularly teaches other constitutional law courses and has published numerous articles on constitutional law for scholarly journals and for publications aimed at more general audiences. Professor Smith regularly speaks about constitutional controversies in media interviews and speeches. A Root-Tilden scholar at New York University School of Law, Professor Smith received his juris doctorate in 1978. He earned a Master of Laws degree from Georgetown University Law Center. From 1979 to 1983, he served as a legal counsel to the United States Senate Governmental Affairs Committee.

Dedication

From Melissa: To Zohar, my partner in life, liberty, and the pursuit of happiness.

From Glenn: To my wife, Diane.

Authors' Acknowledgments

From Melissa: This book exists because of my friend and former colleague Patty Fusco, an extraordinary attorney who connected me with my brilliant co-author Glenn Smith and his wife Diane, who generously shared her editorial expertise. To my mom, Bonnie Brenner, my siblings Holly and Danny Gross and Andy Brenner, I feel your love and support in everything I do, and I feel dad's too, even after all these years. To my children, Jake and Allie, and their partners Katie and Nolan, thanks for keeping your dad busy so I could get this book done.

From Glenn: Glenn Smith thanks his wife for her support as always! He also offers a huge thanks to his co-author extraordinaire; this book could not have been written without Melissa's legal expertise, experience and organizational skills, combined with her positive attitude and compassion.

From both of us: To our editorial team: Tracy Boggier, Laura K. Miller, Thomas Hill, and Ajith Kumar, thanks for your guidance and support in helping us get from idea to publication.

Publisher's Acknowledgments

Executive Editor: Tracy Boggier

Development Editors: Thomas Hill, Laura K. Miller

Copy Editor: Laura K. Miller

Managing Editor: Ajith Kumar

Production Editor: Magesh Elangovan

Cover Image: © W.Scott McGill/stock.adobe.com